"This is not a book for reading. It's a book for practicing. Jared Boyd graciously invites us to practice new ways of being present to God, ourselves, others, and creation, for and with the younger children (or childlike ones) in our lives. Not surprisingly, we are all transformed in the process. By gently making room and time for creative listening, imagination, and revelation of God's very good news of lavish love, children young and old together come to know God by experiencing this love that surpasses knowledge.

Cherith Nordling, associate professor of theology, Northern Seminary

"In the age of social media, so many of us struggle to be present to those closest to us and to God, who is an ever-abiding presence with us. Jared Boyd's extraordinary book *Imaginative Prayer* introduces us to a way of learning to be present to those closest to us—our children—and together with them to learn to use our imaginations to become more attentive to God's presence with us. Read this book slowly and carefully, and experiment with it: you, your family, and your church will undoubtedly be transformed!"

C. Christopher Smith, founding editor, *The Englewood Review of Books*, coauthor of *Slow Church*

"As a spiritual director, I understand the importance of formational experiences with Jesus rather than knowledge about Jesus. As a mother, I have struggled to find language and resources to transcend my own awkward efforts to help my daughter know right things about God and instead establish a real, lived relationship with God. Jared Boyd's work in *Imaginative Prayer* is a gift to my mother's heart and, I believe, a gift to the body of Christ as a whole.

Tara M. Owens, president and spiritual director, Anam Cara Ministries, instructor, Benedictine Benet Pines Monastery, former senior editor, Conversations Journal

"As the wise ancients have made clear, prayer is not part of life; it is life. But to pray—to live with God in the world as God lives and to be formed in the image of our older brother Jesus—necessarily requires the marshaling of our imagination. And it is our imagination that leads to the neuroplastic change—flexible alterations in our neuron firing patterns—to which St. Paul was referring when speaking of the renewal of our minds. With *Imaginative Prayer*, Jared Boyd has given us a treasure that reveals not only what children need to flourish in their spiritual formation but, even more, what we adults need—we who are woefully undernourished in the practice of truly, robustly imagining God living with us. If the deeper, more joyful, more resilient life is what you seek for your children (and for yourself), then look no further to find what perhaps has been just beyond your imagination but now expectantly awaits your discovery of it."

Curt Thompson, author of *The Soul of Shame* and *Anatomy of the Soul*

"I loved this book! If only it were around thirty years ago, when our family was exploring devotions! This book is an imaginative game, a devotional guide, and a theology text all rolled into one. It will nurture your own spiritual formation as much as your child's. The guided prayers that form the core of this book are well constructed, creative, and simply delightful. Boyd is not afraid to introduce difficult questions, but he helps me as a parent talk about them with my children. *Imaginative Prayer* develops essential skills of Christian spiritual formation—skills that are often neglected in the training of our children. I would recommend this book to parents, Christian education workers, and theology professors. We all need to imagine the gospel!"

Evan B. Howard, author of *Praying the Scriptures, A Guide to Christian Spiritual Formation,* and *The Brazos Introduction to Christian Spirituality,* and coauthor of *Discovering Lectio Divina*

"In this book of depth and whimsy, Jared Boyd inspires the imagination with new ways of engaging children in the work of the Spirit. I will be using this book for years to come, not only with the ministry leaders I teach, but with my own children! Jared's book speaks to a deep need felt within the church and within the lives of parents to help our children learn new and creative ways to engage with what the Holy Spirit is doing in their lives and in the world today. The result is a book that is practical and reflective: a deep reflection on a way of approaching the inner spiritual life of children."

Beth M. Stovell, assistant professor of Old Testament, Ambrose University, national catalyst, Vineyard Formation (Theological and Spiritual Formation), Vineyard Canada

"Jared Boyd has given Christian families a gift with this imaginative and practical guide to Bible study and prayer. While attending the same church as Jared, I saw firsthand the ways that his masterful storytelling and simple ideas for next steps excite children and adults alike with the message of Scripture, inspiring them to live out the story of the Bible in their own families."

Ed Cyzewski, author of *A Christian Survival Guide* and *Coffeehouse Theology*

"We are shaped not primarily though information-gathering but through practices and experiences that work their way into us, forming our appetites and kindling our imaginations. Many of us want to invite our kids into the miracle of knowing God in prayer and through the Scriptures, but we often aren't sure where to start. *Imaginative Prayer* is a great gift to parents (or godparents, aunts, uncles, and anyone who loves children) because it offers a guide for us grownups to engage our kids with the gospel holistically—not just their minds but also their hearts and imaginations. These prayer exercises are theologically rich yet elegant, even refreshing, in their simplicity. Here is an invitation to wonder, to surprise, to creative engagement with God. Walking through these practices with our kids was delightful and nourishing, not only for our kids but for us parents as well."

Tish Harrison Warren, Anglican priest, author of *Liturgy of the Ordinary*

imaginative
prayer

A YEARLONG GUIDE FOR YOUR
CHILD'S SPIRITUAL FORMATION

Jared Patrick Boyd

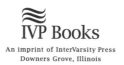

IVP Books

An imprint of InterVarsity Press
Downers Grove, Illinois

InterVarsity Press
P.O. Box 1400, Downers Grove, IL 60515-1426
ivpress.com
email@ivpress.com

InterVarsity Press® is the book-publishing division of InterVarsity Christian Fellowship/USA®, a movement of students and faculty active on campus at hundreds of universities, colleges, and schools of nursing in the United States of America, and a member movement of the International Fellowship of Evangelical Students. For information about local and regional activities, visit intervarsity.org.

Scripture quotations, unless otherwise noted, are from The Holy Bible, New International Version®, NIV® Copyright © 1973, 1978, 1984, 2011 by Biblica, Inc. Used by permission. All rights reserved.

Scripture quotations from The Message: Copyright © 1993, 1994, 1995. Used by permission of NavPress Publishing Group. All rights reserved.

While any stories in this book are true, some names and identifying information may have been changed to protect the privacy of individuals.

"All Things Rise" lyrics by Sam Yoder, ©2015 Mercy/Vineyard Publishing (ASCAP), admin. by vineyardworship.com, CCLI#7051263, used by permission.

Cover design: Cindy Kiple
Interior design: Daniel van Loon
Images: child silhouette: © VectorSilhouettes/iStockphoto
colorful swirls: © OliaFedorovsky/iStockphoto
Image of girl and bucket: TanyaRu/iStockphoto

ISBN 978-0-8308-4625-2 (print)
ISBN 978-0-8308-9229-7 (digital)

Printed in the United States of America ∞

Library of Congress Cataloging-in-Publication Data

Names: Boyd, Jared Patrick, 1978- author.
Title: Imaginative prayer : a yearlong guide for your child's spiritual formation / Jared Patrick Boyd.
Description: Downers Grove : InterVarsity Press, 2017. | Includes bibliographical references and index.
Identifiers: LCCN 2017010364 (print) | LCCN 2017016956 (ebook) | ISBN 9780830892297 (eBook) | ISBN 9780830846252 (pbk. : alk. paper)
Subjects: LCSH: Prayer—Christianity. | Imagination in children | Imagination—Religious aspects—Christianity. | Christian education of children. | Children—Religious life. | Spiritual formation.
Classification: LCC BV214 (ebook) | LCC BV214 .B69 2017 (print) | DDC 248.8/45—dc23
LC record available at https://lccn.loc.gov/2017010364

| P | 23 | 22 | 21 | 20 | 19 | 18 | 17 | 16 | 15 | 14 | 13 | 12 | 11 | 10 | 9 | 8 | 7 | 6 | 5 | 4 |
| Y | 36 | 35 | 34 | 33 | 32 | 31 | 30 | 29 | 28 | 27 | 26 | 25 | 24 | 23 | 22 | 21 | 20 | 19 | 18 |

For my girls

contents

Imaginative Prayer
Creedal Poem

The most important part of the story is that God loves so many things.
That he loves *me*.
That when I am lost, he will come looking for me.
That when I am sick, he wants to heal me.
And when I make mistakes, he will always have grace on me.
There is nothing that can separate me from the *love* of God.

God invites us to live a life of love.
Love looks like being patient and kind and not making a list of
     people's mistakes.
Love looks like inviting people who may be left out.
Love looks like taking care of people when they need help.
We love others with the love that God pours into us.
People will know that we are followers of Jesus because of our love for
     each other.

Forgiveness means we can have peace with God.
Forgiveness means God welcomes anyone.
Forgiveness means God takes away our sin.
Forgiveness means we can forgive the sins of others.
When we forgive, we will be forgiven. When we give, it will be given to us.
Love and forgiveness make room for reconciliation.

Jesus is the King who came to undo the power of death.
Jesus is the King who came to defeat the power of sin.
Jesus is the King who came to defeat the power of the Accuser.
Jesus is a faithful King, even when we don't have faith.
We have life with God through the faithfulness of Jesus the King.
Love and forgiveness: this is how God became King.

God made a new promise, and it comes to us through Jesus.

The good news of God comes to us through the *words* of Jesus.

The good news of God comes to us through the *life* of Jesus.

The good news of God comes to us through the *death* of Jesus.

The good news of God comes to us through the *resurrection* of Jesus.

We receive the promises of God when we choose to follow Jesus.

When we follow Jesus, we join the mission of God to bring his love into
the world.

The mission of God is to make everything in the world good again,
to bring all things under the reign of King Jesus,
to bring peace and reconciliation to everything.

The mission of God is to take away the veil that covers up the presence of God.

God is at work all around us: open your eyes and join God in his mission to
the world.

Introduction

*Christianity is not an intellectual system, a collection
of dogmas, or a moralism. Christianity is instead
an encounter, a love story; it is an event.*

POPE BENEDICT XVI

*What if education . . . is not primarily about ideas and information,
but about the formation of hearts and desires? The education of
desire . . . requires the pedagogical formation of our imagination.*

JAMES K. A. SMITH,
DESIRING THE KINGDOM

THIS BOOK IS ABOUT CONNECTION. As a father of four girls one of my greatest desires is to pass on to them a deep understanding and awareness of the *experience* of God. My hope is that they would feel connected to God and the story God is unfolding in their lives and in the world around them. Will they see themselves as part of God's story? Will they feel close and connected to God as they navigate decisions that come their way and pursue risks on the horizon? Will they say yes to all that God is inviting them into? This book is about *connection* because of the way Jesus asks us to imagine our life with him—he is the vine, his Father is the gardener, and we are *connected* to him. This is how we bear fruit. This is the image he gives us. This is what he asks us to imagine.

This book is also about formation. "Spiritual formation . . . is the intentional and God-ward reorientation and re-habituation of human experience."[1] Or, more simply defined by M. Robert Mulholland Jr., spiritual formation is "the process of being formed in the image of Christ for the sake of others."[2] Whenever we're intentionally doing something to shift our experience or understanding of God, we're involved in spiritual formation. When we're working, in response to God's grace, to shift our thoughts, the patterns of our relationships, and our actions toward a greater alignment with the life and teachings of Jesus, we are doing the work of spiritual formation.

And when we help others in their journey of formation, we become connected to them and their story.

We share in their experience, and we too are formed by it.

This book is an invitation to connection with your child and to your child's spiritual formation.

PARENTING, CONNECTION, AND FORMATION

In my late twenties, as I tried to settle into adulthood (and feeling quite unsettled), I began meeting with a spiritual director—someone with formal training in helping me pay closer attention to my conversation with God and the movements in my soul.[3] I began to notice the story of my own formational journey, which took me all the way back to childhood. This wasn't therapy. It was a form of prayerful attentiveness to how God has been present to me throughout the seasons of my life. It is an attentiveness that seeks to name God's activity and my responses. One glaring observation was that while I had a powerful encounter with the love and grace of God when I said yes to Jesus at age ten, my next *experience* of God, the next time I felt the *nearness* of God, didn't come until I went to a worship service at a Vineyard church six years later.

I have a lot of questions about those six years in between. I remember being asked, at baptism, what I *believed* about God, about the Bible, and about the cross. What I don't remember is anyone asking me what my conversation with God was like. Or what my experience of him was like. Or what he might be inviting me into. I think, looking back now, that I would have loved to talk more about Jesus and my experience of him. I think somewhere along the way, someone would have heard me say out loud what I was thinking and feeling. Perhaps someone would have heard in my answers that my experience of God was filled with guilt and shame. And I think someone would have helped me see it differently.

The truth is that the church tradition I grew up in wasn't really asking these kinds of questions. Spiritual formation and the contemplative stream in the evangelical world of the 1980s was just being birthed with Richard Foster's *Celebration of Discipline*, published in 1978, the same year I was born. It took the next thirty years for that contemplative stream to broaden enough to begin widely quenching the thirst of evangelical adults.[4] And now those adults are parents and pastors (myself included), raising and forming children the best we know how. It's second nature to raise a child in the way we were raised. It takes a ton of work to take the lessons we are learning and, in real time, think about how to recontextualize some of that learning for the little ones among us. When I started to sense a shift in my own formational journey, I didn't have any idea how to offer my children a drink from the contemplative stream. I think I'm beginning to scratch the surface of what has been for me a big shift in my focus as a pastor and a parent. And that is why you are holding this book. This book is my attempt at helping to contextualize a spiritual formation for children.

And here is why.

As I set out to do some of that hard work of allowing my own formational journey to shape my parenting, I noticed something that felt unsettling to me as a pastor; I had spent nearly a decade meeting with a spiritual director, I had been trained as a spiritual director myself and offered a listening ear to dozens of people each month as part of my pastoral ministry, and yet I seemed to only be using rudimentary tools for nurturing the spiritual formation of my own children. I had grown in paying attention to my own conversation with God. I was even getting pretty good at helping other adults pay attention to their life with God. But when it came to these kinds of conversations with my own children, I quickly reverted back to asking questions about belief in God, the Bible, and the cross.

I was reading stories from the Bible and answering questions that my girls would bring up. I was trying to ask some questions I had learned through my spiritual direction practice, but I was having a hard time facilitating for them the kind of connection to God that I seemed to be experiencing in my own life. I was still focused on getting them to *understand* and *believe* the right things. And then I read a book by James K. A. Smith, a philosopher at Calvin College. Smith writes, "Human beings are not only, nor even primarily, 'thinkers.' We are not as defined by what we know, as we are but what we *love*—what we long for."[5]

We are defined by our *longings*, and what we long for is at the root of spiritual formation.

I was having trouble connecting with my children around issues of faith because I was no longer focused on making sure I had everything figured out. I wasn't really concerned with the questions and answers we typically think are important to pass along to our offspring. I had learned to embrace more mystery and tension than I was willing (or capable) of leading them into. I still, of course, believed things about God, the Bible, and the cross. But I was no longer connected to those things the same way; it seems that I had become connected to the vine, and all those questions that nagged my *thinking* self remained unanswered, though no longer central. My life with God had shifted from the importance of *knowing* to paying attention to what I was truly longing for. And what I longed for was the experience of God himself.

I wanted my children to connect with God, and I also wanted to connect with them in their experience of him. And yet we didn't really have a *shared vocabulary* or a *shared experience*. I was reading Thomas Merton and Dallas Willard and finding that Wendell Berry was speaking to me as much about the gospel as anyone else had been. I had experienced some deep shifts in my understanding of my experience of God in places of silence, solitude, and imaginative prayer. I knew that I couldn't expect my girls to become little mystics and plunge the depths of consolation and desolation. There are stages of faith to walk through, often with a more contemplative expression showing up later developmentally.[6] We need seasons of certainty as much as we need what follows, which is often the tragic anguish when what we once held certain begins to trickle out the cracks in the façade of self.

But surely, I thought, *there is a way to nurture them toward an awareness that God is present and can speak to them.* Surely it was possible for my own children to experience God in ways similar to how I was experiencing him. How can I introduce my children to bite-sized pieces of the contemplative life and the experience of God? How could I give my children a memorable experience of growing in their awareness of what God is like? How might I help aim their desires toward becoming the kind of people who intuitively understand the world in light of the gospel?[7]

These were the kinds of questions I was asking, not only for my own parenting but as a pastor overseeing a kids' ministry of close to one hundred third- to sixth-grade children. I was trying to think through how to reorient our kids' ministry toward nurturing a *connection with God* and teaching parents how to ask the right kinds of questions so that our efforts as a church and parents' efforts at home would reinforce each other. We were trying to create a culture in which parents understood that they were the most important spiritual influence in their child's life. How do we help them connect in meaningful ways with their child's spiritual formation? These kinds of questions led me to meet with Sam.

MY CONVERSATION WITH SAM

Sam was a typical fifth-grade boy. This is not to say that all fifth-grade boys are alike. Sam was unique, but he was typical—high energy, low attention span. Sam's parents were also typical, though both had been in ministry positions in the past, which means they had a little extra insight into why we were all sitting around this table on a Sunday afternoon. Sam was their oldest of three children, and they were tired parents. They had that after-church kind of tiredness that most parents of children can tell you about. We all were on our second or third cup of coffee. Sam's parents seemed a bit hesitant about some of my efforts to introduce contemplative practices in our church service and community groups. They were hesitant but curious.

Sam was all over the place during the first part of our meeting. His parents had informed me prior to our meeting that Sam had a healthy dose of ADHD. And this is exactly the reason I wanted to meet with Sam. If we can't figure out how to pastor parents of kids like Sam, and if we can't figure out how to pastor Sam—to help him grow up to be someone who is intrigued by Jesus and wants to follow the kind of life that Jesus invites us to—then we need to keep trying. Sam was just as much a part of our church as his parents were. And I felt like I wasn't doing a great job of nurturing his formation. I wasn't interested, however, in trying to get Sam's attention. I couldn't compete with video games or a high-budget youth program. I went into my meeting with Sam convinced that getting him to get a glimpse of what it feels like to *experience* God would be a good place to start.

"Sam, I want you to try something for me. I want you to close your eyes and listen to a story I am about to tell you.

"Sam, I want you to imagine that you are a crippled beggar. Sam, you can't walk. All you can do is sit on the side of the road and beg for food. Imagine that you are on the side of a dusty road, Sam. Imagine it in your mind as though you are watching a movie.

"Now, imagine with me, Sam, that some friends of yours come and pick you up. They've brought something like a stretcher to carry you on. They are taking you to a house down the street because someone said that Jesus is there.

"Keep your eyes closed, Sam, and imagine that your friends carry you all the way to a house down the street—they're going to ask Jesus to heal you. They think Jesus can say the word and make it so you can walk again."

I've got my eye on Sam. He's got his head down. His feet are fidgety—but he's quiet. He's really listening.

"Now imagine, Sam, that you get to the house down the street where Jesus is. Imagine that the house is completely full and there is no more room. You can't even squeeze through a window because there are so many people in the house listening to Jesus talk. I wonder what he's talking about. Imagine that you too are wondering what Jesus is talking about that has so many people listening so intently.

"Sam, I'm going to ask you a question, but it's just a question for you to think about—you don't need to answer me: Sam, what does it feel like for there not to be any room for you to get in to be healed by Jesus?"

I pause for just a bit. Long enough to give Sam some space, but not too long.

"Now, imagine with me, Sam, that your friends decide to do something crazy. They pick up the mat you are resting on and begin to climb the stairs that go up to the roof of the house. This house has a flat roof that can be walked on. You are now on top of the roof and your friends begin digging into the roof with their hands. The roof is made of mud and straw—and so little bits of the roof begin to crumble and you can see a small hole beginning to form. Suddenly, you and your friends are getting all the attention. Everyone is staring up at the roof from inside the house. Some men are down below yelling up at your friends—but your friends don't stop digging.

"And you won't believe what they do next, Sam. They tie a rope around you and they begin to lower you through the hole in the roof. Imagine, Sam, that everyone in the room down below is looking at you as your friends lower you to where Jesus is standing. The room is quiet, and everyone is looking at you. What do you feel as you are lowered down to Jesus?"

Again, I pause here. There is silence. Sam's feet are no longer fidgety. Sam is now sitting upright, silent, with his eyes closed; he's still. Something is happening here.

And then Sam says out loud, "I feel embarrassed. I feel embarrassed that everyone is looking at me."

"Sam, imagine that Jesus looks right at you. How do you feel when Jesus looks at you?"

Sam's eyes are still closed, but he smiles. "I don't feel embarrassed anymore."

"Imagine that he kneels down beside you and he takes your hand and says to you, 'Get up and walk.' Imagine that you stand up and walk for the first time in a long time."

We get to this point and I'm not quite sure what to do next. It ends quite a bit more awkwardly than I wanted it to, but I knew that what had just happened with Sam was what I was looking for. I knew it. His mom knew it. And I think Sam knew it too. I asked Sam what he would think if we did this kind of thing on Sunday mornings at church.

"What if we could use our imagination? To watch the story inside our head as though we're watching a movie? Sam, what would you say if we did some of that?" I asked.

He said, "That'd be cool."

But I had no idea how I was going to make it happen.

IMAGINATIVE PRAYER

The Christian imagination plays a great role in the spiritual development of the soul.

St. John of the Cross

There is something mysterious and perhaps more than moral about the power and call of imagination.

G. K. Chesterton

What I had stumbled across that afternoon with Sam goes quite a bit deeper than just *pretending* to be a part of a scene that includes Jesus. I remember hearing a story that Eugene Peterson told in one of his lectures. One of his grandchildren crawled up on his lap and said, "Tell me a troll story, Grandpa, and put me in it!" He used this story to illustrate our desire to get into the story—that there is a way for us to read and experience Scripture that puts us in the story. It turns out that there is a rich tradition of reading Scripture and *imagining* ourselves in the story as a way of prayer. St. Ignatius of Loyola, the founder of the Jesuits, was converted through an *imaginative* experience of God.

In 1521 Íñigo López de Loyola, while serving as a commander under the Duke of Najera, was severely wounded when the French invaded the city of Pamplona, Spain. After a surgery to repair one of his legs, which was struck by a cannonball, he spent nearly ten months in bed with nothing to do except read two books that were handed to him: *De Vita Christi* (*Life of Christ*) by Ludolph of Saxony (a fourteenth-century Carthusian monk), and a collection of biographies known as *The Lives of the Saints*. His conversion experience happened in the loneliness of his convalescence, and through the adventure that he lived in his fantasies about what it might look like to emulate people like St. Francis of Assisi and St. Dominic. When he read about the lives that these men lived, and when he imagined living as they lived, he found that his desires, his *longings*, began to shift away from daydreaming about becoming a hero in battle and winning the hand of a wealthy girl. His imagination, and thus his *desires*, began to shift toward following the person of Jesus—doing great things for the greater glory of God.

It was in that daydreaming and in his imagination where conversion took place. At first, he began to imagine himself in a story whose plot included him laying aside his life of wealth and privilege. It began as a fiction in his mind. But eventually, as this fiction was nurtured through contemplation and prayer, he felt compelled to make it true. As soon as he was able to walk, Ignatius began a pilgrimage to Jerusalem, giving his fancy clothes to a poor beggar and taking for himself a linen robe of poverty. Ignatius imagined his way toward a life of complete devotion to Christ. And then he enacted what had first taken place in his imagination.

St. Ignatius's own conversion experience would later inform his method of spiritual direction for those who were looking to join the Jesuit order, as well as those looking to deepen their experience of God. In the *Life of Christ*, Saxony encourages his readers to place themselves within the scenes of the Gospel story and to make that imaginative exercise a prayer. He recommends the reader to look at the events of the life of Christ as though they were actually taking place. This method of prayer would become the center of the *Spiritual Exercises* (a series of prayers, meditations, and other mental exercises) that St. Ignatius wrote shortly after laying his sword and shield, in true chivalrous fashion, at the feet of a statue of the Virgin Mary.

My conversation with Sam was rooted in a practice that goes back nearly five hundred years. We were daydreaming together *for the greater glory of God*. I provided the scene for Sam, giving him a setting and directing his attention a little, but his imagination and the Holy Spirit did the rest. I never could have planned for Sam to feel embarrassed while imagining being lowered through the roof with everyone looking at him. I certainly couldn't have forced the natural smile on his face when his attention turned to the face of Jesus. What happened inside Sam's daydream is nothing that we could recreate or even fully describe—it belongs to him. It's a gift. I've become convinced that in the spiritual formation of children we are looking for little movements like this. We can go back and help Sam name what he experienced. We can even help point to other stories in the life of Jesus that might bring up a similar response—Zacchaeus being called down from a tree, Peter walking on water, Joseph holding the newborn Messiah—but we can't see what Sam sees. And we can't predict where Sam will make a connection to the life and story of Jesus.

It's his alone.

Now I had a connection to Sam. We had a *shared vocabulary* of experience. I know a little about what he experienced that day because I have had similar experiences.

A few months before my conversation with Sam, I had a profound experience with imaginative prayer. I was working through the preparatory exercises before beginning my own journey through the *Spiritual Exercises* of St. Ignatius.[8] After a brief time of slowing down and inviting God's presence to be with me, I began to read through the passage found in Matthew 20 where Jesus is telling a story about workers and wages. I first began to imagine myself as one of the workers who came to work early in the morning. I imagined working all day long, sweating in the hot sun, and watching other workers show up throughout the day. I paid attention to the anticipation I felt for receiving my wages when the work was complete. I watched as the manager began to hand out cash to each worker. And I felt the sting of receiving the same wage as those who had slept in that morning, taken a long lunch, and showed up just a few hours before the work was finished. Finally, I started over and reviewed the whole story by imagining myself in the shoes of the latecomer.

The one who missed the morning call to work.

The one who overslept.

The one just squeaking by.

What if God's love and grace were like this? What if he wasn't paying so much attention to how hard I was working or what great thing I was trying to accomplish? What if the grace and love of God were simply a gift? Could I rejoice that others received the same as I? Could I allow myself to receive the abundance of the gift, knowing that I was undeserving?

Something happened in my mind that morning as I sipped coffee during my morning prayer. I wiped away tears as I felt the love of God wash over me. (In fact, I'm wiping them away now at the memory of it.) I closed my eyes and imagined what response I might have to Jesus as he tells the story. I imagined what it might be like to walk away with a pocketful of cash after just a few hours of work. I recognized that I was drawn toward Jesus, that I could see the grace of God, and that God was more generous than I had imagined.

All of this happened because I had a story to jump into, a little guidance from a book, and some time allotted to use my imagination in a way that didn't come naturally to me. In fact, when I first started out in imaginative prayer, it felt quite clunky. I'm not by nature a very playful person. I studied philosophy in college, and I studied a lot. Most of the books I had read up until a few years ago were nonfiction. Stories, science fiction, and make-believe have never been my strong suit. But there was no denying that something happened in me that day. I had experienced God's presence and something shifted.

As I continued to work my way through the *Spiritual Exercises* I began to wonder whether my children might be able to enter into some of what I was doing. I watched them playing dress-up and make believing all sorts of things. They had no trouble imagining themselves as one of the characters in Louisa May Alcott's *Little Women*. Certainly they could put themselves into a Jesus story. Perhaps in *pretending* to be with Jesus, they might experience firsthand what it was like to see him bring the kingdom.

For a few weeks I began to sit quietly with one or more of my daughters. I would help them create the scene of one of the stories of Jesus in their imagination. It was simple: I would pick a story from one of the Gospels and begin to narrate what was happening in the story.

But here is what happened that convinced me we were onto something. One evening during our bedtime routine that includes a time of connection with each of our four girls, I was trying to explain to one of my daughters, who was then eight years old, that God is present to us whenever we need him, that he sees us and knows us and even though we cannot see him, we can know him. "What do you mean?" she asked. She was curious enough and engaged enough that I knew she wanted to know more; I just didn't know how to explain it. I couldn't quite put it into words because I don't think I fully understood it myself.

I invited her to close her eyes and began to rub her back. How do I explain to an eight-year-old that God is present with her? I started to speak.

"Imagine with me that you are lying in bed and are about to go to sleep. Imagine that Jesus comes into your room and is rubbing your back and singing you a song, just like Daddy does each night. Imagine that right now it is Jesus who is rubbing your back."

I paused briefly.

"What would you ask Jesus if he were here? What would you say to him?"

I paused again, not even knowing if she was still awake. There was a long enough pause that I assumed that she had fallen asleep. But just as I stopped rubbing her back, and as I stood up to leave the room, she said, "I would ask him to hold me while I sleep." I knelt beside her bed and quickly said to her in a whisper, "And what do you think he would say back to you?"

"He would say yes."

··

How to Use This Book

*[Knowing] God is mediated through formation, imitation, affectivity,
intuition, imagination, interiorization, and symbolic engagement.*

AMOS YONG, *THEOLOGY AND DOWN SYNDROME*

HOW CAN WE USE OUR child's imagination in the process of their
spiritual formation?

Let's go back to the story of Sam from chapter one. I can't describe Sam's
experience for you, but I can describe what I witnessed: nothing less than
Sam dipping his toe into the contemplative stream of Christian experience.
Instead of rehearsing some abstract doctrine, Sam had an experience of
Jesus. Instead of reciting something that someone wrote over five hundred
years ago, Sam left that day with a *memory* of something that happened to
him. Instead of sitting through another Bible lesson, Sam climbed into the
story and imagined what it would be like to be healed by Jesus. We helped
Sam make a connection to Jesus through a real experience of God. This
experience created a memory. And this memory can be drawn upon in the
future. This memory will represent (literally re-present) Jesus to him at some
point in the future.

This book is written to help you have a full year of spiritual formational
experiences with your child.[1] This book is written to provide a new *shared
vocabulary* of the experience of God. When both you and your child can
imagine your way into the story, you each have your own experiences. And

though you aren't experiencing the exact same thing, you share the context and the story. If you've ever had an opportunity to stand in front of a Van Gogh painting or have viewed the Rocky Mountains from the top of a "fourteener"—when you meet someone who has also had that experience, you have a connection and a shared vocabulary.

Children are unique little creatures. You may find that your child seems engaged in the imaginative prayer sessions. Or not. Or maybe it's a little of both, and there isn't any rhyme or reason to it from one week to another. I have four girls with differing personalities and abilities. Each of them has experienced imaginative prayer in her own way, and I've experienced some level of connection with each of them as we engage in the practice. The conversations that follow these experiences are where the real gold is. I'm tempted, as I think many parents are, to try to figure out what works. Part of what it means to go down a path of a more contemplative approach of spiritual formation is to embrace the mess and leave behind the part that wants to quantify the progress. Let me set you at ease: the Holy Spirit will do the heavy lifting. And this kind of formation takes time.

SLOWING DOWN

Our lives are busy. Most of us struggle to pay bills, do laundry, make repairs, and put healthy food on the table. Evenings are filled will homework and housework, play practice, soccer practice, dishes, baths, and getting ready for the next day. When are you going to find time to lead your child in imaginative prayer? It's unlikely that you'll be able to add something else into your schedule.

The question is, what can I take out of my schedule to make room for this?

In order to take on this spiritual formation journey with your child, you'll need to make room for it. While some of what is in this book can happen on the margins of your life (we've planned for that), going all the way back to the desert fathers a general attitude pervades the literature on spiritual formation: nothing good happens in a hurry. Dallas Willard, one of the fathers of the evangelical contemplative stream, suggested that you should "ruthlessly eliminate hurry from your life."[2]

This book is not a guide for *busy parents*. It's an invitation for *busy parents* to slow down, take some deep breaths, and recognize that you are the most important person in your child's life and spiritual formation. There is no environment your church can create to compete with the kind of connection that you are able to nurture with your child. Spend some time together as a family thinking through your weekly schedule. This book asks for one thirty-minute time slot each week, and ten minutes of conversation each day. Anything else that comes out of that is a bonus.

We'll be exploring six themes together over the next nine or ten months. In truth, given the rhythms of many of our lives, while there are forty-two weeks worth of material here, it might take a full year to journey through.[3] Once you have found a spot in your calendar for the thirty minutes of imaginative prayer each week, guard that time slot. Even this commitment, and your intention to keep it, will be a place of formation for your child. The habit you form in the practice of these sessions will do as much formative work as the prayers themselves.[4] This book tends to build on previous weeks. If you set it aside for long periods of time, the continuity won't be the same. But by all means give yourself some slack, and ask God for the grace to gently bend your life in this direction.

My hope is that you'll keep this book in a special place on your bookshelf or end table, along with a journal, which you can use to facilitate some reflection with your child through drawn pictures and written prayers.[5]

HOW IS THIS BOOK LAID OUT?

Each of the following six parts explores a theological theme: *"God's Love," "Loving Others," "Forgiveness," "Jesus Is the King," "The Good News of God,"* and *"The Mission of God."*[6] Each part is made up of seven sessions with six imaginative prayer sessions and a seventh session set aside for a week of review. Some of you will be reading this book as part of a larger initiative at your church where the imaginative prayers will be introduced during your child's class, while others will be leading your child through the imaginative prayer yourself at home. Either way, each week you'll have some guiding questions to help you stay in touch with your child's experience of the theme for that week's session. These questions are designed to deepen your child's understanding and experience, as well as to help facilitate a greater connection between you and your child. These are the questions you'll throw into the natural rhythm of your day. Each session has five sections.

 Each session begins with "Connection and Formation." This section is meant to provide the theological framework and the purpose behind that session's imaginative prayer. It includes imaginative prayers that borrow from and build on themes from previous sessions. I try to point these out to help you see the connection. There are also some sessions in which further theological reflection might be helpful. Of course each of the themes we explore could be addressed in several volumes. I've tried, in less than a page, to say *why* this particular imaginative prayer contributes to the formation of your child. My hope is that part of the formation process will include some age-appropriate theological reflection. Again, the goal isn't knowledge, but for you as a parent it'll be helpful to see how the imaginative prayers contribute to a holistic understanding of the experience and work of God.

Each session also has a "Question and Answer" section. This is a throwback to the style of *catechism* the church has used historically. From the late Middle Ages up to the present, the church has focused on knowledge and understanding of the articles of Christian faith through a question and answer format initially popularized in Luther's *Small Catechism*. In a traditional catechism, a parent (or tutor) asks a child (or student) a series of questions like, "What is the chief end of man?" and "What is thy only comfort in life and death?"[7] This question-and-answer format is still used today in church traditions that participate in a formal catechism. And, while it's true that the answers to these questions are important—men and women gave their lives for some of the answers—this book has attempted to approach spiritual formation through the use of other (more contemplative and formative) avenues. Sometimes the patterns of pedagogy need to be revisited, modified, and reimagined.

This book began as an effort toward *reimagining* catechism for the twenty-first century. I believe the traditional question-and-answer format is still a valid form to help remind children of larger concepts. I've kept this remnant of traditional catechism in hopes that the questions and answers provided in each chapter will serve as signposts to the memories that we hope to create along the way. Each question-and-answer coupling is a stand-in for the imaginative prayer, which I hope will itself be a stand-in for your child's experience of that prayer. I've shared a story in "Buckets of Water" (see below) of how I've seen this get fleshed out in our own experience. When you stitch together the answers to these questions, they make up a thirty-six line creed that can be memorized along the way. This can help maintain continuity throughout the year and serve as a tool for gathering up these memories once the year is completed. I see the use of this creed more like a poetry slam than any sort of test for proficiency or rite of passage. I do think the church needs ceremonial events for children as they pass from one stage to the next. Though I'd love to see these events as a celebration of a child's life and experience of God rather than a demonstration of what they know or have learned about God.

BUCKETS OF WATER

An imaginative prayer in chapter eleven stands out to me as a good example of how the memories created in imaginative prayer can be drawn upon later.

In session eleven we are led to imagine that each time we fill with water the empty buckets of our neighbors, we find that our own bucket is made full again. Each time we see a thirsty neighbor (in an area where there is little access to water) and share our water, by some strange mystery  we find that once we return to our own home the bucket is filled again. The point of the lesson is that *we love others with the love that God pours into us*. It is a lesson about how the work of the kingdom comes as a result of first being filled up with God's own love for us. The resource we have to give, namely, our love for others, comes from what God gives to us. This lesson also sets us up for future conversations about the work of the Holy Spirit.

During the week that this particular lesson was at the forefront of our conversation, one of my daughters was planning to attend a playdate. She had everything packed for the day. The playdate was with a longstanding friend, though by looking at her you wouldn't know it. I could sense that something was off, and so I asked her about it.

"What's wrong, sweetie?" I probed.

She told me that she and her friend had been experiencing some conflict recently. She was having a difficult time with something unkind her friend had said. We talked about forgiveness and then about love.

"What would it look like for you to love her right now?" I asked.

It's a simple question that got her thinking. This question opened up even more conversation. She was having a hard time thinking what it would look like to love, because she felt hurt.

"What would it look like to take buckets of water with you?" I asked.

I smiled. So did she.

This question helped her understand that her friend was just like a neighbor in our imaginative prayer—someone who was thirsty and in need. This question reminded her that there is a deeper well she could draw from. We talked about what it might look like to get filled up before she left. We prayed together briefly. And she left for her playdate with visions of full buckets in her imagination.

The image of buckets of water was a signal of a larger story she had already participated in through imaginative prayer. She had a memory of that practice. The story itself was a stand-in for a bit of spiritual theology and formation—that we give to others out of the overflow of our life with God and what he provides. This is rooted in Jesus' own experience of receiving the love of the Father (Mt 3:16-17), being filled with the Holy Spirit, and ministering to others with what God has already provided (Acts 10:38). Each imaginative prayer in this book is meant to work like this. We are looking for spiritual formation of our heart and desires through experience rather than knowledge. Your child may memorize the answers to poignant questions throughout this material, but the content they memorize is meant to be a trigger for the larger imaginative experience. Memorization is in the service of remembering.

 **IMAGINATIVE PRAYER**   The "Imaginative Prayer" is pretty straightforward. If you are leading your child through this material alone (without partnering with your local church),[8] each week you'll want to find a twenty- to thirty-minute time of quiet (not at bedtime) to lead your child through the imaginative prayer. I've written the exercises in such a way that you should be able to read each session out loud, slowly, and prayerfully, following the prompts—(*pause 8 seconds*)—for silence and cadence.[9]

Feel free to adjust the language for your household. Some of these prayers try to address themes (e.g., lust, racial injustice) that may feel a bit much for where your own child is in his or her experience or development. I've taken risks in introducing some important topics because true spiritual formation is rooted in the real world around us. You'll want to be aware of your own child's sensitivities and possible triggers that may be present in their emotional life. The imagination is a powerful tool and can often evoke emotions on par with real-life events.

Before each imaginative prayer, there is a short welcome of God's Spirit. I like to take three long, deep breaths before I begin, and I encourage the child to join me in those breaths. My hope is that you and your child will marinate in each theme and revisit that week's theme a little each day, even just for five minutes at the end of the day.

 **FOR THE PARENT OR MENTOR**   The "For the Parent or Mentor" section is meant for your own reflection and devotional life as a parent. This is where you can create that *shared vocabulary* of the experience of God. I encourage you to share openly with your child about your own interaction with the imaginative prayer and the questions that it might provoke for you. Your own vulnerability here will go a long way in forming the connection this volume intends.[10]

As you lead your child through this book, my hope is that you too will go deeper in your life with and experience of God. I've provided questions that are meant to help in your own formational life (as well as some further invitations for you to consider). I believe that most of what we pass on to our children comes out of who we are and our own experiences. In short, it's hard to lead someone where we ourselves haven't gone. If you want your child to experience the wealth of God's grace and forgiveness, it will go a long way for you to experience these first. You may have picked up this book with a desire to deposit some good things into your child. My prayer is that you too will see these next nine to twelve months as a journey in your own spiritual formation.

Suggested questions and conversation starters are found at the end of the section for parents or mentors. I've tried to provide more suggestions than you likely will be able to implement. The list of questions during the review week may seem particularly long. Just choose a few questions. Once you get going, your natural instincts will take over. These example questions are there in case you are stuck and need a quick reference.

These questions, and your own experience of the material, provide ever-so-brief moments of dialogue throughout the week (doing errands around town, walking to the school bus, eating meals). These moments will continue to solidify your child's experience as well as create more places of connection for both of you. You might be surprised by the conversation that opens up, though don't be discouraged if your child seems occasionally to lose interest. The goal is not to master the material. The material and exercises are here to foster connection and experience. If this starts feeling like a chore for you or homework for your child, something has gone off course.

 **FOR THE JOURNAL** At some point during the week you are encouraged to carve out fifteen to twenty minutes to encourage your child to write down some thoughts or draw a picture related to that week's imaginative prayer. Many adults have found that keeping a journal has aided tremendously in their spiritual journey and formation. Additionally, articulating their thoughts and emotions on paper can either make something more concrete, in the case of writing (which comes from the more literal and analytic left side of our brain) or can open up a richer emotional experience through drawing (which helps us access the more intuitive, emotive, and nonlinear right side of our brain). Just fifteen minutes once a week can help make that particular formational experience *stick*.

YOU ARE READY

You are now ready to dive in! But let me leave you with one last thought. Even with another nine months worth of material—which is currently being planned—I wouldn't be able to include every important scriptural theme or experience that you might hope to convey to your child about God's good news for the world. I've made no attempt here to be comprehensive.

As you work your way through these imaginative prayers with your child, you may wonder why *this* is included or why *that* is left out. There are even some imaginative prayers that aren't directly pulled from Scripture, but rather attempt to put your child in a make-believe setting in order to help them experience the deeper truth of a theological principle and experience of God, which may be the root of a larger theme of spiritual formation. Aslan on the stone table and the "deep magic" of Queen Jadis are two examples. There is no stone table in the Bible, but the image comes through, the scene does some heavy lifting, and there is something about that imagery that makes some things true of God's kingdom stick. Fiction does more than ask someone to believe something. "When we tell a story," and when we put ourselves into a story, "although we may hope to teach a lesson, our primary objective is to produce an imaginative experience."[11] These imaginative experiences, and the conversations that follow, I believe, will begin to do the work of spiritual formation in your child.

PART 1

God's Love

1

The most important part of the story is that God loves so many things.

2

That he loves *me*.

3

That when I am lost, he will come looking for me.

4

That when I am sick, he wants to heal me.

5

And when I make mistakes, he will always have grace on me.

6

There is nothing that can separate me from the *love* of God.

1

God loves so many things

 **CONNECTION AND FORMATION** The purpose of this imaginative prayer is to help your child experience how vast and wonderful the world is. Your child lives within God's ongoing creation. "It is the visual, fragrant, audible, touchable, and tastable manifestation of God's love, the place where God's desire that others be and be well finds earthly expression."[1] This creation is part of God's revelation, it is full of beauty, and God loves every bit of it.

We are trying to help your child find his or her place in a world that is deeply loved by God. This is the opening session of part one, which explores God's love. He is rich in love. He is not stingy. There are so many things that God loves.

Where we begin the formational journey can often determine where we end up. How we begin to tell the story can determine what kind of story we're telling. And here we begin with beauty and love. Scripture begins with a story about God placing Adam and Eve in a beautiful garden and inviting them to work in it and enjoy it. He placed them in a place where they would develop habits and rhythms that would allow his creation to do the work of forming them. We begin spiritual formation immersed in the beauty of God's creation, receiving it for the gift it was intended to be. What is the most important thing you hope your child will learn through these prayers? What is your intention as you enter into these formational prayer exercises?

St. Francis of Assisi also used his imagination when he considered God's creation. He imagined that God was the Creator and parent of all living things, and that all creatures were brother and sister to one another. Toward the end of his life, St. Francis of Assisi wrote a creation canticle demonstrating how he saw God's love incarnate in all of creation.

Be praised Good Lord for Brother Sun
who brings us each new day.
Be praised for Sister Moon: white
beauty bright and fair, with wandering
stars she moves through the night.
Be praised my Lord for Brother Wind,
for air and clouds and the skies of every season.
Be praised for Sister Water: humble,
helpful, precious, pure; she cleanses
us in rivers and renews us in rain.
Be praised my Lord for Brother fire:
he purifies and enlightens us.
Be praised my Lord for Mother Earth:
abundant source, all life sustaining;
she feeds us bread and fruit and gives us flowers.
Be praised my Lord for the gift of life;
for changing dusk and dawn; for touch
and scent and song.
Be praised my Lord for those who
pardon one another for love of thee,
and endure sickness and tribulation.
Blessed are they who shall endure it in
peace, for they shall be crowned by Thee.
Be praised Good Lord for sister Death
who welcomes us in loving embrace.
Be praised my Lord for all your
creation serving you joyfully.[2]

Question: What is the most important part of the story?
Answer: The most important part of the story is that God
loves so many things.

Say out loud to your child:

Close your eyes and let's take a few deep breaths together.

God, I pray that you will release our imagination and help us to hear you speak to us during this time together. We open our hands to you. We open our ears to you.

(pause 8-10 seconds)[3]

Come, Holy Spirit.

Close your eyes and imagine with me that you have the ability to fly into the air. Imagine with me, that you can fly like Superman. Where would you go? What would you go and see?

(pause 5 seconds)

Imagine that you fly into the air and that you watch as the ground gets farther away from you. You feel the wind pressing against you as you fly faster and faster. Imagine that you begin to notice how beautiful things are. You notice how beautiful and green the grass is. You notice the leaves, and you look across and see a great number of trees blowing in the wind. Off in the distance you see a body of water—the ocean—and you make your way toward the coast.

Imagine now that you dive into the water—and somehow you are able to breathe under water. You are swimming with thousands of fish. There are bright orange fish all around you, and they are beautiful. You swim past an octopus, a sea turtle, and a group of dolphins. You are captivated by the beauty around you. And then you see a big blue whale swim right in front of you.

You are surrounded by God's beautiful creation. There are so many things here beneath the water that God loves.

(pause 5-8 seconds)

Imagine now that you swim to the surface of the water and fly into the air. As you fly, you feel the warm sun dry off your body and you begin to think about where you should fly to next. Fly fast! Fly fast across the ocean and visit the beautiful mountains of France and Switzerland. Fly to the beautiful Victoria Falls in Zambia. Fly to the great rainforests in Brazil.

There are so many places in this world. There is so much beauty, so much of God's creation. There are so many things and places that God loves.

(pause 5 seconds)

Imagine now that you fly straight up into the air, breaking through the atmosphere like the space shuttle. Imagine looking back and seeing the earth get smaller and smaller. And it is beautiful. Look back at this planet. See the blue and the green. Find the reddish brown land of the southern part of Africa and the white polar icecaps. All the people who have ever lived have lived on this little planet. And they have been loved by God from the very beginning.

Keep your eyes closed and imagine that you are floating in outer space. You see the planets. You see the bright red glow of Mars, the perfect rings of Saturn, and a million zillion stars shining their light. Everything here is beautiful. There is so much that God loves.

(pause 5-8 seconds)

Fly now down to earth. Fly as quickly as you can. And go to your favorite forest. Imagine that you are in a forest with tall trees and there are beautiful flowers that line the forest floor.

Listen to the birds sing to you. Watch as little animals gather around you. Squirrels and foxes. Owls and rabbits. Imagine walking through the forest along a path, and imagine that the path is coming to an end. You reach the end of the path and there are two roads to choose from, one to the right and the other to the left. Stand there where the path splits into two.

(pause 5-8 seconds)

Which way do you want to go? Pick a trail: the one to the right or the one to the left. Imagine heading down that trail and you can see that the path is coming out of the forest and into a clearing. As you get closer to the clearing, you can see that it is a giant field of purple and yellow flowers, nearly as tall as you are. Imagine walking into the flowers. Notice their beauty. Pick a flower, smell it, and take in the smell.

(Parent: pretend to pick a flower and smell it. Breathe a deep breath into your nose so that you can hear your breath as you smell the flower.)

What does the flower smell like?

What does it feel like to be surrounded by such beauty?

(pause 5-8 seconds)

Imagine walking through the field of flowers. Feel the cool breeze blowing through. Notice how blue the sky looks.

This world is a good place. There are so many beautiful things here.

There are so many things to explore about the story of God in the world.

The most important part of the story is that God loves so many things.

 Question: What is the most important part of the story? *Answer:* The most important part of the story is that God loves so many things.

 What do you love about the world? Where is your favorite place? What beautiful places in the world have you visited? When is the last time that you simply looked at a flower? A butterfly? A tree? Many of our children have a nature deficit in their lives. Sometimes our lives are surrounded by plastic and metal and well-trimmed lawns and we can forget about the wild things. The invitation to your child to think about creation and notice the beauty in it is also an invitation to you. Help your child experience the wonder of beauty by nurturing the same in yourself.

Ask your child this question:

"What are some things in the world that you think are beautiful?"

Wait for it. Listen. Engage.

And then ask:

"Is there anything about that thing (the answer to the first question) that tells us something about what God is like?"

O Check out this book from the library: *Natural History: The Ultimate Visual Guide to Everything on Earth*, Smithsonian Series (New York: DK Publishing, 2010). Brew some hot tea or sit with a bowl of ice cream. Sit on the couch with your child and look at the book. Make this part of your routine (once a month?). Take a closer look at all the wonderful things in the world that spring forth from God's power to speak things into life. There are so many things that God loves.

O A few nights this week, as you tuck your child into bed, ask the question, "What did you notice today that was beautiful?" Help your child reflect on the day. Help him or her see the beauty in it.

O Take a long walk through the woods, the prairie, or along the ocean. Make a special trip someplace out of your everyday context, just to see a different part of God's beauty in the things he has made.

O Find a quiet place to sit and read out loud St. Francis's "Canticle of Creation" (see p. 36).

 **FOR THE JOURNAL** Set aside twenty minutes just once this week to sit with your child while he or she writes or draws in a journal. Ask them to spend just a few minutes thinking and writing or drawing an answer to this question: "What did you notice this week that was beautiful?"

2

....

He loves me

This week's imaginative prayer continues with the theme of God's love, but moves toward focusing the love and creativity of God specifically toward your child. Yes, God loves so many things. But more importantly, in terms of the way we experience God firsthand—he loves *me*. With this imaginative prayer we are providing an imaginative experience of being created with great care and detail. Right from the start we are giving your child an image and memory of the tender hands of Jesus, and his creative work in us (Col 1:16).

There is nothing more important to growing in Christlikeness (which is the goal of spiritual formation) than fully embracing God's love for *you*. Before doing any ministry in the world, before being *released* to do the work that the Father set out for Jesus, the Father blessed Jesus with these words: "This is my Son, whom I love; with him I am well pleased" (Mt 17:5). If we are going to set Jesus up as a model of how to follow after the heart of God, then we would do well to begin our journey where Jesus began it—receiving the love of the Father. "Divine love is absolutely unconditional, unlimited and unimaginably extravagant."[1]

God's love is something we learn about in hymns and songs and books of theology. But to experience God's love personally is different. And until we know it through experience, the whole story of Scripture feels like something for other times and other people. It may feel a bit self-focused to say that the most important part of God's story is his love for *me*. But this is the part of the story that makes sense of the rest of it. If it's not good news for *me*, it's not good news.

The root of Christian love is not the will to love, *but the faith that one is loved.* The faith that one is loved *by God.* The faith that one is loved by God although unworthy—or, rather, irrespective of one's worth![2]

 Question: Of all the things that God loves, what is the most important thing, to you?
Answer: That he loves *me.*

Close your eyes and let's take a few deep breaths together.

God, I pray that you will release our imagination and help us to hear you speak to us during this time together. We open our hands to you. We open our ears to you.

(pause 8-10 seconds)

Come, Holy Spirit.

Close your eyes and imagine that you see two hands knitting. Imagine there are two hands in front of you with a great ball of yarn sitting next to those hands. What color is the yarn? Is it all one color, or is it different colors? If you were to knit something special, what color yarn would you choose?

(pause 5-8 seconds)

Watch as the hands begin to shape the yarn into something. The yarn loops around the knitting needles and first begins to form a shape that you recognize. You aren't sure exactly what it is yet, but you have the sense that the person knitting is taking great care and paying attention to every detail. The hands that you see in front of you are strong hands, but they gently hook and loop the yarn so carefully.

You notice now that you begin to see a set of feet being formed. They are perfect feet and they seem about the same size as your feet. *(pause)* Suddenly you notice that these feet are no longer made of yarn; they seem to be real live feet, and yet the hands continue to knit more. This is very strange, indeed! But wait—it gets even stranger. It isn't just that these feet look like your feet, they *are* your feet! You can tell by looking at them. You know your own feet when you see them, and those are definitely your feet! What do your feet look like? Try to notice what you see.

Watch as the knitted legs turn into real legs. Your legs are right there connected to your feet. Someone is knitting with great detail and care, and everything they are knitting is coming to life. Watch as your body is knit together and formed. Your arms. Your hands. Your fingers. Imagine the hands that are knitting you pause a moment and reach out and grab one of *your* hands.

Are you wondering who this is? Who is knitting you and forming you from the ground up?

Let's continue to look closely. Watch as these hands knit your neck and begin working on your chin. Nobody's chin is like anyone else's. You have a unique chin.

Next, your lips. (*pause*) Your nose. (*pause*) Your cheeks. (*pause*) Your ears.

And finally your eyes. Imagine now that your whole body is almost formed and someone is knitting your eyes into place. Suddenly, you can see. You see the hands that are knitting you, you see the yarn lying next to you. You blink. And then you open your eyes to see that the hands are the hands of Jesus—they are bringing you into existence, bringing you into life. He knits. And you are created.

Think for a moment about who you are. Who God has made you to be. What do you notice about yourself?

What are you good at? (*pause*) What makes you laugh? (*pause*) What makes you cry?

When do you feel strong and confident? What activity makes you feel like you are doing something you were meant to do?

And when do you feel weak and maybe a little bit insecure? Are there things that you try to do that are hard for you?

God has knit you together to be just the way you are!

Can you think of anything that makes you uniquely *you*?

(pause 5-8 seconds)

Listen to these words of David, who wrote many psalms. He says:

> Oh yes, you shaped me first inside, then out;
>   you formed me [knit me (NIV)] in my mother's womb.
> I thank you, High God—you're breathtaking!
>   Body and soul, I am marvelously made!
>   I worship in adoration—what a creation!
> You know me inside and out,
>   you know every bone in my body;
> You know exactly how I was made, bit by bit,
>   how I was sculpted from nothing into something.
> Like an open book, you watched me grow from conception to birth;
>   all the stages of my life were spread out before you,
> The days of my life all prepared
>   before I'd even lived one day. (Ps 139:13-16 *The Message*)

Of all the things that God loves in the world, the most important thing to pay attention to is that he loves you.

The most important part of the story is that God loves so many things, and that he loves you in particular.

 Question: Of all the things that God loves, what is the most important thing, to you?
Answer: That he loves *me*.

 FOR THE PARENT OR MENTOR When it comes to God loving you, that *you* are the one being loved means that you are the object of God's affection. It means God loves you for you. Not for what you do or can do, not for what you can become, but just for who you are right now. Even our sin doesn't stop God from loving us, not merely because love is God's nature but because God cares about us that much. God loves you because you are you. God loves you for you. Pray that into your heart today: "You love me for me."[3] Your ability to teach your child how much God loves them will in large part depend on your own ability to receive God's love.

Ask,

○ What do you like about yourself? What are some things you like about who God has made you to be?

○ Help your child notice his or her distinct characteristics, both in their physical appearance as well as their personality. "You've got a dimple right there on your cheek. You are the only one who has *your* dimple." "You really enjoy reading don't you? God made you that way!" "I notice that you like to climb trees. You know, not every kid likes to climb trees."

○ Read Ephesians 3:14-19 with your child. Make it into a prayer. Pray it. Pray with your child that he or she would understand the richness of God's love for them. Ask your child to pray the same for you. Teach them to place their hand on your shoulder and pray for you. Receive it. Let your child feel the nature of a powerful prayer.

○ Remind your child: "Do you know that God is absolutely in love with you?" Then ask, "Why does God love you?" The answer will reveal a lot. Remind your child that God would love them under any circumstances.

○ One night this week make your bedtime reading Psalm 139. Read it slowly. Talk it through. Ask, "What does it feel like to know that God knows everything about you?"

 **FOR THE JOURNAL** "Together, let's make a list in your journal of things that are unique about *you*." Spend fifteen to twenty minutes this week helping your child jot down some thoughts and observations about what makes them unique. Make it fun and goofy. Pay attention to what your child notices—this could be a moment that you'll want to remember. What they say about what makes them unique could reveal something that you didn't know.

3

When I am lost,
he will look for me

 This imaginative prayer is meant to create an experience of *lostness* for your child. We all have had the feeling of being lost. It's lonely and it's scary. Jesus tells a great story about three things that get lost: the lost sheep, the lost coin, and the lost (prodigal) son. You can read the passage from Luke 15 this week with your child. Here, we are setting the stage for your child to begin to experience what Jesus is saying in Luke 15: God is seeking those who are lost. God loves us so much that he comes looking for us.

We grow in our love for God out of the recognition that he first loved us (1 Jn 4:19). Your child has likely yet to experience the sense of lostness of the prodigal son. But I wonder if he or she has experienced what it might be like to be trailing behind? To be off course in some way? We are hoping to create a memory of being rescued by Jesus. God does not leave us behind when we stumble. God does not walk quickly ahead of us, waiting for us to find our own way or catch up. He leaves the ninety-nine others and comes looking for us.

Q+A *Question:* What will God do for you if you get lost?
Answer: When I am lost, he will come looking for me.

IMAGINATIVE PRAYER

Close your eyes and let's take a few deep breaths together.

God, I pray that you will release our imagination and help us to hear you speak to us during this time together. We open our hands to you. We open our ears to you.

(pause 8-10 seconds)

Come, Holy Spirit.

Imagine with me that you are on a walk with some friends—lots of friends. Imagine that there are one hundred of you walking through the countryside, over hills, crossing streams. You are on a nature hike someplace in the wilderness. Imagine that you are feeling very safe. You are surrounded by a group of people. And you aren't really worried about where you are headed right now—somebody is leading you, and you are following the crowd as it walks through a grassy field. Though there doesn't seem to be a trail to follow.

Next, imagine that you spot something colorful at the edge of the forest. It looks like a bright spot in the middle of the brown tree trunks and the green leaves. You want to take a closer look to see what the bright and colorful spot might be. It isn't very far away from everyone else, so you leave the crowd of friends, just for a moment, to take a closer look at what you have discovered.

(pause 5-8 seconds)

You are walking now all by yourself as you head toward the edge of the forest. You can still hear the others chatting as you continue toward the bright spot in the trees. However, as you walk, you discover that the bright spot is much farther away than you had thought.

(pause 5 seconds)

You arrive now at the edge of the forest. The bright spot is nothing more than an old orange hunter's hat—bright orange—that was left behind by someone a long time ago. You notice that it is stuck on the end of a branch. It looks old and worn out, so you leave it where you find it.

As you turn back to join your friends you notice that they are pretty far off in the valley. You can see them turning a corner off in the distance, and they head into the forest. You begin to run as fast as you can in order to catch up, but you realize that you are in a bit of trouble as you watch the last one head into the forest. You continue to run fast in order to catch up. But by the time you reach the place where they entered into the forest, they are nowhere to be found.

You are alone. You are lost.

(pause 5-8 seconds)

Imagine that as you stand here, all alone, at the edge of the forest, you begin listening for voices. Though you can't see your friends, you wonder if you are really quiet and listen hard enough perhaps you will hear them. And so you wait.

(pause 5 seconds)

You don't hear anything and so you begin to go down a path through the forest. You notice that it is getting darker, and the wind begins to pick up. It's also getting colder. The sun is setting.

You are alone. You are lost.

And then, to make matters worse, it begins to rain.

You find some shelter underneath a hemlock tree. You begin to wonder how this could happen. How could you have gotten lost? *(pause)* There are ninety-nine others somewhere in this forest, and you are the only one who is lost. You are the one who is alone.

(pause 5-8 seconds)

What does it feel like to be alone and lost? Imagine what it would be like to be cold, wet, and in the dark.

(pause 5 seconds)

You begin to shiver, and as you reach for some leaves to cover you up, suddenly, you hear a gentle voice calling out your name.

You crawl quickly from underneath the tree to look around for the voice.

Imagine looking up to find that it is Jesus. He wraps a blanket around you to keep you warm. You walk through the woods and come out into an open clearing where the whole group is standing. They had been looking for you all along. They noticed that you were missing, and they stopped walking in order to look for you. What does it feel like to be noticed?

To be looked for?

To be found?

(pause 5 seconds)

What does it feel like to be the one that Jesus came looking for?

There are so many things in the world that God loves.

Of all the things he loves in the world, the most important is that he loves you. He loves me.

He loves you so much that when you are lost, he will come looking for you.

 Question: What will God do for you if you get lost?
Answer: When I am lost, he will come looking for me.

FOR THE PARENT OR MENTOR   When is the last time you took some time to *remember your own story?* When was the last time you reflected on your own sense of lostness throughout your life? Be reminded this week that you are engaged in a process of sharing with your child a story of God's great love. You are investing in your child because someone once invested in telling their God story to you. Spend some time this week reflecting on your own spiritual journey. How does remembering your own story make you feel? Where do you see the kindness of God in it? When were the periods in your life where you felt God seeking after you?

O Ask your child to tell you about a time they felt lost (or actually were lost). Share with your child a story from your own life about a season when you felt lost—perhaps a time when you didn't have life with God. How did God come looking for you? Tell the story to your child. Tell some of your story!

○ This week read Luke 15:1-10 several times together. Your child should feel the familiarity of the story because their imaginative prayer from this week put them exactly in the same spot as the lost sheep. Remind them that this is a story Jesus told when the religious leaders were complaining that Jesus was spending too much time with people who weren't following God. Jesus tells two stories about people looking for something that was lost. God looks for lost people. Imagine Jesus eating with people who don't have life with God: this is what it looks like when God is looking for lost people.

○ Talk with your child this week about the reality that some people are not connected to God. Ask your child, "How do you think God feels about this? What do you think Jesus was trying to say when he told the stories about the lost coin, the lost sheep, and the lost son?"

○ Ask, "Do you know anyone (at school, in the neighborhood, on your sports team) that maybe doesn't have life with God?" Pray with your child for the person(s) that come to mind.

 **FOR THE JOURNAL** Encourage your child this week to take fifteen minutes to make a list of people in their life who seem lost. "Who do you know that doesn't have life with God?" Sit with your child as they make a list of those people. Pray for those people with your child. Thank God together for *looking* for you when you were lost. Ask God to seek the people on this list. Encourage your child to ask God how they may participate in extending God's love and invitation to the people on this list.

4

....

When I am sick,
he wants to heal me

**CONNECTION AND FORMATION** This week we are im-
mersing your child in a
story of being healed from blindness, based on the Mark 10 passage where
a man named Bartimaeus receives his sight. God wants to heal sickness and
disease. Jesus lived in a rhythm of life where he consistently participated in
this kind of *kingdom* work. This lesson is primarily about God's love—he
loves us so much that when we are sick he wants to heal us. However, when
we pray for people they often don't get well, and this creates some tension.
We want to be upfront about the tensions in our faith and life with God.
These tensions create space for conversation. And the conversation about
the reality that God heals some people while others remain sick is a conversation that creates connection.

One of the most challenging areas of spiritual formation are questions
we hold that remain unanswered. We begin to gather these questions at a
young age, far before there are natural contexts to wrestle through them.
While this week's imaginative prayer will lead your child through an example of when someone did receive healing, it's also likely that your child
knows someone who hasn't received healing. Perhaps your child is sick or
suffering in some way. As children imagine themselves in the story, we're
trusting that they can make an emotional connection to the way Jesus moves
toward Bartimaeus.

Question: What does God want to do for you when you get sick?
Answer: When I am sick, he wants to heal me.

 **IMAGINATIVE PRAYER**

Close your eyes and let's take a few deep breaths together.

God, I pray that you will release our imagination and help us to hear you speak to us during this time together. We open our hands to you. We open our ears to you.

(pause 8-10 seconds)

Come, Holy Spirit.

Close your eyes and imagine you are blind. Imagine you can't see anything at all. Imagine you always need to be led from one place to another.

What would it be like for you in school if you were blind?

Would you be able to play baseball?

Soccer?

Video games?

How would it feel to not be able to see?

(pause 5-8 seconds)

Imagine you couldn't see the faces of the people you love. Imagine you didn't know what your mom or dad looked like. What would it be like to only be able to recognize that your friends are in the room by the sound of their voices?

(pause 5-8 seconds)

If you were blind, would you want to see?

(pause 5-8 seconds)

Imagine you are living in a time when blind people had to beg for food. Picture in your mind that you are sitting on the side of a dusty road in the center of a small town. You have a metal cup in your hand. And from time to time, people drop coins into your cup. This is how you live. Every day you beg for food and money.

You also have a bowl next to you. This bowl is for food. Because you are blind, you are poor. You have no one to take care of you, and so you beg for food each day, and from time to time people bring you a cup of rice to eat. Or, when you are lucky, a nice big piece of pizza.

What would it feel like to beg for food and money? To not see the faces of the people taking care of you each day but to only hear their voices?

(pause 5-8 seconds)

Imagine smelling the rice as someone brings some by for you. You are grateful for the warm rice. You are grateful you can eat today.

Suddenly, off in the distance you hear a large crowd coming down the road. You know that a crowd is coming because you can hear all the feet shuffling. There are more people walking your way than usual, and there are more voices. Everyone is moving toward one section of the street. Someone, it seems, is leaving town, and a great crowd is following. You begin to wonder who might attract such a crowd.

(pause 5 seconds)

And then you hear that it is Jesus. Imagine your heart begins to race and you feel a great rush of excitement come over you. You have heard Jesus pass this way before. You remember that the last time Jesus passed this way people were rejoicing when someone was healed of a great sickness.

Imagine that you begin to crawl toward the crowd, and in your excitement you call out the name of Jesus.

(with enthusiasm) Jesus! Jesus! Son of David! Have mercy on me, Jesus! Jesus! Have mercy on me!

Over and over and over again, you call out the name of Jesus.

Jesus, have mercy on me! Jesus!

Imagine that some people are telling you to be quiet. Some people are rebuking you for causing such a scene. The crowd is starting to notice you, and people are looking at you. They are telling you to be quiet.

Jesus! Jesus! Jesus! Have mercy on me!

What does it feel like to call out for Jesus?

(pause 5 seconds)

Then the crowd grows quiet and it sounds as though everyone has stopped. You hear someone coming toward you, and someone says to you, "It's your lucky day! Get up! He's calling you to come!" (Mk 10:49 *The Message*).

Imagine rising up to your feet. Someone is leading you toward Jesus. You can overhear him talking to others. What does it feel like to hear the voice of Jesus? Listen as Jesus begins to talk with you.

He asks you a question: "What do you want me to do for you?" (v. 51).

What does it feel like for Jesus to reach out and take your hands and ask you a question?

Oh how you have longed to look someone in the eyes, to see their face. Imagine what it would be like to say these words: Jesus, I want to see.

And in an instant, Jesus speaks again and your eyes are opened.

"Your faith has healed you," he says (v. 52).

Look at the face of Jesus. Look around you at the crowd that has gathered. Look at people's faces. They are amazed.

God loves you so much that when you are sick he wants to heal you.

(pause for a longer time of reflection—maybe 15-20 seconds)

The most important part of the story is that God loves so many things . . .

That he loves you.

That when you are lost, he will come looking for you.

That when you are sick, he wants to heal you.

Question: What does God want to do for you when you get sick?
Answer: When I am sick, he wants to heal me.

 FOR THE PARENT OR MENTOR As you are out and about with your child, spend some time this week looking for where God might be at work around you. For example, as you walk into the grocery store, pray out loud with your child, "God, will you show us anyone in the grocery store that needs to receive your healing." Talk with your child about what it might look like to pray for someone in the grocery store. Follow the lead of the Spirit. If he leads, pray for someone. Your faith will be a model for your child. What resistance do you feel to this? Where do you feel God's welcome into this kind of partnership?

○ Engage with your child with these questions: "Is there anything you would like to ask God to heal you of?" This question can begin with the obvious bumps and bruises, but can also open up some questions about hurts in the heart. "Is there anything that you are sad about that we could pray about together?" Listen well. Pray. Lay hands on each other and pray.

○ Together read the passage in Mark 10:46-52 a few times this week.

○ What do you notice about Bartimaeus? Ask your child some questions that will help them look at what is going on in this story. Invite your child to observe the scene unfolding. What else do you see going on in the story?

○ Spend some time this week talking with your child about something happening in the world that God wants to heal. Is there someone you know that has cancer? Is there an outbreak of some disease in a distant country? Engage your child in conversation this week about sickness and disease.

○ Is there anyone you know who is sick? Take a few minutes each day to pray for that person. Does your church have a hospital-visitation ministry? Take your child along to pray for someone in the hospital.

 **FOR THE JOURNAL** Encourage your child to pick one person they know and write a prayer requesting God to heal that person. Is someone at your child's school in a wheelchair? Is there someone you know that has to go to the hospital often? Is there anyone you know that is fighting cancer? Invite your child to look at this situation, to really engage the suffering that might be going on in someone else's life. Encourage your child to write a prayer in their journal specifically related to the situation you talk about.

5

When I make mistakes, he will always have grace on me

CONNECTION AND FORMATION This week's imaginative prayer revisits the story of the prodigal son (Lk 15). Like the story of the lost sheep and the lost coin, the story of the son who leaves the safety of his father's estate to make his own way in the world highlights what God thinks of those who are spiritually lost—even when the lostness is of their own doing. Your child will learn that God's love means that God is gracious, every time. He is like the father who is waiting for his son's return. This week we will focus on God's grace and the culture of *grace* and *forgiveness* in your home.

God's love for children doesn't depend on whether they ever do anything right or holy or excellent. The love of God for your child is full and complete and perfect. This imaginative prayer is meant to be a playful way of helping your child experience one of the key stories that define what God is like. The journey of spiritual formation progresses as we become increasingly aware of sin, and of God's grace and forgiveness. There are seasons when our sin is highlighted and we experience its weight.

Children experience many emotions and changes in their lives. You may be unaware of how your child's own awareness of wrongdoing may be affecting their connection with God. Children can carry their own shame in secret and quiet places in their young souls and bodies. Their spirit can feel the guilt and shame of wrongdoing (and even simple mistakes) without having the words or sense to name those feelings for what they are. Grace and forgiveness can never be overdone, particularly in a culture of much scrutiny and perfectionism.

Question: How does God respond when you make mistakes? *Answer*: When I make mistakes, he will always have grace on me.

Close your eyes and let's take a few deep breaths together.

God, I pray that you will release our imagination and help us to hear you speak to us during this time together. We open our hands to you. We open our ears to you.

(pause 8-10 seconds)

Come, Holy Spirit.

With your eyes closed, imagine with me that you are part of a very wealthy family. Imagine that you have everything you could possibly want. Your family is very rich. Imagine you are the younger of two children. You have an older brother. And you and your brother both work in the family business. Your father has built the family business over many years, and your family is a well-known and very successful family.

(pause 5-8 seconds)

Imagine one day your father is talking about what will happen in the future when he can no longer manage the business. You and your brother will divide the business between you. Your brother will get part of the business and you will take another part. It is a large business with a great deal of wealth involved. What would it be like to know that you will inherit a great deal of money someday?

(pause 5-8 seconds)

How does this make you feel?

(pause 5-8 seconds)

Now imagine that something happens. There is some conflict that arises between you and your brother and you and your father. Imagine something happens that makes you want to run away from home, and imagine you are actually old enough to do it. It seems better to first get the money that is coming to you before you leave home.

Imagine going to your father and asking him for your share of the inheritance. Tell your father that you want your inheritance right now.

(pause 5 seconds)

Your father is a kind and reasonable man. Imagine that after giving it some thought, he agrees that you should leave. Your father sells part of his business in order to give you the portion of the inheritance he has promised to you. You notice also that some of the things your family owns are now gone. Your father has sold them in order to keep his promise to you. Your father is busy for weeks in order to gather up enough money for your inheritance.

Imagine your father comes to you one morning and hands you a bag of money, gives you a hug, and lets you know that you are free to go out into the world. He hands you your inheritance. What does it feel like to have this new freedom? Where would you like to go first? What do you want to do with all that money?

(pause 5-8 seconds)

Imagine that you are old enough to drive. You hop into a new car and drive away to seek a new life. You stop first at your favorite ice cream store. Imagine getting the biggest ice cream sundae you have ever had. You eat it quickly rather than how you usually eat ice cream, which is slowly, savoring each and every bite. You have enough money in your backpack to eat an ice cream sundae every day for the next few years! Who needs to savor the ice cream when you can have another one tomorrow?

Next you stop at a restaurant and the movies and the comic book store or your favorite place to buy new clothes. You stop at all the places you love to visit, and you begin to spend the money that your father gave to you. What does the freedom feel like? What does it feel like to be able to have anything you could possibly want?

(pause 5-8 seconds)

Imagine you live like this for quite some time. You travel far from where you live. You go to Disney World and meet new friends. You watch all the new movies in the theater. You eat ice cream every day. And you do all of this for a long time. Sometimes you miss home. Sometimes you miss your mom and dad. And yes sometimes you even miss your older brother. But you are having a lot of fun! You buy everything you want and go everywhere you could possibly go to.

But then everything changes.

The money runs out.

Your new friends leave you.

And you are far away from home.

What would you do if this happened? How would you have money to eat?

(pause 5-8 seconds)

You realize that perhaps you have made a mistake.

Now you are sleeping on a park bench at night. You have a blanket to cover you, but that's it. You are completely out of money. There is no one to turn to. Imagine how lonely you would feel so far away from home.

Imagine you find a job. Someone feels sorry for you and offers to pay you to pick up dog poop in the park. People love to walk their dogs in the park, but dogs poop and somebody needs to clean it up. Today, that somebody is you! All day long you pick up dog poop at the park so you can have enough money to buy something to eat.

Imagine that one night, as you feel chilly while trying to sleep on the park bench, you remember what it was like to sleep in your bed at home. You remember what it was like to eat breakfast with your family. You remember playing hopscotch and riding a skateboard with your friends. You remember how much time your dad and mom spent with you playing games, taking you to the park, working alongside of you, teaching you new things. You realize that your life would be better if you went home. But how could you possibly tell your father that you spent all the money?

(pause 5-8 seconds)

Imagine that you wake up the next morning and you go to the train station to catch a train home. It will take you a couple of days to get home, but you are convinced that you won't survive unless you do. At the very least, you think, you could work in your father's business. Even if he is angry with you, he will hire you to work in his company.

Imagine what you will say to your father when you see him.

How could you even begin to explain where all the money went? You realize that you have made a terrible mistake. You have been mean and disrespectful and unkind. As you ride the train home, you begin to cry. Do you feel sad? Angry? Embarrassed?

(pause 5-8 seconds)

You wake up the next morning as you pull into your neighborhood.

You begin to walk home, rehearsing what you think you might say to your father. You have been preparing a speech—an apology. You've been trying to figure out what to say so that your father might take you back and not be angry with you.

But just as you begin making your way onto your street, you see your father.

Imagine your father sees you from far off and begins to run toward you. He is running toward you and is crying. He is crying and laughing at the same time. Watch your father run toward you. Imagine that he gives you a giant hug; he wraps his arms around you and picks you up and begins to dance with joy. You don't even have a chance to deliver your speech. You no longer feel embarrassed or angry or sad. You feel wanted. You feel special. You feel forgiven.

Imagine your father carries you home on his shoulders. You walk into your home and there is a great feast that has been thrown for you. Someone brings you a new set of clothes to put on and new shoes to wear. You notice all of your friends around, and your family has prepared your favorite food, and yes your favorite ice cream too! Imagine your father raises a glass and the room grows quiets. Through tears and laughter your father says, "I am so happy today. My child who was lost has been found. My child who went away has come home again."

This is what happens when you make a mistake in the kingdom of God.

The most important part of the story is that God loves so many things.

That he loves you.

That when you are lost, he will look for you.

That when you are sick, he wants to heal you.

And when you make mistakes, he will always have grace on you.

Question: How does God respond when you make mistakes?
Answer: When I make mistakes, he will always have grace on me.

FOR THE PARENT OR MENTOR What do you do when your children make a mistake? Or when they are disobedient? Your children's training in the way of Jesus has as much to do with the answer to these questions as it has to do with any set of beliefs or doctrine. Pay attention this week to where you see grace flowing out of you and where it isn't. Ask your children what they feel when they make a mistake. Ask them if they know what *grace* means. The answer to this question will reveal so much. Spend some time this week reflecting on God's grace and kindness in your own life. How does reflecting on this impact your grace and kindness toward your own child?

O   "Did you receive any grace from God today?" The response I have gotten is, "What do you mean?" That's a great question. There is a great image in Hebrews 4:16 about the way we are to receive grace from God. We approach God with confidence to get the grace we need, when we need it.

O   Ask your child, "Did you make any mistakes today? Were you impatient or unkind to anyone?" Your child will most likely answer yes. "Well, if you made mistakes today, talk to God about it, approach him with confidence to get the grace you need." Help your child understand that mistakes and grace are part of each day. Help them begin the habit of thinking through their day, acknowledging the mistakes, and getting the grace they need. Reread the passage from Hebrews 4:16.

○ "But where sin increased, grace increased all the more" (Rom 5:20). Read this verse to your child. Show your child a small pile of laundry, one that has just a few items in it. "Let's pretend that this is all the sin in all the world. And that one sock, that's your sin. That sock represents all your disobedience, all your mistakes, all your impatience and unkindness." Now, get the fullest basket of laundry that you have, one piled high over the edge. "This basket of laundry is like the grace of God. It's filled to the brim. It is overflowing." Dump the big basket of laundry on the small pile. "Where sin increased, grace increases more!"

 **FOR THE JOURNAL** Encourage your child to take a few minutes to write in their journal. Help them make a list of times this week when they really needed God's grace and forgiveness. As you review the week together, don't rehash old conflicts from the week. Resist the temptation to point out faults that your child didn't bring up. Give your child some space to reflect and say out loud areas where God's grace is needed this week. Be the extra encouragement to them that they may need. God always is gracious to us when we make mistakes.

6

There is nothing that
can separate me from
the love of God

This week our imagi-
native prayer takes on a
slightly different form. We're picking up on one image the apostle Paul gives
us in Romans. Paul makes a list for us in Romans 8 to help us understand
there is nothing that can separate us from the love God has for us. One of
the images that Paul uses is *heights and depths*. The greatest height and the
greatest depth would of course be separated by a great distance. Paul says
that the greatest distance we can imagine can't separate us from the love of
God. This week your child will experience separation from God's love by
imagining being on one side of a large canyon and that God's love is off in
the distance. The separation and distance gets closed by the *presence* of Jesus.
This final lesson on God's love will prepare us for part two, where we explore
what it looks like to love others.

Nothing can separate your child from the love of God. And yet so many
children feel unloved and unlovable. Unworthy. Disconnected. What if in
spite of all the back-of-the-bus name calling and all the inner torment that
some experience in middle school, at the end of the day your child knew
and experienced the presence of Jesus filling up the great canyon of darkness
that is disconnection?

God's love is full and complete and able to reach to your child even when
your own tank of love feels dry and overwhelmed. And as much as we would
like to think our love for our child is complete and unending, it isn't. We
have limits. Limits are a gift to us and to our children in ways that make

space for the real and complete love of God to make up the difference. Our love for our child is but a matchstick to the fierce flame of God's love.

 Question: What can separate you from the love of God? *Answer*: There is nothing that can separate me from the love of God.

 **IMAGINATIVE PRAYER**

Close your eyes and let's take a few deep breaths together.

God, I pray that you will release our imagination and help us to hear you speak to us during this time together. We open our hands to you. We open our ears to you.

(pause 8-10 seconds)

Come, Holy Spirit.

Imagine you are standing on the edge of the Grand Canyon. Imagine you are on one side of the Grand Canyon and everything that you love—your friends and family—are on the other side of the canyon. Imagine looking across a great big giant hole that separates you from everything that you love.

Now imagine that this canyon completely surrounds you. It isn't just in front of you, but it's also behind you and to your left and right.

Picture in your mind the deepest canyon you can imagine.

You are surrounded on all sides by a giant canyon.

Your mom and dad are on the other side of the canyon. You turn around and look the other direction and see that all of your friends are on the other side.

Everything is so far away. What is the widest and deepest canyon that you can imagine?

(pause 8-10 seconds)

What does it feel like to be so separated from everything you love?

What does it feel like to be so far away from everything?

(pause 8-10 seconds)

What else do you picture, other than your friends and family, on the other side of the canyon?

Maybe some books that you would like to read. A beautiful flower. A mysterious forest that you would like to explore. A warm blanket to cover you. Picture all the things you enjoy sitting on the other side of this canyon.

What does it feel like to have all of those things so far away from you, across the widest and deepest canyon you have ever seen?

(pause 8-10 seconds)

Now imagine that you turn around and see something beautiful way off in the distance. You are not sure what it is, but you get the sense that the thing is a big box. It looks like a giant treasure chest. And you badly want to know what is inside that chest. Except that it is so far away that it looks like a toy LEGO treasure chest.

And standing between you and that treasure chest is the deepest and widest canyon that you can imagine.

Whatever is inside the chest is something that you desire, and yet you aren't quite sure what is in it. You want it so badly that you can feel yourself drawn to the treasure chest, almost like it's a magnet. The force is so strong on you that you nearly slip down the cliff trying to stay on your feet. You grab onto a tree next to you so you won't fall, and then you notice that sitting next to the tree is your book bag. You remember, all of a sudden, that you have a pair of very powerful binoculars inside that bag.

You take out the binoculars and focus them on the chest to see if you can see any clues as to what might be in the chest.

There is a sign on the chest and the sign says this: *(pause)* Inside this treasure chest is the love of God.

God's love is inside this chest. And you can feel yourself being pulled toward the chest.

But there is this very deep and wide canyon between you and the chest.

How does this make you feel?

(pause)

In a letter to one of the churches the apostle Paul writes, "I'm absolutely convinced that nothing—nothing living or dead, angelic or demonic, today or tomorrow, high or low, thinkable or unthinkable—absolutely *nothing* can get between us and God's love because of the way that Jesus our Master has embraced us" (Rom 8:38-39 *The Message*).

Nothing can separate us from the love of God.

(pause 8-10 seconds)

So imagine now that Jesus has joined you on this island of land surrounded by a deep canyon. He holds out his hands and something happens to the canyon. It starts filling up with land. The canyon gets filled up with beautiful grass and flowers. It's magical to watch the earth spring forth out of nothing. Jesus is filling in the space between you and the treasure chest.

The chest full of God's love is starting to feel closer to you. And it is drawing you closer and closer.

It's as though the force of it pulling you closer is getting stronger.

Jesus is standing right next to you and takes your hand. He leads you onto the land of flowers where the canyon used to be. The land is soft on your feet, and Jesus has your hand. You are walking with Jesus toward the chest, and when you get to the chest imagine that Jesus takes you by the shoulders and invites you to stand right in front of the chest.

(pause 5 seconds)

Get this picture in your head: you are standing in front a beautiful chest that has inside it the love of God.

Now Jesus is bending down. He is on his knees waiting to open the chest. He looks up at you, and you can feel the power of what is inside that chest.

Jesus opens the chest, and out of the chest flows the love of God onto you. It feels like a warm bath without the water. Your heart feels warm, and you feel completely loved. What does it feel like to experience the love of God?

(pause)

What does God's love look like as it comes out of the chest?

You have your eyes closed and you are standing there as God's love pours out all over your body. You open your eyes and realize that Jesus is no longer sitting next to the chest but has his arms around you. He is hugging you.

And the love of God keeps flowing out of the chest.

God's love is flowing out of the chest right onto you.

(pause 30 seconds)

The most important part of the story is that God loves so many things.

That he loves you.

That when you are lost he will look for you.

That when you are sick, he wants to heal you.

And when you make mistakes, he will always have grace on you.

There is nothing that can separate you from the love of God.

Question: What can separate you from the love of God? *Answer*: There is nothing that can separate me from the love of God.

FOR THE PARENT OR MENTOR What do you do when you feel separated from God? When you—or perhaps God—feels distant? When we find our experience of God is not what we want it to be, it is important to notice what might be going on around us and in us that could be causing the spiritual distance. Sometimes it is a result of our own inattentiveness toward prayer or our lack of awareness of God's work in our life. Other times it has nothing to do with us. St. Ignatius reminds us that sometimes God's *distance* from us is a form of grace that reminds us of how truly good it is when we experience the nearness of God. Sometimes we experience God as distant and far away not because there is anything wrong but because he is maturing us. He's growing us up by nurturing a dependence on him and reminding us that we are forever in need of God's grace.

And yet.

We desire closeness to and the nearness of God. And there is nothing that can separate us from him in the real world, where our imagined distances fade away and the stories we tell ourselves always line up with how things really are rather than how we often (wrongly) imagine. We do experience distance, but there is the reality that God is still right there loving us.

With nothing in between.

○ Spend some time this week at bedtime helping your child review their day. Try to pay particular attention to helping your child think about times when they may have felt unloved that day. Ask, "What was going on when you felt unloved?" "When today did you feel loved?" And "When did you feel loved by God?" Listen well. Give some hugs. Encourage gratefulness and thankfulness. As you make emotional connections with your children, you are teaching them to pay attention to what is going on inside.

○ Help your child pay attention to when and how they feel loved. "What felt good about your day today?" Paying attention to these kinds of things will help nurture awareness.

○ Have a conversation with your child about James 1:17. Read it out loud together. Every good thing comes from God. Repeat that: "Every good thing comes from God." Ask your child if anything good happened today. Help them find at least one thing; this good thing is a gift from God. This is God reminding us of his love for us.

 **FOR THE JOURNAL**   Encourage your child to spend fifteen minutes thinking about things in their week that made them feel loved. Write at the top of a new page in their journal: "I felt loved this week when . . ." Remind your child that oftentimes God's love comes to us through the people around us. Moms and dads, brothers and sisters, friends and teachers—they are all gifts from God to us. This kind of reflection can sometimes be hard for kids. God's love can feel so intangible. Help them make the connection. Don't give up too easily, and don't let them give up. If they are having a hard time thinking of things that made them feel loved, name some ways you feel loved. Ask them about some specific things from their week. "When grandma came over and brought cookies, did that make you feel loved? Okay, let's write that down on your list."

The most important part of the story is that God loves so many things.
That he loves *me*.
That when I am lost, he will come looking for me.
That when I am sick, he wants to heal me.
And when I make mistakes, he will always have grace on me.
There is nothing that can separate me from the *love* of God.

CREEDAL QUESTIONS AND ANSWERS

Question: What is the most important part of the story?
Answer: The most important part of the story is that God loves so many things.

Question: Of all the things that God loves, what is the most important thing to you?
Answer: That he loves *me*.

Question: What will God do for you if you get lost?
Answer: When I am lost, he will come looking for me.

Question: What does God want to do for you when you get sick?
Answer: When I get sick, God wants to heal me.

Question: How does God respond when you make mistakes?
Answer: When I make mistakes, he will always have grace on me.

Question: What can separate you from the love of God?
Answer: There is nothing that can separate me from the love of God.

QUESTIONS AND ACTIVITIES

O Spend time this week reviewing each of the past six weeks through everyday conversations and observations.

O Ask some good questions or make some suggestions that might stimulate reflection. For example:

- What are some beautiful things you noticed this week?

- Is there anything in creation that you are currently enjoying? What?

- Let's pay attention this week to the way we feel loved by God through other people.

- How is God loving you this week?

- Tell me something about you that makes you unique. How do you feel about that?

- Do you know anyone who you might want to ask God to look for? Is there anyone (at school, in the neighborhood) that seems a little *lost* right now? Tell me who they are.

- Let's be on the lookout this week for people we can pray for.

- How have you experienced forgiveness this week?

- Have you received God's grace this week for anything? Did you give grace to anyone this week? If so, who?

- Has there been any time this week when you have felt close to God? Will you share this with me?

○ Review the portion of the creedal poem that corresponds with part one. Help your child memorize these first six lines. Again, think poetry slam! We're not testing here for proficiency but a little hard work to make these stick will pay off in the end.

PART 2

Loving Others

7

God invites us
to live a life of love

CONNECTION AND FORMATION This week's imaginative
prayer leads your child
through the experience of sitting with the apostle Paul's description of *love*
in 1 Corinthians 13. We all are tempted to boast. We often take pride in our
abilities and gifts. We tend to measure our lives by external indicators like
status, power, and affirmation. It shows up in the church too. And when our
focus is on measuring our lives by external indicators like spiritual gifts or
even spiritual disciplines, we can overlook more important issues of moti-
vation, intention, and desires. Paul's message is simple; it doesn't matter how
great you are at anything—what matters is love. Every other way we try to
impress people simply fades. And yet love lasts. It alone remains.

Our prayer this week is more rooted in the practice of *lectio divina* and
may feel slightly different from other more *image-based* and imaginative
prayers in this book. Lectio divina is Latin for "spiritual reading" and has
been practiced in the church since the first century. In lectio, we read a se-
lected text slowly, "chewing on it" and sitting with it in a way that welcomes
God's instruction and invitation.[1]

Paul's description of love is a handy reference for reflecting on our need
for the grace of God to empower our love. God's invitation to us is to love.
And we spend a lifetime learning to do it. How do we teach our children to
love when our own example often falls so short? While I am growing in my
patience as a father, the honest truth is that I am often not very patient.
Sometimes I'm not gentle. Reflection on 1 Corinthians 13 can open up
conversation about the kind of love God has, and how he is inviting us to
love others with that same kind of love.

Encourage your child this week toward an understanding that the kind of love spoken about in 1 Corinthians 13 is what we lean toward. Loving in this way can only happen when we let God love through us. Like anything else worth doing, love requires learning.

Question: What is God's invitation to us?
Answer: God invites us to live a life of love.

Close your eyes and let's take a few deep breaths together.

God, I pray that you will release our imagination and help us to hear you speak to us during this time together. We open our hands to you. We open our ears to you.

(pause 8-10 seconds)

Come, Holy Spirit.

With our eyes closed, imagine with me that you are one of the smartest people in your school or your neighborhood. Imagine that everyone looks to you because you are so smart. Imagine you are invited to all the birthday parties. And when a game is being played, you are always the first one to be picked. Imagine when your teacher asks a question that no one else knows the answer to, you raise your hand and answer it.

(pause for 10 seconds)

Imagine people always ask you how to do something. They always invite you over to help them with their projects because you are so smart. And you also play sports. Imagine you are good at sports. And everyone wants you on their team.

What if you did everything just right?

Imagine you always do the right thing. That you listen to your mom or dad, and do what they say. And you serve in your community; you are always helping people. Imagine you give all your allowance money to the poor. Maybe you give all your money away that you earn for chores around your house. Imagine you give it all away to orphans living in Cambodia or India or Syria.

What would it feel like to be good at so many things? To do the right thing so many times? To always be liked? To always be invited? To always be picked first to be on a team?

(pause 8-10 seconds)

The apostle Paul tells us that even if all of these things were true, none of it would matter if we didn't love people. Jesus came to show us what it means to love.

The apostle Paul wrote a letter to people just like you and me living a long time ago. He's trying to help them understand that love is the most important thing.

(read slowly and meditatively)

> If I speak in the tongues of men or of angels, but do not have love, I am only a resounding gong or a clanging cymbal. If I have the gift of prophecy and can fathom all mysteries and all knowledge, and if I have a faith that can move mountains, but do not have love, I am nothing. If I give all I possess to the poor and give over my body to hardship that I may boast, but do not have love, I gain nothing.
> Love is patient, love is kind. It does not envy, it does not boast, it is not proud. It does not dishonor others, it is not self-seeking, it is not easily angered, it keeps no record of wrongs. Love does not delight in evil but rejoices with the truth. It always protects, always trusts, always hopes, always perseveres.
> Love never fails. (1 Cor 13:1-8)

Imagine that you can speak in a special language. And imagine that you could hear what God wanted to say to people, and that God was speaking to you some things that he wanted you to tell other people. Have you ever felt like God was speaking directly to you? Imagine again that God has given you a very generous heart. Imagine what it would feel like to give all your money and all your toys to children around the world who don't have money or toys of their own.

Imagine that you had all of these gifts:

The gift of a special language.

The gift of hearing God's voice.

The gift of a very generous heart.

Imagine that you had all of these things but you didn't know how to love.

What do you think it would be like to not know how to love?

God invites us to live a life of love.

Listen again to the same passage with slightly different words.

(read slowly and meditatively)

If I speak with human eloquence and angelic ecstasy but don't love, I'm nothing but the creaking of a rusty gate.

If I speak God's Word with power, revealing all his mysteries and making everything plain as day, and if I have faith that says to a mountain, "Jump," and it jumps, but I don't love, I'm nothing.

If I give everything I own to the poor and even go to the stake to be burned as a martyr, but I don't love, I've gotten nowhere. So, no matter what I say, what I believe, and what I do, I'm bankrupt without love.

Love never gives up.

Love cares more for others than for self.

Love doesn't want what it doesn't have.

Love doesn't strut,

Doesn't have a swelled head,

Doesn't force itself on others,

Isn't always "me first,"

Doesn't fly off the handle,

Doesn't keep score of the sins of others,

Doesn't revel when others grovel,

Takes pleasure in the flowering of truth,

Puts up with anything,

Trusts God always,

Always looks for the best,

Never looks back,
But keeps going to the end.
Love never dies. (1 Cor 13:1-8 *The Message*)

God invites us to live a life of love.

Question: What is God's invitation to us?

Answer: God invites us to live a life of love.

 FOR THE PARENT OR MENTOR What do you give your attention to in your household? What do you notice? What would your children say is the most important thing to you? A clean room? No burps at the table? Getting good grades? This is a worthy question to consider. You may not actually know what you give the most attention to. Your children may not actually be able to name it. But it is forming them. We read in 1 Corinthians 13 that love is valued most. How are you demonstrating in your home that this is also your top value? Do you pay as much attention to how your child is growing in their love for others as you do to how they are growing in their ability to follow your instructions? How much time do you spend investing in the external accomplishments of your child (sports, grades, extracurricular activities)? What would it look like for you to give as much attention to nurturing the growth of *love* in your child as you give to nurturing growth in other areas?

How do you teach and model patience in your home? Kindness? Gentleness? Self-control?

These qualities are fruits of the Holy Spirit's work in our lives. We don't become more patient by trying to be more patient. Self-control doesn't come to us as a result of some kind of resolution to get more of it. For better or worse, there are no shortcuts to becoming the kind of person who loves as Paul describes in 1 Corinthians 13. But we can practice it. We can attend to it. And we can become increasingly aware of patterns that are the opposite of love. As we grow in our self-awareness we can grow in our ability to ask for God's help in specific circumstances. "God, give me the grace to be more patient during our morning hustle and bustle in getting ready."

Spend some time this week asking God to help you pay attention to the most important things—and let the other stuff slide a bit.

○ Spend some time this week at bedtime helping your child review the day. Try to pay particular attention to helping your child think about times when they had an opportunity to love. Ask, "Where did you notice yourself loving others today?" "What was your favorite way of loving someone today?" And "Tell me about what loving others looked like for you today." Try to catch your child in the act of love this week. "Wow! That was really loving of you to give up your seat like that." "I noticed you loving your sister today when you were outside playing. I like what I saw there."

○ Help your child pay attention to opportunities to love others. When, for example, your child doesn't want to share with a sibling, try saying, "This looks like an opportunity to love—don't miss it!"

○ Read out loud with your child the love passage in 1 Corinthians 13. Talk about each aspect of love. Help your child imagine taking on that trait and learning it like learning a new language. Remind your child that this is what love looks like when it's perfect; this is the kind of love we are growing into as we follow Jesus.

 **FOR THE JOURNAL** Encourage your child to spend ten to fifteen minutes writing a brief story or description of a time when they recently felt a desire to love someone else. Maybe you could help your child by noticing a recent event when they demonstrated love. Ask your child to describe what they did that was loving and what they felt or experienced while they were doing it. Encourage your child to go back to that situation and use their imagination to replay the scenario. Encourage your child to pay attention to what it felt like to love.

8

Love is patient and kind, and does not make a list of people's mistakes

 **CONNECTION AND FORMATION** This week's imaginative prayer helps your child come before God with a question: Who do I need help loving? This lesson is focused on patience, kindness, and love for those we have the most trouble loving: brothers, sisters, neighbors, and friends. Your child will have a chance to ask God to bring someone to their mind—someone specifically who your child is having trouble loving.

One of the simplest ways to teach your child how to hear from God is to help your child ask God specific questions about their life. Even when an answer comes back unclear, the act of asking is an act of reaching out to God. It's an intentional act of connection.

One of the disciplines of spiritual formation is a regular *examen* of conscience.[1] Simply put, we wonder in God's presence about what's going on in our interior life. We notice emotions, thoughts, and take note of our conversation with God. Self-reflection does not come naturally for a child, but they can learn it. Questions like, "How do you feel about that?" and "You seem quiet, what are you thinking about right now?" can help your child learn the art of reflection. When this reflection includes God, it becomes a form of contemplation. We can build on the everyday questions of reflection about things that happen at school or home, and we can change those questions slightly to begin to nurture a contemplative posture in our child's awareness of God. "What do you think God feels about that?" or "I wonder what God thinks about this?" in response to a news story on TV—these kinds of questions and wondering can be formational, even if your child is only overhearing you ask those questions out loud. Eventually, these questions can be turned inward and formed into habits and practices of reflection as your child grows older.

Question: What does love look like?
Answer: Love looks like being patient and kind and not making a list of people's mistakes.

Close your eyes and let's take a few deep breaths together.

God, I pray that you will release our imagination and help us to hear you speak to us during this time together. We open our hands to you. We open our ears to you.

(pause 8-10 seconds)

Come, Holy Spirit.

Take a moment and ask God to bring someone to your mind that you, perhaps, are struggling with right now. Is there someone you get frustrated with? Is there someone you have a hard time being around because you don't like the way they act? Is there anyone in your life right now that is difficult for you to love?

(pause 5-10 seconds)

Maybe it's a brother or a sister. Or a neighbor. Or someone in your class at school. Is there anyone in your life right now you have a hard time loving? Is there anyone that you are having a hard time being patient with? Is there anyone that you sometimes treat unkindly? Again, maybe a brother? A sister? A friend? Mom or Dad?

Ask God to show you someone's face that he wants you to think about.

(pause 10 seconds)

Do you have someone in mind? Nod your head yes if you can see someone in your mind that maybe you have been impatient with or unkind to.

(pause 5 seconds)

What does it look like when you are unkind? What do you see yourself doing when you get impatient with others?

What does it look like when you are frustrated with this person?

(pause 10 seconds)

Do you raise your voice? Maybe you stomp your feet. Maybe you want to call them names. Maybe you do call them names.

What has happened between you and this person that makes you want to be unkind to them?

Is there anything that you hold against this person? Are you still angry about something?

(pause 5-6 seconds)

Do you need to forgive them for something that they have done, or for some way they have wronged you? Have they made a mistake that you are holding against them?

(pause again)

Imagine that you have a piece of paper and a pencil in your hand. Write down on the paper a few things that come to mind, ways that this person has wronged you, made you angry, or annoyed you. Can you remember any of their mistakes? If so, write them down.

(pause 10-15 seconds)

As you look at this list, as you think about ways it is hard for you to be patient with this person, or hard for you to be kind to them, ask God for help in forgiving this person.

Say to God, "God, please help me forgive this person. Help me be patient with them. Help me be kind to them. Help me not to worry or think about the ways they have been unkind to me, or hurt me."

What does it feel like to ask God for help in loving this person?

Do you believe that God will help you?

Now imagine that you look at your list where you wrote some things down, and the list is blank. Imagine there is no longer anything written there. Your list has vanished. You turn the paper over to see if it is on the other side, and it isn't there either. The paper is blank. The list is gone.

Think again of the person God brought to your mind. Imagine now being patient with that person. Imagine smiling at them when they annoy you. Imagine going out of your way to be kind to them.

What would it look like for you to be patient and kind to this person?

(pause 8-10 seconds)

What would it look like to love them?

(pause 10-15 seconds)

Picture yourself doing something that is loving, kind, and patient to this person.

God invites us to live a life of love.

Love looks like being patient and kind and not making a list of people's mistakes.

And with your eyes still closed, listen to me again read from the letter that the apostle Paul wrote to a church when he was talking about love:

> Love is patient, love is kind. It does not envy, it does not boast, it is not proud. It does not dishonor others, it is not self-seeking, it is not easily angered, it keeps no record of wrongs. Love does not delight in evil but rejoices with the truth. It always protects, always trusts, always hopes, always perseveres.
> Love never fails. (1 Cor 13:4-8)

Question: What does love look like?
Answer: Love looks like being patient and kind and not making a list of people's mistakes.

FOR THE PARENT OR MENTOR Love does not keep a list of wrongs. It means not tracking and cataloging people's mistakes. As a parent, this is often difficult. The temptation is to point out to children the things they are doing wrong, their transgressions. The temptation is to keep track of the areas where our kids are struggling. This, of course, can come out in impatience. We get impatient when we've reached our capacity to bear with them, to accept them. Sometimes the reality of daily life presses us toward full capacity.

But consider the possibility that your impatience with your child may be the result of a hidden list you are keeping—a list of the things frustrating you about your child's behavior. Spend some time this week trying to notice when you get impatient with your child. What is at work below the surface? What are the conditions in your heart toward this particular child? Try to replace the secret list of mistakes with a list of moments when your child is at their best, their most loving, their most affectionate, their most respectful.

Father Jacques Philippe reminds us of God's patience: "We must reason as follows: if the Lord has still not transformed this person, has not relieved him of such and such an imperfection, it is because He puts up with him as he is! He waits, with patience, for the opportune moment. Then I must do likewise. I must pray and be patient. Why be more demanding and impatient than God?"[2]

- ○ Spend some time this week at bedtime helping your child review the day. Try to pay particular attention to helping your child think about what opportunities they may have for loving others.

- ○ Ask, "Is there anyone you had trouble loving today?"

- ○ "Who were you able to show kindness to today?"

- ○ "Is there anyone whose mistakes you are holding onto? Is there anyone you need to ask God to help you be gracious to?"

- ○ Help your child remember to throw away the list they may be keeping of others' offenses.

- ○ Read out loud with your child the love passage in 1 Corinthians 13. Talk specifically this week about *patience, kindness,* and *not keeping a list of people's mistakes.*

 **FOR THE JOURNAL** Set aside about twenty minutes and ask your child to remember the imaginative prayer from this week. Ask them to try to recall who it was that first came to mind when they asked God to help them see the face of someone they are having a difficult time loving. Encourage them to write a prayer to God specifically about loving that particular person.

9

Love invites people
who may be left out

 **CONNECTION AND FORMATION** This week's imaginative prayer is based loosely on the parable of the great banquet found in Luke 14. Jesus tells a story about a man who is preparing a great banquet and invites a great number of guests, and all of them have excuses for why they cannot come. The man in the story instructs his servant to go onto the streets and invite anyone he can find. While the main point of the story is about the coming of the kingdom of God and of God's Messiah, one of the underlying implications is that the invitation to the banquet of the coming kingdom is extended to *everyone*. This is a picture of God's love for the world; it is a picture of what love looks like. Here, your child can experience that the love of God is a model for how to love others. This imaginative prayer creates an experience for your child of extending the welcome and invitation to those who may often feel left out. There is great joy in inviting those on the margins and seeing them have fun at a great banquet. This was God's joy and his pleasure in extending the invitation to us. And now we have an opportunity to extend smaller versions of the same invitation to others in our daily lives.

Our life with God exists because of God's invitation to us. With God, there is always welcome. When we experience God's welcome and inclusion, it's unlikely that we'll be able to exclude others without feeling the dissonance.

 Question: What does love look like?

Answer: Love looks like inviting people who may be left out.

IMAGINATIVE PRAYER

Close your eyes and let's take a few deep breaths together.

God, I pray that you will release our imagination and help us to hear you speak to us during this time together. We open our hands to you. We open our ears to you.

(pause 8-10 seconds)

Come, Holy Spirit.

Imagine with me that you have been put in charge of throwing a great big party for a very special occasion. Imagine there is going to be a great feast. And all your friends are going to be invited. Imagine the best party that you have ever been to—it's going to be like that, only ten times better.

(pause 5-8 seconds)

Imagine that you have nearly unlimited money to spend on throwing the greatest party. What would you do at the party? What kind of food would you serve? Would there be ice cream? Pizza? Cookies? Cakes? Imagine a long table with some of your greatest food.

What about entertainment? What would you want to do at this party? Would you play games? Watch movies? Imagine you could have anything you wanted at this party.

(pause 5-8 seconds)

And next imagine who you would invite. Who are your best friends? Who are the people you would want to be sure could make it?

Imagine preparing nice invitations for them and having the invitations delivered to your friends' houses. Imagine what it would feel like to invite all of these people to the greatest party anyone has ever been to.

Remember—you are in charge of the party. Someone has asked you to organize the party and to make sure that lots of people will show up.

Imagine now that a few days before the party, the host of the party—the person who has put you in charge—asks you how the party planning is going.

All of the preparations are going just fine, you say. All of the food is prepared. The table is set. The fireworks are ready.

"And what about the guests?" the host asks. "Is there anyone who has said they will be there?"

"No," you reply.

Imagine trying to explain to your host that everyone is busy. Imagine you have spoken to each person who has received an invitation, and they have said they will be unable to make it to the party.

What does it feel like to be throwing the greatest party ever and not have anyone who is able to come?

(pause 5-8 seconds)

How does this make you feel?

What do you think you should do?

(pause 5-8 seconds)

Imagine now that you are meeting with the host of the party to explain to him that no one is able to make it to the party. And the host asks, "Is there anyone else we could invite? Is there anyone who we may have left out?"

(pause 5-8 seconds)

Suddenly, people's faces begin coming to your mind. They are not people who are really friends of yours, but you know their faces. You have seen them at school or at the park while playing. In fact, these are kids who often get left out. These kids are the last ones to be picked for a team. These are the kids who other kids sometimes make fun of.

Who do you know at your school or in your neighborhood who maybe isn't as popular as others? Is there anyone you know who often gets left out? Is there anyone who comes to mind that doesn't get invited to parties?

(pause 5-8 seconds)

Next, the host says to you: "Go out and find the people who we haven't yet invited. Go find all the people who we left out."

And so you go.

Imagine making special invitations for these kids who haven't yet been invited.

You go to school or you spend the day at the park, or you walk through the neighborhood looking for these kids.

Imagine what it would feel like to invite these kids to a party—many have never even been to a party.

It's the day before the party and you have just spent the entire day working hard to deliver all the invitations. Everyone who you invited said they would come. Some of them got so excited just for being invited that they gave you a giant hug.

What does it feel like to be able to invite people who usually get left out? What is it like to see these kids feel good about being included?

(pause 5-8 seconds)

Now it's the day of the party. The table has been set with a feast. There is a mountain of ice cream ready to be eaten. The music is playing. The games are all set up.

And then they all begin to show up. Everyone invited who had initially been left out begins to show up. You smile as people arrive at the party and have fun. The host, too, is smiling. He's laughing. He is pleased. For all of these kids who you hadn't considered inviting, this is the best party they have ever been to.

This is what love looks like.

Jesus tells a similar story that goes like this:

There was once a man who threw a great dinner party and invited many. When it was time for dinner, he sent out his servant to the invited guests, saying, "Come on in; the food's on the table."

Then they all began to beg off, one after another making excuses. The first said, "I bought a piece of property and need to look
it over. Send my regrets."

Another said, "I just bought five teams of oxen, and I really need
to check them out. Send my regrets."

And yet another said, "I just got married and need to get home
to my wife."

The servant went back and told the master what had happened.
He was outraged and told the servant, "Quickly, get out into the city
streets and alleys. Collect all who look like they need a square meal,
all the misfits and homeless and wretched you can lay your hands
on, and bring them here."

The servant reported back, "Master, I did what you commanded—
and there's still room."

The master said, "Then go to the country roads. Whoever you find,
drag them in. I want my house full! Let me tell you, not one of those
originally invited is going to get so much as a bite at my dinner
party." (Lk 14:16-24 *The Message*)

Jesus is telling a story about a feast and inviting people who may have
been left out, because this is what love looks like. This is what the
kingdom of God is like.

God's invitation to his feast is for everyone.

Love looks like being patient and kind and not making a list of people's
mistakes.

Love looks like inviting people who may be left out.

 Question: What does love look like?
Answer: Love looks like inviting people who may be left out.

 **FOR THE PARENT OR MENTOR** We all have our own
group of friends we
enjoy hanging out with. We also all have people who annoy us a little—
people we don't invite to the party, neighbors we avoid because they talk too

much, coworkers we hide from for fear we'll hear another long story or perhaps another unwarranted complaint. What are ways that you unintentionally leave others out? One of the best ways for children to learn about how to do hard things is to watch their parents do hard things. Invite that neighbor over for dinner or a drink. Spend some time with your coworker who isn't part of the workplace social scene. Share some of your process with your child. Let them know this picture of God's welcome may be challenging to you. Let them in on your own process. When we share with our children the times when we are choosing love in the hard things, this helps place them in a narrative and gives them a picture of what love looks like in real life.

○ Spend some time this week at bedtime helping your child review the day. Try to pay particular attention to helping your child think about what opportunities they may have for loving others, specifically by including them. Ask, "Did you notice anyone feeling left out today while you were playing?" "How did it feel to include _____ in your game today?" The goal is to nurture awareness of the need to include others and being on the lookout for times when kids may feel left out.

○ In the normal rhythm of your day, begin brainstorming with your child a list of people in their life who may often feel left out. Are there kids at school who are in the minority racially, culturally, or in their religious beliefs? Are there children with disabilities who maybe can't participate in the same way other kids can? Spend some time this week helping your child notice people who may be on the margins.

○ Ask your child if they ever feel left out, on the margins. Help your child imagine the *welcome* that God offers in his kingdom.

○ Spend some time this week talking with your child about the world's current refugee crisis. Help your child do some research on what it is like for refugees throughout the world to be without a home and often feel unwelcome in another country.[1]

○ Read out loud with your child the passage in Luke 14 about the great banquet. Ask some good questions about the story. Help your child see the welcome of God in the story. Ask, "Why do you think Jesus is telling this story?" "Who is initially invited to the feast?" "Who ends up coming to the feast?" "Why do you think God wants to welcome everyone at his banquet?"

 **FOR THE JOURNAL** Set aside twenty minutes and ask your child to remember the imaginative prayer from this week. Ask your child to spend some time thinking about a time they felt left out, or a time when they noticed someone else feeling left out. Help your child write a simple prayer that they can pray when they are noticing someone feeling left out. For example, "God, help me to always include others." Or "God, help me to love the people who are left out."

10

Love takes care of people when they need help

CONNECTION AND FORMATION This imaginative prayer does two things: first, it creates space for your child to imagine hearing the story of the good Samaritan firsthand from Jesus, and, second, it helps your child imagine following Jesus' command to "go and do likewise"—not alone, but with Jesus by their side. What does love look like in everyday life? In stories like the good Samaritan, Jesus is trying to help people imagine what love looks like. In this case, a man is wondering, *Who is my neighbor?* The man asking this question is trying to distance himself from doing the hard work of loving others. Jesus tells a story that describes the opportunity we have to be a neighbor to anyone in need. We don't need to wait for others to be defined as our neighbor before we love and care for them. The people we love become our neighbors. This imaginative prayer is practice for the real thing. We are creating an imaginative experience for your child in order to help remove some barriers to responding to someone in need. Sometimes imagining it first helps make a path for doing it in real life.

Silence is a key feature of spiritual formation. And it's in short supply in most teaching environments for children. We are not quiet often enough and long enough to allow silence to become a thing of its own rather than only the absence of something else. There is a quality to silence that can be awkward and unnatural. But half of being in conversation with someone is when we're not talking but listening. There is a full two minutes of silence and undirected time during this lesson. You will introduce your child to this extended silence and ask your child to allow their imagination to finish the story. Be lighthearted if your child finds this difficult. Every bit of silence is good, even if the full time allotted feels like it's too much.

 Question: What does love look like?
Answer: Love looks like taking care of people when they need help.

 **IMAGINATIVE PRAYER**

Close your eyes and let's take a few deep breaths together.

God, I pray that you will release our imagination and help us to hear you speak to us during this time together. We open our hands to you. We open our ears to you.

(pause 8-10 seconds)

Come, Holy Spirit.

In the Gospel of Luke we read a story about a man who had an important question for Jesus. The man wanted to know what he must do to have the kind of life that God wanted him to have—a life that is full of goodness and abundance and love.

Imagine that you are listening in on the conversation. Imagine that you are standing right next to Jesus.

(pause 5-8 seconds)

The man asks Jesus, "What must I do to have the best kind of life?"

Jesus, seeing that the man was religious, gave him a very straightforward answer. He said, "You know what kind of life God invites you into, don't you? Tell me, what's your understanding?"

The man gave a pretty good answer. He said this: "The good life comes to those who love God with all their heart and energy, and also love their neighbors as well as they love themselves."

"That's a good answer," Jesus replied.

But then the man had another question: "And who is my neighbor?"

Jesus answered him by telling a story.

Imagine you are sitting with Jesus as he tells this story. Imagine you are right next to him.

(pause 5-8 seconds)

Jesus begins the story and says,

> "There was once a man traveling from Jerusalem to Jericho. On the way he was attacked by robbers. They took his clothes, beat him up, and went off leaving him half-dead. Luckily, a priest was on his way down the same road, but when he saw him he angled across to the other side. Then a Levite religious man showed up; he also avoided the injured man.
>
> "A Samaritan traveling the road came on him. When he saw the man's condition, his heart went out to him. He gave him first aid, disinfecting and bandaging his wounds. Then he lifted him onto his donkey, led him to an inn, and made him comfortable. In the morning he took out two silver coins and gave them to the inn-keeper, saying, 'Take good care of him. If it costs any more, put it on my bill—I'll pay you on my way back.'
>
> "What do you think? Which of the three became a neighbor to the man attacked by robbers?"
>
> "The one who treated him kindly," the [man] responded.
>
> Jesus said, "Go and do the same." (Lk 10:30-37 *The Message*)

Imagine you are sitting next to Jesus as he finishes the story. Jesus reaches out his hand for yours and offers to go on a walk with you.

Imagine he says your name and takes your hand.

(pause 5-8 seconds)

And then Jesus begins to ask you some questions. He begins to ask you about the story you have just listened to.

He says to you, "Who do you relate to in the story?"

Think for a moment about the people in the story that Jesus has told.

There is the man who was robbed and beaten. There were two people who passed him by. And there was the man, the Samaritan, who stopped and helped the beaten man.

Continue to imagine that you are with Jesus and you are having a conversation with him about the story. "Who are the people in your life that sometimes need help?"

(pause 10 seconds)

Who comes to mind?

What are some ways that Jesus may be inviting you to be like the Samaritan in this story?

(pause 5-8 seconds)

Who are the people you have an opportunity to be kind to? Who do you have an opportunity to love?

Is there anyone that comes to mind?

Imagine now that as you walk with Jesus, you notice there is someone on the side of the road who seems to be in need. It is a man who has been badly beaten, and someone has torn his clothes.

What do you want to do when you see the man?

(pause 5-8 seconds)

Imagine running over to the man, with Jesus right by your side. Imagine helping the man up, and offering him a drink of water. What does it feel like to have Jesus by your side as you help this man?

Take a few moments of quiet, and try to imagine what happens next as you and Jesus are helping the man.

Ask Jesus right now to help you finish the task of love in this story. How would you finish the story?

(take about 2 minutes of silence)

God invites us to live a life of love.

Love looks like being patient and kind and not making a list of people's mistakes.

Love looks like inviting people who may be left out.

Love looks like taking care of people when they need help.

Question: What does love look like?
Answer: Love looks like taking care of people when they need help.

 FOR THE PARENT OR MENTOR Our lives are busy. Crowded. Sometimes uninterruptable. Love looks like taking care of someone who needs a little help. Who are those people in your life? Do you notice them? Jesus tells the story of the good Samaritan to a man who is trying to figure out what he has to do to have the kind of life that God promises as the "good life." *Eternal life* isn't really about how long you will live in God's new creation. The man in the story isn't asking a question about how to "go to heaven when he dies." *Eternal life* is specifically about a certain *kind* of life—the abundant life. The question the religious leader is asking is about what constitutes the good life, a life blessed by God and a life lived to the fullest of God's desire for us. Jesus' response is brilliant: the good life comes to the man who goes out of his way to express love. He gives his time, he crosses cultural barriers, he loves when it is difficult. What are some ways you are doing this as a family? The best way to have the kinds of kids that end up following Jesus is to take them along with you as you follow Jesus. Spend some time considering how you might participate more in this kind of love. This is the best kind of life, says Jesus.

○ Spend some time this week at bedtime helping your child review the day. Help your child this week be on the lookout for ways to respond to someone in need. "Did you see anyone at school today who was having a hard day?" "Is there anyone we know that could use our help today?"

○ With your child at your side, try to care for someone who needs help. Is there a neighbor that lives alone and perhaps needs some extra help around the house? Is there anyone near your neighborhood or some-place close to where you live that seems to be in need?

○ Have you ever been with your child when someone on the street has asked for money or food? This is a great opportunity to go out of your way and help.

○ Take your child to a place in your city where you know you'll en-counter someone who is in need, maybe a beggar or a homeless person. Together, spend time with that person trying to figure out a way to love them. If you need some help navigating this kind of scenario, get in touch with a local organization that works with the homeless pop-ulation in your city.

○ Read out loud with your child the passage in Luke 10 about the good Samaritan. Ask, "Why do you think Jesus is telling this story?" "Why do you think some people pass on the other side of the road?" "Let's brainstorm together how we can be good Samaritans to people this week!"

 **FOR THE JOURNAL** Set aside about fifteen minutes and ask your child to remember the imaginative prayer from this week. Ask your child to spend some time thinking about who in their life is currently in need of some help. Encourage them to ask God how he might be specifically in-viting your child into a life of love for that person. Encourage your child to write down what they sense God is asking them to do.

11

We love others with the love that God pours into us

 **CONNECTION AND FORMATION** This is an exciting week in our imaginative prayer journey. In 2 Corinthians Paul gives us an example of what love looks like in practical terms. He tells of the Macedonians' earnest love for those in need, and he hopes this example might excite the same kind of practical love in the Corinthian church. Paul wonders if the Corinthians will also be compelled to give generously, not out of a sense of obligation but with the understanding that they have abundance already—that they can give out of an overflow of the love and the grace of God in their lives.

He writes:

> And now, brothers and sisters, we want you to know about the grace that God
> has given the Macedonian churches. In the midst of a very severe trial, their
> overflowing joy and their extreme poverty welled up in rich generosity. . . .
>
> I am not commanding you, but I want to test the sincerity of your love by
> comparing it with the earnestness of others. (2 Cor 8:1-2, 8)

This week's imaginative prayer is meant to open up conversation about the source of our love for others. We love others out of the abundance of God's love in our own lives. We love others with the love God pours into us. We are empty buckets ready to be filled with God's love. And yet we often feel compelled to serve God or others without first recognizing our own need to receive. We see Jesus receiving the love of his Father in the waters of baptism before he goes into the desert. We see Jesus preparing his disciples for service in the world not through a pep talk but by getting on his knees and washing their feet in loving service. Jesus had learned that in order to give we must first receive. It's why he told the disciples to wait for the Holy Spirit to come at Pentecost before going out to build the church. The best kind of love overflows from our experience of being loved.

Finally, this week's imaginative prayer continues to nurture conversations of justice and mercy. There are 783 million people in the world who do not have access to clean water.[1] There are so many needs in the world that we can often feel overwhelmed by our little capacity. We have, maybe, five fish and two loaves for a whole hillside of hungry people. We have the capacity to love others to the degree that we have taken the time to notice and receive the love God has for us. He multiplies because he loves.

Question: Where does our love for others come from?
Answer: We love others with the love that God pours into us.

Close your eyes and let's take a few deep breaths together.

God, I pray that you will release our imagination and help us to hear you speak to us during this time together. We open our hands to you. We open our ears to you.

(pause 8-10 seconds)

Come, Holy Spirit.

Imagine with me that you are living in a part of the world where there is very little water to drink. Imagine that each day you only have one small cup of water to drink. That you are often thirsty. Imagine sitting outside under the hot sun, wanting so badly to have a drink of water.

(pause 5-8 seconds)

Do you know that there are places in the world where there is not very much water to drink? There are places all over the world where people simply do not have enough water. The water in the rivers and streams is too dirty to drink, or the rivers and streams are all dried up. Imagine that you live in one of these places.

(pause 5-8 seconds)

Imagine you are so very thirsty.

(pause 5 seconds)

Imagine that each day you walk with a bucket for an hour to get water for your family. Your mother and father and any brothers or sisters you have also take a bucket and walk an hour to fetch water for your household. With this water you do all your cooking and bathing and drinking. Imagine what it would be like to walk each day to fetch the littlest bit of water.

As you walk home with your bucket of water, you notice that some of your neighbors aren't able to gather enough water for their family. Actually, there are quite a few families in your neighborhood who don't even have buckets for gathering water. Some families' mom and dad are both sick, and the children are too little to carry the heavy buckets.

Imagine that you have set your bucket of water down at your home. Your family begins to cook dinner and drink water and wash their hands. The water is running low, so you decide to take one more trip to the place where you gather water, which again is an hour's walk away.

Imagine walking home with a heavy bucket of water. And on your way home you see a family in their home with no water at all.

What does it feel like to see this family?

What do you want to do?

(pause 5-8 seconds)

Imagine that you make the choice to give your bucket of water to this family. It's heavy in your hands, but as you set it down on their front porch, and as you watch them come for the water and drink it, you know that you've done something good.

You have done something loving.

Imagine now that you go back home and see that all your buckets of water are filled.

There are five buckets full of water at your house and they are filled right up to the top, but nobody knows how they were filled. In fact, they are overflowing. Water is spilling out of the top of the buckets and onto the ground.

What do you want to do with the water?

(pause 5-8 seconds)

Imagine that the other families in your neighborhood come to mind. You remember that there are so many families that need water. Imagine that you take some of the water from your home, one bucket at a time, to some of the families around you. Imagine taking a bucket of water from your home and pouring it into the bucket at your neighbor's home. You come back to your home with an empty bucket and grab another full bucket to take to another family. You pour this water into a bucket at a house next to you—and again you return to your house with another empty bucket. You grab a third bucket of water and take it to the neighbor down the street who hasn't been able to get water for quite some time.

What does it feel like to be able to give away so much? What is it like to be able to give something away, to love people?

(pause 5 seconds)

Imagine now that you come back to your house with an empty bucket. You know that you have one full bucket left, and you have someone in mind that needs this bucket of water.

As you drop off your empty bucket, you notice that all the buckets are full again.

Imagine it.

Every single one is completely full—even the bucket you just brought back empty. The one you just set down on the ground is full. They aren't just full; they are overflowing. Something is happening here that you can't explain. You live in a place where water is hard to come by, and yet every time you empty a bucket, somehow it is filled back up.

Imagine that you take another full bucket of water to someone who is thirsty.

What is it like knowing that you are giving because you have so much to give away? That every time you give away, every time you empty a bucket, more water comes?

This is how we love.

(pause 5-8 seconds)

We love because we are overflowing with God's love for us. We love because we are so full.

Imagine right now being filled with the love of God.

(pause)

Hold out your hands in front of you and receive God's love—let it fill you up.

(pause 10-15 seconds)

Let God's love for you fill you up like an empty bucket.

Love looks like being patient and kind and not making a list of people's mistakes.

Love looks like inviting people who may be left out.

Love looks like taking care of people when they need help.

We love others with the love that God pours into us.

 Question: Where does our love for others come from?
Answer: We love others with the love that God pours into us.

 FOR THE PARENT OR MENTOR There is an old saying in the tradition of Ignatian spirituality: You cannot give what you do not have. St. Ignatius instructed his members of the Society of Jesus to first get filled up before they went out onto their mission. In fact, Ignatius would keep his new members in spiritual exercises for up to two years before sending them out into the world. As parents, we notoriously have a tendency to run on empty. Often, we become so busy in the activities we think will make our children feel loved that the stress of it all takes a toll on our emotional life. Your greatest impact on your child will be the way you love them. If they learn from you that it is okay to run yourself ragged in service of others, then they too will one day do the same. Look at Jesus. He constantly pulled away to get filled up before going out and loving. He served and loved out of an overflow of his life with the Father. His instruction to us is to remain in him. For he is the vine and we are the branches. How filled up are you in your own life with God? What things can you do to help you get a full bucket of God's love this week? How are you experiencing God's love for you?

○ Spend some time this week at bedtime helping your child review the day. Help your child be on the lookout for ways to be thinking both about God's love for them and their love for others. "When did you feel God's love today?" "When did you feel filled up?" "What are some things that help you feel filled by God?" "Is there anything we can do right now that would help fill your buckets? Could we pray?"

○ Try to pepper the week with conversation about full buckets and over-flowing water. At least once a day help your child do something to bring their attention back to the idea of being filled with the love of God. Put your hand on your child's shoulder every morning this week and pray that God will fill them with love. Pray that God would let them feel filled up.

○ When you talk about loving others this week, speak in terms of letting love overflow. Say, "How can we let God's love overflow onto that person?" Or "What could we do to have our love buckets overflow onto that person?" Every time we speak of love in this manner, we're reinforcing the idea that our love for others isn't something we give out of a dry place, but rather it is channeling the overflow of God's love onto others. That's how it is supposed to work.

○ Take some time to talk to your child about your own need to be filled up. If you feel filled up, let your kids know. "I feel filled up with God's love today. Is there anything I can do for you?" And when you feel empty, let them know. "I think my bucket is empty today, can I take twenty minutes to be alone with God?" Let them see that this is on the forefront of your mind, that you pay attention to whether you're filled or empty.

○ Do some research with your child on issues of poverty and clean-water access. Help your child begin to understand and contend with the reality of needs in the world.[2]

○ Read out loud to your child Luke 6:43-45, and spend some time talking about this passage. Help your child understand the concept of a particular fruit coming from a particular tree. An apple tree produces apples. A pear tree brings forth pears. What is the connection between this passage and the idea of loving others from an overflow? "The mouth speaks what the heart is full of."

 **FOR THE JOURNAL** Set aside about fifteen minutes and ask your child to remember the imaginative prayer from this week. Ask your child to spend some time thinking about what it feels like when they are full of God's love. Teach them how to ask God to fill them up. Encourage them to write a prayer to God asking that God will fill up their heart with love so that they can allow that to overflow onto others.

12

People will know that we are followers of Jesus because of our love for each other

 **CONNECTION AND FORMATION** This imaginative prayer blends a normal childhood experience and a key lesson from Jesus. Children intuitively know what it means to belong to a special group or team. In this imaginative exercise your child will be immersed in a familiar experience in their own time and place (belonging to a special club), and then we'll stitch this experience to the concept of being identified as one of Jesus' followers.

The early church, even in spite of Jesus' teaching, struggled to know what marked them as followers of Jesus. What was required to get in on this new thing? What set them apart? How would people know they were living in the way of Jesus? Jesus' own words are clear on the matter: "They will know that you are my disciples by the love that you have for each other." This is our identity marker. This is the badge. The uniform. The secret handshake. Loving one another, just as Jesus loves us.

The church is the people who gather together and help each other along in the way of Jesus. Community is vital to the work of spiritual formation because alone we do not have everything we need to reflect the fullness of who God is. You, as a parent, don't have everything your child needs. I chuckled a bit as I wrote that last sentence. A little voice inside me declared "amen!" I imagine hearing your own knowing laughter. It's true. We simply do not have everything our children need.

As children grow within a healthy community, their sense of belonging and of *family* will also grow. At a young age, and during these early stages of faith, a child's sense of belonging can often feel at risk, especially when morality and adherence to particular doctrines are being emphasized. We can be quick to think that our behavior or belief system is what sets us apart from "the world." It's just not so. This kind of thinking can be dangerous, especially for children. Churches that set up behavior and doctrine as boundary markers can produce an underlying system of comparison and judgment.

The distinguishing mark of the Christian is love empowered by the Holy Spirit, who himself is a gift from God to help us on the way.

 Question: How will people know that we are followers of Jesus? *Answer*: People will know that we are followers of Jesus because of our love for each other.

 **IMAGINATIVE PRAYER**

Close your eyes and let's take a few deep breaths together.

God, I pray that you will release our imagination and help us to hear you speak to us during this time together. We open our hands to you. We open our ears to you.

(pause 8-10 seconds)

Come, Holy Spirit.

Imagine with me that you are part of a club.

(pause 5 seconds)

Imagine you are part of a club, but it isn't a secret club—it's a club anyone can join. There are no secret passwords. There are no secret handshakes. There are no secret knocks on the door of a treehouse. Everyone is welcome.

In fact, there are no T-shirts. There are no special things for you to buy to be a part of this club. There are no monthly dues to pay.

Imagine you are at a club meeting where a discussion is going on about how to let people know that you are part of the club. Some people suggest that everyone wear green scarves. Imagine being in a club where everyone had to wear a green scarf. That seems funny to you and to others. Imagine that everyone is having fun thinking about the suggestion of wearing a green scarf.

Everyone decides that this is a fun idea, but it's probably not the best way to let people know you are part of the club.

Other people suggest hats. Still others suggest a special bracelet or a necklace.

What do you think should be the thing that sets your special club apart? What do you think club members should do to let everyone else know that you are part of this special club?

(pause 5-8 seconds)

Do you think it should be about something you wear? Or maybe it should be something that you all do? Perhaps you could all learn the same dance or have a special song that everyone sings.

Imagine with me that someone has drawn a picture of a badge— almost like a police badge. Imagine this person wants everyone to wear a badge on their shirt to let everyone else know that they are a part of the club. This is another good idea, but there still is something missing. It just doesn't seem to fit.

Some people want to create a list of rules for the club. They want to say that members of the club can't wear the color orange, for example. One person wants all the members of the club to only eat with their hands—no forks, no knives, no spoons. Just hands.

Another person suggests that everyone get a tattoo on their arm. Imagine what it would be like to have to get a tattoo on your arm, just to be in a club. This seems to be getting out of hand!

What would you suggest? How would you want everyone to be identified as part of the club?

(pause 5-8 seconds)

Imagine now that someone stands up in front of everyone else. You are curious what this person might say, and you are curious because this is the leader of the club. This is the person who started the club in the first place.

Imagine that everyone is quiet and silent, waiting for the leader of the club to speak.

(pause 5 seconds)

Imagine that the leader begins to speak:

(read slowly) "I know that many of you are wondering what sort of badge or mark or special handshake we might have for our club. I too have been thinking about this—and I have an idea.

"What if people could know we all belong together and are all a part of the same club simply because of our love for each other? What if we loved each other so well that people would notice? What if when people saw us loving each other, they would know that we are members of the club?"

Think about this for a moment. What would it feel like to be a part of a club where the special thing that held you all together was your love for each other?

(pause 5-8 seconds)

Imagine everyone in the club is thinking about this suggestion. The people with hats take off their hats. The people with green scarves take off their scarves. The people who are drawing badges set down their art supplies. Everyone is listening to the leader who begins to speak again.

"Imagine if all of us simply love each other so well that people will want to join the club. Imagine if we welcomed everyone."

(pause 5 seconds)

Imagine that everyone in the club begins to love each other really well.

That love becomes your badge of membership.

You see people around you serving each other, helping each other with chores, sharing snacks, taking turns, and saying nice things about each other.

This is the command that Jesus gave us when he invited us all to follow him.

He said:

> Let me give you a new command: Love one another. In the same way I loved you, you love one another. This is how everyone will recognize that you are my disciples—when they see the love you have for each other. (Jn 13:34-35 *The Message*)

Love looks like being patient and kind and not making a list of people's mistakes.

Love looks like inviting people who may be left out.

Love looks like taking care of people when they need help.

We love others with the love that God pours into us.

People will know that we are followers of Jesus because of our love for each other.

 Question: How will people know that we are followers of Jesus? *Answer*: People will know that we are followers of Jesus because of our love for each other.

 Who among your neighbors and co-workers knows that you are a follower of Jesus? If they do know, what is it about you that they would notice? Take these questions before God in prayer this week. Sit with them. Ask God to answer this question for you: Are there any unhealthy criteria by which I judge myself as better than those who aren't following Jesus? These comparisons can be subtle. Are there behaviors that you notice in unbelievers that make you feel better than them? These small micro-judgments can be a window into a deeper

assumption about what God is most concerned about. As you reflect in prayer on this, and as God brings things to your attention, ask God to forgive you for these judgments. Ask for the grace to allow love to be the indicator of your belonging.

○ Try an experiment in your home this week. Encourage the members of your family to ask to be served. You read that right. Encourage each family member to ask to be served by another member of the family one time each day. For example, "Would you serve me by getting me a glass of milk?" or "Would you serve me by clearing the table?" Watch what happens when you go out of your way to create opportunities to love. Make this fun. And make sure that everyone knows that they can say no to a request. Love isn't love if it is forced.

○ Read out loud with your child Paul's instructions in Colossians 3:13-15. Talk briefly about how this verse describes love as something we "put on." Throughout the week playfully encourage your child to "put on love." If you find some conflict this week between you and your child or between your child and a sibling, encourage some reflection: "Let's put on our love and try this conversation again." Pretend to "put on love" as you would a pair of pants or a raincoat.

○ Encourage your child this week to reach out to one or two people in their Sunday school classroom or youth group, perhaps someone who is new, or someone who isn't as connected.

○ Reflect on ways in which your faith community has blessed you over the past few months. Share with your child examples of how people in your faith community have loved your family. Do this together with your child.

 **FOR THE JOURNAL** Set aside about fifteen minutes and ask your child to remember the imaginative prayer from this week. Ask your child to spend some time thinking about what it means to be a part of your faith community. Encourage your child to notice ways they feel loved by the people in your community. Suggest to your child that this week's journal time be spent making a list of people and things your child is grateful for, specifically friends who share their faith in Jesus.

REVIEW WEEK

God invites us to live a life of love.

Love looks like being patient and kind and not making a list of people's mistakes.

Love looks like inviting people who may be left out.

Love looks like taking care of people when they need help.

We love others with the love that God pours into us.

People will know that we are followers of Jesus because of our love for each other.

CREEDAL QUESTIONS AND ANSWERS

Question: What is God's invitation to us?
Answer: God invites us to live a life of love.

Question: What does love look like?
Answer: Love looks like being patient and kind and not making a list of people's mistakes.

Question: What does love look like?
Answer: Love looks like inviting people who may be left out.

Question: What does love look like?
Answer: Love looks like taking care of people when they need help.

Question: Where does our love for others come from?
Answer: We love others with the love that God pours into us.

Question: How will people know that we are followers of Jesus?
Answer: People will know that we are followers of Jesus because of our love for each other.

QUESTIONS AND ACTIVITIES

○ Spend time this week reviewing each of the past six weeks.

○ Ask some good questions. For example:

  ○ Where do you see God at work around you?

- What are some things you'd like to see God working on in the world? Is there something about the way the world works that bothers you? If so, what is it?

- Is there anything you see going on in the world that makes you feel sad? Would you share this with me?

- If you could choose one place in the world to work to bring peace and reconciliation, what would that place be?

- Let's talk about the big party in the world with King Jesus. What do you think it would be like if everything came under the reign and rule of Jesus?

- What most excites you about Jesus' reign?

- Are there any relationships that feel like they aren't going well for you? Is there anything about those relationships you'd like to share with me? If so, what?

- Do you think any of our neighbors need to experience the love of God? How do you think God is loving them? How might we join in what God is doing?

- Tell me about how God has recently spoken to you.

- Have you had any interesting dreams that might be God speaking? If so, what are they?

- What are some ways you have received God's love this week?

- How has God filled up your bucket this week?

- Have you been able to bring buckets of water to anyone this week? Explain how you did this.

- What are some of the things you are praying about right now?

- What are you talking to God about?

- What are you asking from God?

- Where do you want God to do something?

- Review the portion of the creedal poem that corresponds with part two, "Loving Others." Help your child memorize these next six lines. Review the creedal poem from part one. See if you can string them all together.

PART 3

Forgiveness

13

Forgiveness means we can have peace with God.

14

Forgiveness means God welcomes anyone.

15

Forgiveness means God takes away our sin.

16

Forgiveness means we can forgive the sins of others.

17

When we forgive, we will be forgiven.
When we give, it will be given to us.

18

Love and forgiveness make room for reconciliation.

13

Forgiveness means we can have peace with God

The purpose of this week is to give your child the experience of being in conflict with God, of having icky feelings toward God, and of being unable to experience God's love. Ignatius of Loyola refers to this feeling as *desolation*—when God seems distant and inattentive. Desolation is a normal part of the spiritual journey that we often forget to explain to children. We experience the highs and lows of connection with God as adults. We find ourselves feeling disconnected from God and learn to pray through it. But these periods of desolation and disconnection can come as a surprise to many people. Normalizing this kind of disconnection—where God seems absent—and fostering some self-reflection will help your child to recognize these inner movements of the soul.

This imaginative prayer is a symbolic story, both for our enmity toward God prior to our conversion as well as our occasional struggle to be at peace with God throughout our spiritual journey. As followers of Jesus our difficulty with God is a residue we live with due to the fact that the whole world is in a process of moving toward *shalom*.

Most children are too young to have experienced a real and lasting disappointment with God. If your children haven't had this experience yet, they will. Prayers will go unanswered. Perceived needs will go unmet. And the feelings that arise during these seasons can be confusing and, well, icky.

Here, we are trying to begin to demonstrate that the disconnection and ickiness can be recognized and brought to Jesus. Jesus can help us navigate the disconnection and feelings of separation. This imaginative prayer will open up conversations about what it looks like to let the grace and love of Jesus bring peace with God—both for our first reconciliation to God through faith and for our ongoing need for forgiveness and relationship. Spiritual formation is an ongoing work of responding to the grace of God.[1]

 Question: What does forgiveness mean?
Answer: Forgiveness means we can have peace with God.

 **IMAGINATIVE PRAYER**

Close your eyes and let's take a few deep breaths together.

God, I pray that you will release our imagination and help us to hear you speak to us during this time together. We open our hands to you. We open our ears to you.

(pause 8-10 seconds)

Come, Holy Spirit.

Think back over the past few months and remember some of what we have been imagining about God's love and how God's love helps us to love others.

What does it feel like to know that God loves you and that there is nothing that can separate you from the love God has for you?

(pause 8-10 seconds)

Imagine God's love for you is so great, and imagine God's love is like a light that is all around you.

You can feel it and see it and even smell it, because the love of God is also like a fragrant aroma.

Imagine that it smells like a sweet-smelling flower. Imagine that God's love is like the warmth of the sun coming through the window on a chilly morning. Or it feels like a cool mist on a hot day.

Ask God, right now, to let you feel his love.

(pause 10 seconds)

Now, take a moment and try to bring to mind what it has felt like to be in conflict with someone. Is there anyone at home, at school, or in the neighborhood who you have been angry at or hurt by? Try to remember what that felt like.

(pause 5 seconds)

Now imagine what it might feel like to be in conflict with God. Imagine that you and God have just had an argument, and you feel icky toward God. You feel distant. Imagine that you are frustrated and angry, and feel as though something just isn't right.

Have you ever been frustrated with God? Have you ever been angry with God?

Imagine that you and God are having an argument about something.

"This isn't fair!" you say.

And then some kind of scales start forming all over your body—like the skin of a snake or a dragon. Your body begins to grow scales.[2]

First your arms, and then your chest and stomach. The scales are now running down your legs and then up your neck and over your face—like a mask.

Imagine that you are now completely covered in scales.

You can't see the light of God's love around you.

You can't smell the sweet aroma of God's love, and the scales are blocking the warmth of God's love on your skin.

It's like you are in a cocoon. God's love is all around you, and yet you can't feel it. Something hard has grown over your skin, over your heart, over your eyes, your nose and your ears. You can no longer feel God's love or hear God's voice.

What does it feel like to be separated from God like this?

Try to imagine what this might be like. Imagine you are in the same room as God—and yet you feel so far away.

(pause 8-10 seconds)

This is what life is like without Jesus.

(pause 8-10 seconds)

And now imagine that you are in this room, wanting so badly to experience the love of God. And Jesus walks into the room with a bucket of water and some towels. He looks at you and dips the first towel into the water and begins to wet the scales that cover your eyes. After a few moments you can now see Jesus because he has washed off the dragon-like scales from your eyes.

You watch now as Jesus returns the towel to the bucket of water, rings it out, and moves to washing your neck and shoulders. He reaches down and picks up a bottle of oil. It smells like lavender flowers, and he pours the oil over your head so that the scales come out of your hair. Imagine the oil dripping down the side of your face.

Your eyes are open now to seeing God's love. God's love fills the room like a cool mist. And your ears are open too, and you can hear God's voice and the sweet song he is singing. It's a love song for you. Your nose too is free. You can smell the sweet smell of the oil, and while you aren't sure what the smell is, it is wonderful and soothing.

Jesus continues to drip water over your head and it runs down your body and begins to loosen the scales. The scales pull and tug a bit at your skin as they come off.

But as your body becomes free you can feel once again the warmth of God's love. The scales fall to the ground. Imagine you are standing in a room full of God's love again, with your hands open like you are waiting for a gift. Your eyes are closed and you are soaking it all in.

(pause 8-10 seconds)

The only thing still covered with scales are your feet.

Imagine now that Jesus gets down on his knees and begins to wash your feet. He looks up and smiles at you as the last of the scales fall off.

All the icky feelings, all the conflict you felt between you and God, are gone.

Forgiveness means we can have peace with God.

Question: What does forgiveness mean?

Answer: Forgiveness means we can have peace with God.

 FOR THE PARENT OR MENTOR Sometimes we want to be able to protect our children from all the pain and struggle of the world. Most of our conversations and lessons in church and Sunday school center on how great God is. But what about when he isn't? What about when we feel the lack of God's presence in our lives? Is this something you are grappling with? Where in your life have you experienced a difficulty in faith? What did it look like for you to walk through the pain? Have you ever grieved for ways in which God has let you down? Have you lamented the conflict and pain you have experienced in your life with God? This, I think, is one of the most important things to consider as you invite your children into a life of faith. They need to see that life with God is not only about hope and faith. They need to see that it is also about disappointment and, yes, sometimes grief. Faith is when we let God meet us in that place and bring his peace, his *shalom*.

○ Spend some time this week at bedtime helping your child review the day. Help your child think about what it means to have peace with God. "Can you remember a time that you felt icky toward God?" "Has there been a time when you have been disappointed with God?" "Tell me about it."

○ Share with your child a story about when you had a difficult time in your life with God. Was there ever a time when you felt some frustration or disappointment with God? Did you ever have a crisis of faith? How did God meet you in it? How did the love of Jesus draw you back to a genuine relationship with God? How did he wash away the scales? How might you appropriately share some of this with your child?

○ Read Romans 5:1-11 out loud with your child this week. (Read from *The Message* if you can.) Talk about what true friendship with God looks like. Friendship with God can feel like other friendships in that even though you are friends, sometimes there are things to work through.

One disagreement doesn't nullify the friendship. Highlight for your child that our peace with God—our friendship with God—is a done deal. It's final. Once the scales come off, there is no going back. It's sealed by what Jesus accomplished on our behalf. The scales of sin have been removed for good, but sometimes the ickiness can still get in the way of our experience of God. Sometimes it can feel as though the scales are still there.

O Read Colossians 1:21-23 out loud with your child. Talk to your child about what it means to be without blemish in front of God. Go back to the imaginative prayer and remind your child of the scales that had formed and prevented peace with God. What is this passage saying about the process of being at peace with God? Ask your child, "Do you feel at peace with God?" And "What are some things you are talking to God about these days?" Remind your child of God's great love for them. You can never say it enough!

 **FOR THE JOURNAL** Set aside about fifteen minutes and ask your child to remember the imaginative prayer from this week. Help your child to remember what it was like to feel the ickiness toward God. Help them to remember that the love and grace of Jesus—his gentleness—took away the scales. Encourage your child to write in the journal a prayer of thankfulness for the love and forgiveness of God.

14

Forgiveness means God welcomes anyone

 **CONNECTION AND FORMATION** The purpose of this week's prayer is to invite your child into the experience of being welcomed by God. The story of Zacchaeus is a Sunday school favorite. It demonstrates the heart of God through the willingness of Jesus to pick out the one guy in the crowd who nobody wants to be around—and to invite himself to dinner at that guy's house. This imaginative prayer puts your child in the place of the swindler. Your child will imagine being the one in town who has cheated and lied to people. By identifying with the "sinner" in the story, we are helping your child understand the experience, perhaps, of how their own sin stands in relation to the reality of God's welcome. We want to bring your child to the awareness of personal sin—to realize that they too make mistakes and sin against people—to feel this, to recognize it, and then to have a pathway to experience the welcome of Jesus.

God's posture toward everyone is that of welcome. And yet we often think God is more preoccupied with sin than he is with welcoming sinners. This welcome of God, the kindness of God, leads to repentance. While our imaginative prayer doesn't lead your child through the process of repentance before God (that's next week), we are trying to sew a seed for your child that connects feelings of shame and unworthiness to God's welcome. The natural tendency is to disconnect from God when we feel shame or are confronted with our sin. One of the most interesting things about the story of Zacchaeus is that he wanted desperately to see Jesus. This pursuit of Jesus, even while carrying the awareness of our faults, is an important practice in our spiritual journey.

Question: What does forgiveness mean?
Answer: Forgiveness means God welcomes anyone.

 **IMAGINATIVE PRAYER**

Close your eyes and let's take a few deep breaths together.

God, I pray that you will release our imagination and help us to hear you speak to us during this time together. We open our hands to you. We open our ears to you.

(pause 8-10 seconds)

Come, Holy Spirit.

Imagine you live in a small town where everyone knows who you are.

It isn't that you are popular, but everyone knows who you are because they don't like you. You see, your job requires you to go to people's houses and collect money from them. It's called taxes. Think about the story of Robin Hood. Imagine that *you* are the sheriff of Nottingham. You steal money from the poor and give it to the rich.

Nobody really likes you. You are sort of an outcast. And you feel lonely.

What would it feel like to be this person?

(pause 8-10 seconds)

So you are the village tax collector. And sometimes you are dishonest. You take more money from people than you are supposed to collect. You know that this isn't right, but the temptation is too great. The money is too easy to come by. You have all the power. Nobody really knows that you are being dishonest; they only suspect you of being dishonest, and so you lie to them. You lie to everyone.

You steal from people.

And you lie to people.

And you take their money.

And you have become a wealthy person.

Most of the time you don't really think about it, but sometimes, when you are honest with yourself, your life, and the choices that you have made, it all bothers you.

(pause 5 seconds)

Think now about your own life. Your real life. As a ____ (boy or girl) with _____ (brothers and/or sisters) and friends. Are there any areas of your life that bother you? Are there any choices that you make that cause you to feel sad or ashamed? Do you ever feel like you are an outcast? Do you ever feel like you've done something wrong?

(pause 10-15 seconds)

Imagine you are back to being the tax collector in the village. Remember, you are that village's sheriff of Nottingham character. You notice a crowd beginning to gather as Jesus walks through the town. Everyone wants to be around Jesus. Everyone is pressing in close to him, and you are having a hard time seeing what he is doing and hearing the things he is saying. You try to get through the crowds so you can see Jesus, but people push you out and prevent you from getting through.

You look down the road and see a tree on the side of the road. It looks as though Jesus is going to go right past that tree, so you run ahead of the crowd, climb the tree, and wait for Jesus to pass by. Something about Jesus makes you want to meet him, to talk with him, to hear his voice clearly.

(pause 8-10 seconds)

As you sit in this tree, you have a few minutes to think before Jesus comes by. You think about your life and how much you wish you could change.

As you sit in the tree and think about your life, what comes to mind? What if Jesus looks right at you as he passes you by? What would you say to him? What would you ask him?

(pause 10 seconds)

Jesus is passing by now. And he does look at you. He stops walking, comes closer to the tree, and calls your name.

He says, "Come down from that tree and show me the way to your house. I want to eat dinner with you."

Out of all the people in town, and all the people who are gathered around Jesus, he has chosen you to eat dinner with tonight.

Imagine climbing down from the tree and walking over to where Jesus is standing. He looks at you and smiles.

He knows all about you.

He knows that you are the tax collector.

He knows that you lie.

That you cheat.

He knows that you steal.

And he wants to have dinner with you.

(pause 5-6 seconds)

Forgiveness means we can have peace with God.

Forgiveness means God welcomes anyone.

 Question: What does forgiveness mean?
Answer: Forgiveness means God welcomes anyone.

 How welcomed do you feel by God? At the end of each day this week, ask yourself, "Where did I feel the welcome of God in my life?" Sometimes there are seasons in our lives when we feel like outcasts. We get confronted by the sin in our lives and our response can sometimes be *shame* and *disconnection*. But this isn't the way that people who meet Jesus respond. When we see Jesus pick us out from the crowd and welcome us despite our status as a swindler—a welcome which he offers to

us daily—our response, it seems, should look something like Zacchaeus's response. Notice that Zacchaeus doesn't hide. He doesn't make an excuse for why the Teacher should go to someone else's house. He doesn't make comparisons of his life (and behavior) to others' lives. He doesn't view others as more deserving. He just welcomes the welcome of Jesus. Our ability as parents to receive the welcome of God will directly affect our ability as parents to extend the welcome of God to our children.

- Spend some time this week at bedtime helping your child review the day. Help your child think about what it means to be welcomed by God. "Where did you feel welcomed by God today?" "If you could have Jesus invite himself to do something with you today, what would it be? Play Legos? Swing at the park? Toss the ball?" Help your child imagine what it would be like for Jesus to invite himself to play.

- Gently help your child think about the ways they are like Zacchaeus. You might want to consider sharing some ways you have noticed your own sin. What are some ways you have experienced the welcome of God in the midst of being aware of your own sin and brokenness?

- Read the Zacchaeus story this week in Luke 19:1-10. Ask, "Why do you think Jesus wanted to go to Zacchaeus's house for dinner?" "What do you notice about how Zacchaeus responds to Jesus?" "Why does this seem significant?" "How could our response be like Zacchaeus's response?" "In what ways can we respond to the welcome of Jesus?"

- Read Luke 7:36-50. Remind your child of this story. Pay attention to Jesus' response to the woman in the story. Help your child see that people who make mistakes respond to Jesus with gratitude—not hiding, not fear, not shame. Their lives are changed by grace, not punishment.

 **FOR THE JOURNAL** Set aside about fifteen minutes and ask your child to remember the imaginative prayer from this week. Help your child remember what it was like to be Zacchaeus in the story. Encourage your child to make a list of things from the past week that they would like to talk

to Jesus about. "Are there any mistakes from this week? Any ways in which you hurt someone? Lied to someone? Spoke unkindly to someone?" Encourage your child to have a conversation with Jesus about these things. "Spend some time imagining Jesus inviting himself over."

15

Forgiveness means God
takes away our sin

 **CONNECTION AND FORMATION** This week we want to help your child experience the negative feelings that can come when we think about sin, as well as help them realize that we don't need to hide our sin. Hiding sin, and hiding our true self from God, is often the first instinct. We hide because of shame. When we feel shame, a little voice inside our head tells us that we're not good enough, that we're defective in some way. Rather than trying to hide our sin where we can't see it (and where other people can't see it either), we need to be able to look right at it with the understanding that forgiveness means God takes it all away.

This imaginative prayer makes a path toward repentance and confession. One of the most important steps in our spiritual formation is to learn true repentance. This includes growing in our ability to allow God to see our darkest and most secret places. "The man who is not afraid to admit everything that he sees to be wrong with himself, and yet recognizes that he may be the object of God's love precisely because of his shortcomings, can begin to be sincere. His sincerity is based on confidence, not in his own illusions about himself, but in the endless, unfailing mercy of God."[1]

 Question: What does forgiveness mean?
Answer: Forgiveness means God takes away our sin.

 **IMAGINATIVE PRAYER**

Close your eyes and let's take a few deep breaths together.

God, I pray that you will release our imagination and help us to hear you speak to us during this time together. We open our hands to you. We open our ears to you.

(pause 8-10 seconds)

Come, Holy Spirit.

Imagine you have a special little box. It's a wooden box. And it is about the size of a shoebox but a little bigger. It isn't really a pretty box. It isn't decorated. It isn't painted. There are no shiny hinges or handles. It's just plain wood.

Try to imagine what your box looks like.

(pause 10 seconds)

This is a box that you keep hidden. That's why it's not pretty. No one ever sees this box. It's a box that only you get into. But you keep it locked, just in case someone finds it.

If you had a box that you wanted to keep hidden where no one would find it, where would you hide it?

(pause 8-10 seconds)

Imagine going to that place where you keep your box, finding the key, and making sure that no one is around you. You open the box to check on the stuff that is inside.

(pause 8-10 seconds)

Inside this box are small pieces of paper with stuff written on them. It's your handwriting.

On these small pieces of paper, you have written all the things you have done that you wish you hadn't done.

Whenever you are mean, you write it down on a piece of paper and put it in the box.

Whenever you are disobedient to your parents, you come to this box and write it down on a small piece of paper—and lock it away.

(pause 5 seconds)

Whenever we do things that aren't God's best design for our lives, the Bible calls these things sin.

And you write your sins on little pieces of paper, fold the paper up a few times, and drop it into the box.

Imagine that you are looking into your box and it is full of little pieces of paper.

What are some things that you have written on your papers?

Have you ever told a lie?

Have you ever hit anyone?

Have you ever been unkind to your brother or sister?

Have you ever shown disrespect to your mother or father?

If you had a box like this, think to yourself now, what are some things you would have written on those little pieces of paper?

(pause 10-15 seconds)

If you could write one or two things right now—maybe a couple of things that happened this week . . .

Maybe a time this week when you acted in a way that was not loving . . .

What would you write on a piece of paper right now if you had a box like this?

(pause 10 seconds)

Now imagine that you have your box open and you are just about to close it and lock it up. And Jesus knocks on your door. You want to slam your box shut and hide it, but you don't. Jesus opens your door and peeks in—he smiles at you through the crack in the door. He whispers, "Can I come in?"

(pause 5 seconds)

Imagine inviting Jesus in. You open the door, and he sits down next to you. He doesn't even notice the box sitting there. He's just looking at you and smiling at you. Imagine Jesus giving you a big hug.

(pause 5 seconds)

You feel like you should show Jesus the box. And so you point it out to him. He looks in and he sees all the little pieces of paper. His eyes are very kind. He isn't angry. He isn't frustrated or mad.

He looks at you and says, "I know all about that stuff. I love you, and I forgive you."

Then he says, "Is there anything written on those little pieces of paper that you would like to talk about?"

Imagine picking up a piece of paper with something written on it. Show it to Jesus. He looks at it and says, "I forgive you." And then the piece of paper disappears.

You pick up another piece of paper and show it to Jesus. He does the same thing. He looks at it and says to you, "I love you and I forgive you." And then the piece of paper disappears.

(pause 5-8 seconds)

One by one you pick up a piece of paper with some sin of yours written on it, and one by one Jesus makes them disappear.

You are half-way through the box now, and it's getting easier.

How do you feel as the papers disappear? What does it feel like to have Jesus look at you and smile, and tell you that he loves you and forgives you?

(pause for 10 seconds)

Imagine now that your box is completely empty. You are sitting there with Jesus in front of your empty box.

Jesus says to you, "Any time you write something down and put it in this box, show it to me, and I'll forgive you. You don't need to hide anything in this box. Just keep the lid open."

(pause 5 seconds)

"I love you. I forgive you."

In Psalm 32 we read:

> Count yourself lucky, how happy you must be—
> > you get a fresh start.
> > your slate's wiped clean.
> Count yourself lucky—
> > God holds nothing against you
> > and you're holding nothing back from him.
> When I kept it all inside,
> > My bones turned to powder,
> > my words became daylong groans.
> The pressure never let up;
> > all the juices of my life dried up.
> Then I let it all out;
> > I said, "I'll [show God all my failures]."
> Suddenly the pressure was gone—
> > my guilt dissolved,
> > my sin disappeared. (vv. 1-5 *The Message*)

Forgiveness means we can have peace with God.

Forgiveness means God welcomes anyone.

Forgiveness means God takes away our sin.

 Question: What does forgiveness mean?
Answer: Forgiveness means God takes away our sin.

 How easy is it for you to confess your sins to God? How easy is it for you when others see your sin? Or when they point

it out? What happens to you when you realize that you have sinned (or are in the process of sinning)? How you answer these questions will ultimately be how your child will one day answer those questions. If we are constantly hiding our sin, if we are slow to recognize even the *small* sins—when we are impatient, unkind, lacking in gentleness—we are modeling to our children that sin is something to hide. But it isn't. As we grow in our awareness of our sin, we actually grow in our experience of God's love because the most radical place of God's love is at the place of our disobedience. If we are hiding our sin in a secret box, it's likely because we are feeling shame. We're trying to avoid punishment. Every way in which you are disobedient before God, he will meet with grace. You can cultivate a culture of forgiveness in your family by being quick to let Jesus see the stuff you are tempted to hide. Let him see it and receive from him the great "I love you." Receive from Jesus the words "I forgive you," and your child will catch onto it. If you are a person who easily receives grace from God, it will be so with your children. You'll no longer feel the need to hide your flaws. And you will be free.

- Spend some time this week at bedtime helping your child review the day. Help your child this week to think about what it means to experience God taking away our sin. "Is there anything from today that you would want to write down and put in the box?" "Is there anything you want to talk to Jesus about right now?"

- Model for your child what confession looks like. Pray together and confess some (appropriate) sins to God alongside your child. For example, "Dear God, I confess to you that I was impatient today and that I spoke with unkind words. Thank you, Jesus, for your love and forgiveness."

- Read Psalm 32:1-5 together this week. Mention to your child that David wrote this psalm. Ask, "How did David feel when he was silent and kept his sin from God?" This question is begging for a great conversation!

- Catch your child bringing sin out in the open. If your child lies to you and later comes to tell you the truth, focus on the truth telling, not the lie. Celebrate the confession and completely ignore the sin. The sin is gone once it is confessed.

○ Read 1 John 1:9 together. Explain that unrighteousness means sin.

○ Find an empty wooden box like the one featured in the imaginative prayer. Give it as a gift to your child. Remind them that it is empty. Ask them if they'd like to decorate it and keep it in their room as a reminder of the fact that we don't need to store our sins in a hideaway place.

○ Remind your child repeatedly this week that forgiveness means God takes away our sin. He makes it disappear.

 **FOR THE JOURNAL** Set aside about fifteen minutes and ask your child to remember the imaginative prayer from this week. Help your child reimagine what it was like to see Jesus look at the little slips of paper and simply say, "I love you. I forgive you." Encourage your child to write a note to Jesus in the journal. "What note would you want to write to Jesus after he tells you about all the forgiveness he has for you?"

16

Forgiveness means we can
forgive the sins of others

CONNECTION AND FORMATION This imaginative prayer continues to unpack what forgiveness means. We're trying to paint a broad picture of ways we can experience forgiveness—between us and God, between God and those who are lost, and between the people we interact with in our daily lives. Next week we'll look into the fruit of forgiveness, which is reconciliation. But this week we're setting the stage for talking about the larger (and systemic) issues of forgiveness and reconciliation by painting a picture of how forgiveness works between your child and someone they know and interact with. We're inviting your child to ask God to bring up whether there is anyone in their life they need to forgive, and then we're giving the child an opportunity to actually do it right away. We're trusting that this process doesn't need to be forced or contrived, but that God's Spirit will lead and help connect the dots. We've invited your child in a previous lesson to bring to mind someone they may need to forgive. We're doing it here again because of how often we actually need to consider this question in our lives.

The goal of spiritual formation is to grow in our likeness of Jesus Christ (Rom 8:29; 2 Cor 3:18). When asked how many times we ought to forgive those who sin against us, Jesus told a story about what it means to unconditionally forgive those who ask for mercy (Mt 18). Your child's formation toward the likeness of Christ is a lifelong journey. It takes a lifetime to learn how to forgive. There is a deep connection between the experience of being forgiven and our ability to forgive others. These go hand in hand, and this is a key connection we're trying to foster here.

Question: What does forgiveness mean?
Answer: Forgiveness means we can forgive the sins of others.

Close your eyes and let's take a few deep breaths together.

God, I pray that you will release our imagination and help us to hear you speak to us during this time together. We open our hands to you. We open our ears to you.

(pause 8-10 seconds)

Come, Holy Spirit.

Take a few moments and think about some of the people in your life. You mother. Your father. Your brothers and sisters. Your friends. Your teachers at school. Kids on the playground.

Is there anyone you know that has sinned against you?

Has anyone ever hurt you? Has anyone ever been mean to you? Or spoken harshly to you?

Take a moment to ask Jesus to bring someone to mind who you perhaps need to forgive.

(pause 8-10 seconds)

Say to Jesus, "Jesus, is there anyone I need to forgive? Is there anyone in my life I am bitter against?"

(pause 8-10 seconds)

Ask Jesus, "Is there anyone who you want me to forgive right now?"

Try to remember what it is that was hurtful to you.

Perhaps someone called you a name. Maybe Mom or Dad were impatient with you? Maybe your brother or sister took something out of your room? Maybe someone said something mean to you?

Is someone coming to mind? Nod your head if there is someone in your mind that you think you might need to forgive for something.

Imagine going to find that person. Imagine you have to look for that person, but you find them. Where do you find them? Are they at your house? At school? At the playground? In a classroom?

Imagine that the person who is coming to mind is standing before you.

Imagine this person standing right in front of you.

You reach into your pocket and pull out a small piece of paper. And written on that paper is the thing this person has done to you, the thing you need to forgive. Reach into your pocket and pull out the paper.

What is written on the paper?

(pause 8-10 seconds)

Imagine reading this paper out loud in front of the person who has hurt you or sinned against you.

Tell them now how they have hurt you.

(pause 5 seconds)

Imagine you are looking the person in the eyes.

Imagine looking right at them, and you say, "I forgive you for this."

Say it again to them: "I forgive you."

Imagine giving that person a hug and smiling at them.

Imagine now that the paper you were holding, the one that you took out of your pocket, has disappeared.

Imagine now that you invite this person to come and play with you.

(pause 8-10 seconds)

There is a story that we hear from the Bible about forgiveness.

Jesus is teaching his followers about forgiveness and says, "If your brother or sister or friend sins, if they do something wrong toward you or toward someone else, go directly to them and tell them. Don't talk to others about that person's sin. Go directly to them."

After the teaching about forgiveness, one of Jesus' followers, Peter, comes to Jesus and says, "Jesus, how many times should I forgive someone who sins against me? Up to seven times?"

Jesus answered, "I tell you, not seven times, but seventy-seven times."

Jesus goes on to tell a story about forgiveness, and he says this:

> The kingdom of God is like a king who decided to square accounts with his servants. As he got under way, one servant was brought before him who had run up a debt of a hundred thousand dollars. He couldn't pay up, so the king ordered the man, along with his wife, children, and goods, to be auctioned off at the slave market.
>
> The poor wretch threw himself at the king's feet and begged, "Give me a chance and I'll pay it all back." Touched by his plea, the king let him off, erasing the debt.
>
> The servant was no sooner out of the room when he came upon one of his fellow servants who owed him ten dollars. He seized him by the throat and demanded, "Pay up. Now!"
>
> The poor wretch threw himself down and begged, "Give me a chance and I'll pay it all back." But he wouldn't do it. He had him arrested and put in jail until the debt was paid. When the other servants saw this going on, they were outraged and brought a detailed report to the king.
>
> The king summoned the man and said, "You evil servant! I forgave your entire debt when you begged me for mercy. Shouldn't you be compelled to be merciful to your fellow servant who asked for mercy?" The king was furious and put the screws to the man until he paid back his entire debt. And that's exactly what my Father in heaven is going to do to each one of you who doesn't forgive unconditionally anyone who asks for mercy. (Mt 18:23-35 *The Message*)

Imagine now that the person is still standing in front of you, and your pockets are now filled with pieces of paper. All of these pieces of paper are ways this person has sinned against you.

Imagine taking each paper, reading it out loud to the person, and saying, "I forgive you."

"I forgive you."

"I forgive you."

"I forgive you."

Each time you forgive this person, a piece of paper disappears.

Forgiveness means we can have peace with God.

Forgiveness means God welcomes anyone.

Forgiveness means God takes away our sin.

Forgiveness means we can forgive the sins of others.

 Question: What does forgiveness mean?
Answer: Forgiveness means we can forgive the sins of others.

 FOR THE PARENT OR MENTOR Forgiveness is power-ful. So is *unforgiveness.* Sometimes it is hard to know where we have unforgiveness in our heart for others. When is the last time you asked God whether there is anyone in your life that you need to forgive? One way you can tell is to notice how you speak about people. Unforgiveness very quickly leads to bitterness, and bitterness has a way of leaking out in the tone of our voice or in harsh words we speak about others. The best way to teach your children about forgiveness is to practice it daily. Look each other in the eyes and say, "I forgive you." Do it often. Do it for the little things. Do it for the big things, and add lots of hugs and cuddling. When your child feels forgiven by you when they are disobedient, for example, they will understand and be able to forgive when someone has hurt them. When was the last time you asked your child, "Is there anything I need to ask your forgiveness for?" Try it. See what kind of dialogue opens up. You might be surprised by the hurt and agitation just below the surface.

○ Spend some time this week at bedtime helping your child review the day. Help your child this week to think about what it looks like to forgive the sins of others. "Is there anything that happened today where you might need to forgive someone?" or "Is there anyone you need to forgive today?" "Let's go back to our imaginative prayer. If you were to reach in your pocket and pull out a piece of paper that records how this person hurt you, what would be written on the paper?"

○ Help your child walk through the process of forgiveness when something or someone comes to mind. Help them to start by naming the thing that needs to be forgiven. For example: "Samantha was unkind to me today." "My sister pushed me." "Dad was impatient with me."

○ Help your child imagine standing in front of the person and saying, "I forgive you."

○ Read Matthew 18:21-35 together once or twice this week. This was introduced earlier in this lesson as well, but it's important enough to spend some more time with.

○ Look at the teaching in Matthew 18. Give a brief overview of what to do when someone sins against you.

1. Go to them directly (this is important; if this doesn't happen it's gossip!).
2. Go to them with another believer.
3. Bring the issue to a larger group of people in the church. (Clearly explain this to your child. Offer to help them if they get into conflicts that aren't resolved by 1. and 2. above.) The spirit behind the third step is not to shame someone but to seek help in resolving the conflict.
4. Treat them like tax collectors. Ask, "How did Jesus treat the tax collectors?" He loved them! He showed them kindness and ate meals with them. Remember, he invited himself over to Zacchaeus's house for dinner.

○ When you ask, "Is there anyone who comes to mind that you might need to forgive?" use this as an opportunity to probe a bit. Talk about how we have to daily forgive people. Talk about how seventy-seven times is simply a way of saying, "Keep forgiving! Don't stop!"

○ Ask your child, "How do you think we do as a family in quickly forgiving each other?" "Do you have any suggestions for how we could do better?"

○ Memorize Ephesians 4:32 with your child.

 **FOR THE JOURNAL** Set aside about fifteen minutes and ask your child to remember the imaginative prayer from this week. Encourage your child to write a prayer to God thanking him for all the people your child forgave this week. Say, "Make a list of people you extended forgiveness to this week. Let's write a prayer in your journal for each of these people." When we are able to bless the people who have hurt us, we know that we've made some progress in the area of forgiveness.

When we forgive,
we will be forgiven

 **CONNECTION AND FORMATION** True generosity is a sure sign of God's work in our lives. In this imaginative prayer we are nurturing the experience of what it is like to be generous and to feel generous toward others. Forgiveness is a work of generosity. Forgiveness is a gift we give away just like anything else. It is an act of generosity because it requires us to shift away from needing to hold onto things like bitterness and our right to be treated well. When we are willing to give generously with material goods, we are often also willing to forgive more easily. It's almost as if we are training the same muscle when we *give* and *forgive*. We don't need to try to answer why these two things are connected, but they seem to be connected for Jesus—so much so that the result of forgiving others is that we will be forgiven. And the result of giving to others is that others will give to us as well.

Jesus further strengthens the connection between the forgiveness of our sins and our ability to forgive others. It is included in his instruction on how to pray: "Forgive us our sins, as we forgive those who have sinned against us." As we are asking our heavenly Father to forgive us, Jesus seems to suggest that we have in mind others we need to forgive. Frederick Buechner says,

> Jesus is *not* saying that God's forgiveness is conditional upon our forgiving others. In the first place, forgiveness that's conditional isn't really forgiveness at all . . . and in the second place, our unforgivingness is among those things . . . that we need to have God forgive us most. What Jesus apparently is saying is that the pride that keeps us from forgiving is the same pride that keeps us from accepting forgiveness, and will God please help us do something about it.[1]

Question: What happens when we forgive?
Answer: When we forgive, we will be forgiven. When we
give, it will be given to us.

 **IMAGINATIVE PRAYER**

Close your eyes and let's take a few deep breaths together.

God, I pray that you will release our imagination and help us to hear
you speak to us during this time together. We open our hands to you.
We open our ears to you.

(pause 8-10 seconds)

Come, Holy Spirit.

Imagine you have a lemonade stand.

(pause 5 seconds)

Actually, it is sort of like a lemonade stand, but you aren't selling
lemonade.

You are selling flour. That's right, *flour*. The white stuff used for baking
cakes and bread.

But it isn't just any flour; it's not like the flour that you buy in the store—it's
kind of like a magic flour.

This flour bakes the best breads and cakes in the world.

This is a very rare flour that when baked into bread makes the best
tasting and most nutritious bread that has ever been invented.

Imagine your flour stand is on the corner near your home. You have
giant bags of this magic flour behind you and a giant bag right near
you where you take a measuring cup and scoop out flour for your
customers.

(pause 8-10 seconds)

There is a line of people waiting to buy flour from you.

Your neighbors.

Your friends.

Your teachers from school.

The bus driver.

Who else can you imagine would want to come buy some flour?

There are many people waiting in line to buy your flour, and as each person approaches your flour stand, you take a big scoop, scoop out some flour, and put it into a bag.

There is one person in line who looks a little tired. Their clothes are a little tattered, and they seem a little sad.

Imagine this person waiting in line.

And now it is their turn to buy flour from you. They are carrying a bowl and ask you to put some flour into their bowl, even though they don't have any money.

They are asking you to give it to them for free.

They say to you, "I don't have any money to buy flour to feed my family. Can you give me some flour for free?"

What would you do?

(pause 5-8 seconds)

Everyone in line has paid for their scoop of flour, but this person wants it for free.

How do you feel about giving it away for free?

(pause 5 seconds)

You can tell that this person is hungry. It seems like they haven't eaten bread in quite some time.

How do you imagine that this person looks?

(pause 5 seconds)

They are standing there with their bowl in hand, waiting for you to scoop out some magic flour for them.

Imagine taking your scoop and reaching deep into your bag of magic flour. You pull the scoop up with flour and you shake the scoop a little to make sure you get as much flour into the scoop as you can.

(pause)

You are just about to pour the scoop into the bowl when you have an idea. If you press the flour down, you might be able to get just a little more into the scoop.

Imagine now that you take your scoop and you press the flour down with your hand, which allows you to get a little more flour into your scoop. The scoop is overflowing with flour.

You smile at the person who wants this flour for free, and you pour the scoop into their bowl. They smile back.

They say, "Thank you." And you are happy that you gave the magic flour away.

There is something about giving it away that makes you feel good. It makes you happy.

This person is leaving, but you tell them to wait. You take your scoop again and scoop out another giant scoop of magic flour. You shake the cup to make more room, you press down the flour into the cup to make more room, and you scoop up some more until the scoop is running over with flour. And again you pour the flour into this person's bowl.

Two giant scoops of free magic flour. You have been generous.

(pause 8-10 seconds)

This is how Jesus says we are to give. Forgiveness is like a gift that we give to someone who has hurt us.

This is what it looks like for us to forgive others.

Jesus says to us:

> Forgive, and you will be forgiven. Give, and it will be given to you.
> A good measure, pressed down, shaken together and running over,
> will be poured into your lap. For with the measure you use, it will be
> measured to you.

(pause 8-10 seconds, then read the passage again, slowly)

> Forgive, and you will be forgiven. Give, and it will be given to you.
> A good measure, pressed down, shaken together and running over,
> will be poured into your lap. For with the measure you use, it will be
> measured to you.

With your eyes closed, imagine now that you are the one who needs
some free magic flour. Imagine that you are standing there with a bowl,
and someone scoops out two large scoops of magic flour.

Imagine someone is filling up your bowl. Imagine they are generous.

What does it feel like to have someone give to you so generously?

Forgiveness means we can have peace with God.

Forgiveness means God welcomes anyone.

Forgiveness means God takes away our sin.

Forgiveness means we can forgive the sins of others.

When we forgive, we will be forgiven. When we give, it will be given to us.

Question: What happens when we forgive?
Answer: When we forgive, we will be forgiven. When we
give, it will be given to us.

FOR THE PARENT OR MENTOR   One of the most powerful teachings of Jesus is that by not judging others, they in turn will not judge us; when we forgive, we get in return forgiveness from others; and when we give, we are often the recipients of generosity. These three themes—judgement, forgiveness, and generosity—are linked. Luke reports in his Gospel that Jesus links these three words within the same paragraph. Are the little judgments we make of others rooted in unforgiveness? Is our unforgiveness rooted in stinginess (or a lack of generosity)? Spend some time this week considering these three themes in your life and the way they may be connected. Even the tiniest of judgments against other people can help reveal some potential unforgiveness in our hearts. How might leaning into generosity in your life prime the pump of forgiveness? Spend some time this week simply asking God to speak to you about these words.

- Spend some time this week at bedtime helping your child review their day. Help your child think about forgiveness as a gift we can give away to others. "Was there anything today that happened where you were able to be generous with forgiveness?" "Have you experienced any forgiveness from someone this week?" "What was it like for you when your sister forgave you?" "That sounds like it was a really hard thing. What do you think it would look like for you to heap some magic flour into that situation?"

- Read Luke 6:37-38 together once or twice this week.

- Look at Jesus' teaching in Luke 6 as a whole.

- Help your child understand what it means to judge someone. When we judge others, we are thinking badly about them and pushing them into a certain mold or way of being that often isn't true.

- Be on the lookout for judgments in your home this week. They're easier to spot among siblings. "She's not . . ." "He's always . . ." It's hard to break the habit of judging each other because we're often judging in order to win an argument or get our way. Help your child understand that when we judge others, it's a sign that unforgiveness is taking root. Jesus' instruction not to judge has the very practical benefit that when we refrain from judging others, we create a safe environment that makes it far less likely that we'll be judged by them.

- Look for ways to encourage your children toward generosity, both in forgiveness and in general. Help them see that when they give, people are likely to give in return out of gratitude.

- Find ways to be generous with your children this week. Show them generosity in your grace and forgiveness. Think of ways you could be generous this week to your neighbors. Bake some cookies, for example, and deliver them to someone on your street or in your neighborhood.

 **FOR THE JOURNAL** Set aside about fifteen minutes and ask your child to remember the imaginative prayer from this week. Encourage your child to write a prayer to God asking for God to give them a generous heart as it relates to forgiveness, as well as the awareness to notice when they are judging someone. Say, "How could we ask God to help us in this area?"

Make a sign or a poster in your house that says, "Forgive, and you will be forgiven. Give, and it will be given to you."

18

Love and forgiveness make room for reconciliation

 **CONNECTION AND FORMATION** The purpose of this week's imaginative prayer is to have your child experience how sin and disconnection from God can create disconnection from others. Historically, this disconnection from others is often witnessed along lines of racial tensions and conflict between men and women. Think about some current conflict in the world and racial or ethnic tension is likely at its root. Your child's spiritual formation is as much about looking at the world and developing empathy and lament for systemic injustice as it is about taking a deeper look at what's happening within them. And this week we're attempting to create a context from which much more conversation can emerge.

One of the challenges laid against a more contemplative expression of Christian faith is that contemplation doesn't help solve the real and difficult circumstances of life. But as we grow in our experience of God we also grow near to the heart of God. And the heart of God will move us into the world.

We are trying to paint a picture of what reconciliation feels like rather than merely talking about the concept. We are hopeful that when your child is faced with conflict, disconnection, and even systemic injustice in everyday life, they might be able to draw on this imaginative prayer of how the love of Jesus has the power to bring forgiveness, peace, and reconciliation.[1]

"Nobody can be a Christian today without being a peacemaker," Henri Nouwen wrote in his book *Peacework*. "There are many . . . urgent tasks to accomplish: the work of worship, evangelization, healing of church divisions, alleviating worldwide poverty and hunger, and defending human rights. But all of these tasks are closely connected with the task that stands above them all: making peace."[2]

Question: What comes as a result of love?

Answer: Love and forgiveness make room for reconciliation.

Close your eyes and let's take a few deep breaths together.

God, I pray that you will release our imagination and help us to hear you speak to us during this time together. We open our hands to you. We open our ears to you.

(pause 8-10 seconds)

Come, Holy Spirit.

Imagine with me that you are playing at the park with some of your friends. You have a lot of friends. Some friends are boys. Some are girls. Some friends have lighter skin and some have darker skin. Some have dark hair, others have light hair. Some have freckles, some have a sun tan from being at the pool. You have so many friends, and everyone is so different—but you all get along.

(pause)

Imagine you are playing a fun game together. Everyone is having so much fun. Everyone is laughing. People are running around and playing. Everyone has brought something to share—some food, some toys. It's a great afternoon picnic at the park.

(pause)

Who is there with you? Who are the people there you are playing with? Try to picture them: laughing, having fun, sharing together.

(pause)

And then something happens. You look around and notice that people are arguing. They are fighting with each other and being unkind. You watch as your friends, who just moments ago were playing and laughing and sharing, begin fighting and arguing and demanding that their toys and games be returned.

What has happened?

You feel frustrated and upset. You notice that all of your friends are choosing sides—everyone is forming small teams, but it isn't a game. Everyone feels hurt and upset, and it seems like everyone is angry at everyone else. You too feel angry at some of your friends. Why is everyone fighting? Why is everyone choosing sides? Why are people separating and standing in small circles?

You too have separated from some of your friends. Some of your closest friends are sitting on a bench underneath a tree. You want to go to where they are, but you can't find the courage to move toward them. There is something icky in your heart that prevents you from smiling at them or talking with them.

(pause 8-10 seconds)

It feels like there is some invisible force, some invisible darkness that separates you from all your friends, except the ones standing right next to you. You feel sad, disconnected. You also feel insecure and wonder why people aren't being friendly toward you.

(pause 8-10 seconds)

You notice now that everyone has divided into smaller groups. You notice that the people you are standing near are just like you. They have the same color of skin you have and the same color of hair. If you are a girl, imagine you are standing near girls. If you are a boy, imagine you are standing near boys. Boys and girls, just like you. Everyone different from you is sitting on another park bench, under a different tree.

You look around the park. Everyone with freckles are standing together, boys on one side, girls on another. Everyone with light skin are standing together, boys on one side, girls on another. Everyone with dark skin are standing together, boys on one side, girls on another. Everyone is separated and disconnected.

And something—some force of darkness—will not allow you to all play, laugh, and share together.

How does this feel to you?

(pause 8-10 seconds)

With your eyes still closed, imagine now that Jesus shows up at the park. Watch him as he walks to each group. He is smiling, though he also seems to be speaking sternly to a few people. There were some people who were bullying others, taking their toys and stealing their lunches. Imagine Jesus convinces them to give those things back.

(pause 8 seconds)

Imagine now that Jesus sits down on one of the park benches, and the kids are sitting and standing around him. You can't quite hear what he is saying, but you can tell he is saying something kind to them. One by one each child around that park bench comes to Jesus and he welcomes them into his arms and gives them a hug.

He offers forgiveness to each one.

Those children Jesus has hugged begin to play together again.

Jesus makes his way to the next group of kids, at the next park bench. The same thing happens. He comes, gives hugs, sets things right, and asks each child to make things right with other children they offended or hurt.

You watch as two small groups of your friends who used to be separate join together to play a game. They are laughing again. They are friends again.

And now Jesus is coming your way. He is walking toward the group of friends you are standing near. Remember, everyone in your group looks like you and different from the other groups. Jesus comes into your group, gives everyone a hug, and sits on the park bench. He talks about love and forgiveness. He talks about sharing. He points to the group of kids now playing together. He asks you if you would be willing to play again with the kids who look different from you.

Everyone in your group nods their head yes. Each of you, one by one, talks with Jesus. And he has instructions for each of you to go make things right with the people you may have hurt.

Imagine you go to a few of your friends and ask them to forgive you for the ickiness in your heart toward them. Imagine receiving forgiveness from someone you hurt.

The icky stuff in your heart disappears and you join all the other kids.

There is something that Jesus has done here. Something bad had happened, and Jesus used his love to fix it.

Forgiveness means we can have peace with God.

Forgiveness means God welcomes anyone.

Forgiveness means God takes away our sin.

Forgiveness means we can forgive the sins of others.

When we forgive, we will be forgiven. When we give, it will be given to us.

Love and forgiveness make room for reconciliation.

 Question: What comes as a result of love?
Answer: Love and forgiveness make room for reconciliation.

 Where is forgiveness and reconciliation most needed in your own life? When was the last time you thought about this? Sometimes we break with old friends, and it seems like too much work to make it right. Sometimes old wounds fester beneath the surface. We are unforgiving toward some of the people we love the most. Our parents. Our spouse. Even our children. Spend some time this week thinking about un-reconciled differences between you and another person. Have you allowed any roots of bitterness to spring up? Unforgiveness has a way of leaking out unnoticed. Ask God to help you be on the lookout for a lack of forgiveness and relationships that are not at peace.

O Spend some time this week at bedtime helping your child review the day. Help your child think about forgiveness and reconciliation. "Are you experiencing any conflict with anyone right now?" "Do you want to talk about it?" "Are there any relationships at school that are hard for you right now?" When there is conflict in your home: "What could happen if we love each other right now?" Or "What do forgiveness and reconciliation look like right now?"

O Ask your child this week if they know what reconciliation means. Spend some time this week thinking through some past scenarios in your home where reconciliation and forgiveness happened. What was the turning point in those situations? Where does conflict require the most work in your home? The most patience? Help your child see that forgiveness and reconciliation require intentionality—it doesn't just happen all by itself.

O Read Galatians 3:28. Have a conversation with your child about conflict and the resulting division. Explain that Paul is writing to a group of people divided along racial and gender lines over some important matters. Have an honest conversation with your child about race and about conflict between people of different colors. Don't shy away from current events where racial tensions are at work. Spend some time helping your child understand that there are systemic issues at work in areas of racial divisions. Encourage your child, for example, to consider the unfortunate history of systemic injustice in the United States (e.g., slavery, Jim Crow laws, police brutality).

 **FOR THE JOURNAL** Set aside about fifteen minutes and ask your child to remember the imaginative prayer from this week. Read Romans 12:18 out loud with your child. Read it together. Encourage your child to sit for just a bit and think about what it means to live "at peace" with the people in his or her life. Ask, "Is there anyone with whom you are currently not at peace?" Encourage your children to write a prayer to God asking for help in pursuing reconciliation and forgiveness for difficult relationships.

Forgiveness means we can have peace with God.
Forgiveness means God welcomes anyone.
Forgiveness means God takes away our sin.
Forgiveness means we can forgive the sins of others.
When we forgive, we will be forgiven. When we give, it will be given unto us.
Love and forgiveness make room for reconciliation.

CREEDAL QUESTIONS AND ANSWERS

Question: What does forgiveness mean?
Answer: Forgiveness means we can have peace with God.

Question: What does forgiveness mean?
Answer: Forgiveness means God welcomes anyone.

Question: What does forgiveness mean?
Answer: Forgiveness means God takes away our sin.

Question: What does forgiveness mean?
Answer: Forgiveness means we can forgive the sins of others.

Question: What happens when we forgive?
Answer: When we forgive, we will be forgiven. When we give, it will be given
   unto us.

Question: What comes as a result of love and forgiveness?
Answer: Love and forgiveness make room for reconciliation.

QUESTIONS AND ACTIVITIES

- Spend time this week reviewing each of the past six weeks.

- Ask some good questions or make some suggestions that might stimulate reflection. For example:

  - How have we grown over the past few weeks in our understanding
    of forgiveness?

○ Where have you noticed conflict at school? Are different groups of people experiencing conflict between them? How could we pray for what's going on at school (or on their sports team or other areas outside the family)?

○ Let's review the steps of forgiveness and reconciliation together. (See week one of this unit.)

○ Do you feel like there is reconciliation between you and God? Tell me more.

○ Remind your child of their standing before God. They are without blemish (Col 1:21-23).

○ Where did you feel welcomed by God today?

○ Have you noticed anyone recently that might need to be welcomed by God (remember Zacchaeus)? Who?

○ Ask your child about shame. Maybe share a story from your own life when you have felt badly about something that you did or didn't do. Remind your child that we all make mistakes and that it's okay to feel bad about making mistakes, but shame is different. A little voice in our head sometimes says, "I'm bad!" That's the voice of shame. Help your child learn to pay attention to when this is happening and have them talk with God about it.

○ Where are you aware of the need for God's peace and reconciliation?

○ Review the portion of the creedal poem that corresponds with part three, "Forgiveness." Help your child memorize these next six lines. Review the creedal poem from parts one and two. See if you can recite them all with your child.

PART 4

Jesus Is the King

19

Jesus is the King who came to undo the power of death

CONNECTION AND FORMATION Over the next several weeks we'll be looking at how Jesus the King wins victory over the power of sin, death, and the devil. The sessions in part four are the most theological of all the sessions in this volume. Dallas Willard said, "Spiritual formation may be thought of as the *shaping of the inner life, the spirit, or the spiritual side of the human being.* The formation of the heart or will (which I believe is best taken as the spirit) of the individual, along with the emotions and intellect, is therefore the primary focus."[1] Part of the spiritual formation journey is the formation of the intellect. Again, we are not essentially brains in bodies, and the goal here is not primarily doctrinal education. But what we think—what your children think—about the work of Jesus will shape the way they experience God. It will shape the way they talk with him.

God became King through love, forgiveness, and entering this world in the life of Jesus, conquering the power of the *Accuser*, who had held us captive to sin and death. Greg Boyd speaks powerfully: "Christ did whatever it took to release us from slavery to the powers, and this he did by becoming incarnate, living an outrageously loving life in defiance of the powers, freeing people from the oppression of the devil through healings and exorcisms, teaching the way of self-sacrificial love, and most definitively by his sacrificial death and victorious resurrection."[2]

This first imaginative prayer in part four is written to help your child to be immersed in the story where the Accuser leads us toward death and away from God. Our separation from God began here. And the result of this separation, for both Adam and Eve, was shame. They hid. This pattern of sin—extending beyond the limits God has set for us, illegitimate desires and willful disobedience—continues to lead us away from God. We hope this imaginative experience begins to help your child experience the pattern of disconnection from God, and through continued conversation, begins to put Jesus' death and resurrection in its proper place as the definitive event making connection to God possible again.

 Question: What did Jesus the King come to do?
Answer: Jesus is the King who came to undo the power of death.

 **IMAGINATIVE PRAYER**

Close your eyes and let's take a few deep breaths together.

God, I pray that you will release our imagination and help us to hear you speak to us during this time together. We open our hands to you. We open our ears to you.

(pause 8-10 seconds)

Come, Holy Spirit.

(Note to the Parent or Mentor: if your child is a boy, have him imagine he is Adam; if your child is a girl, have her imagine she is Eve.)

Imagine with me that you are in the Garden of Eden.

Imagine that you are Adam (or Eve).

This is a beautiful garden. It's a garden God has made in which everything is good. The animals are good. The plants give food and are nourishing to you. You are at peace with everything. You are at peace with God.

Imagine that God is present with you in the Garden. Imagine that everything is good between you and God. God has put you in the Garden and says these words to you:

"You can eat from any tree in the Garden, except for that one tree, over there."

Imagine looking through the Garden and seeing the very special tree, the one that God doesn't want you to eat from. It's in the very middle of the Garden.

What does the tree look like?

(pause 8-10 seconds)

This tree in the middle of the Garden is called the tree of the knowledge of good and evil.

Look again at the tree. Imagine you begin to walk closer to the tree. You want to get a closer look because the tree is very beautiful. The fruit on this tree is so colorful.

Imagine with me that you are getting closer to the tree of the knowledge of good and evil.

(pause 8-10 seconds)

God is there with you. Imagine God reaches out his hand to comfort you. Imagine God is with you, Adam. Imagine God is with you, Eve. He has his arms around you, and you are standing right next to God. And he begins to show you all the trees in the Garden that you may eat from—all the fruit you could possibly want on every tree.

"Look at all of these trees I have made for you," God says. "All of these trees are good and beautiful, and you may eat from every tree in the Garden, except for that one." God is pointing now at the tree of the knowledge of good and evil.

"If you eat from that tree, you will die."

Imagine, Adam, that you are looking at Eve.

Imagine, Eve, that you are looking at Adam.

Both of you are looking now at the tree of the knowledge of good and evil.

This is the one tree you cannot eat from.

(pause 5-8 seconds)

Imagine now that a few months later you are walking through the Garden. Remember, this Garden is not small. It's not like any other garden you have ever seen. This Garden is more like a forest. The trees are tall, the plants are numerous, and there are fruits and vegetables all around you, everywhere, for you to eat.

Imagine you are walking through this wonderful garden forest one day and you are eating fruit from one of the trees.

Guess who shows up: the Accuser.

The Accuser is like an evil supervillain.

The Accuser has an evil power—the power to destroy things that are good.

When God creates, the Accuser tries to destroy.

Where God loves, the Accuser hates.

Where God gives grace and forgiveness, the Accuser brings the opposite of grace and forgiveness.

The Accuser is sometimes called "Satan" or "the devil."

The Accuser is like the witch in the land of Narnia.

The Accuser is like Saruman in *The Lord of the Rings*.

And he is here, in the Garden. He has taken on the form of a crafty and slithering snake.

He begins to speak to you and says:

(with an accusing tone) "Is it true God has said to you that you may not eat of any of the fruit in the Garden?"

Imagine looking at the snake, the Accuser, saying those words.

What does it feel like to have a piece of fruit in your hand knowing that you are allowed to eat it, and to have the Accuser say to you that you are doing something wrong?

"Not at all," you say, calmly. "We are allowed to eat from the trees of the Garden. It's only about the tree in the middle of the Garden that God said, 'Don't eat from it; don't even touch it, or you will die.'"

(pause 5-10 seconds)

(use an accusatory and nasty tone when you read the parts of the Accuser)

"You won't die!" says the Accuser. "God knows that the moment you eat from that tree [*he is pointing at the tree of the knowledge of good and evil*] you will see what is really going on. You'll be just like God, you'll know everything, ranging all the way from good to evil."

The Accuser is looking at you now, and waiting for you to respond.

Imagine looking at the tree of the knowledge of good and evil. It looks so beautiful. Imagine, what would it be like to know everything?

(pause 8-10 seconds)

Imagine now that you go close to the tree. You are standing in the middle of the Garden and you take a piece of fruit from the tree of the knowledge of good and evil.

Imagine the fruit is in your hand. What does it feel like to hold this piece of fruit?

(pause 5-6 seconds)

And now you eat it.

And everything changes.

Adam, you look at Eve, and you feel embarrassed. You feel shame. And you are angry for the first time.

Eve, you look at Adam, and you too feel embarrassed. You feel shame. And you hide behind a tree so Adam can't see you.

You hear God calling out to you in the Garden. But you stay hidden.

Both of you are now hiding from God. What does it feel like to hide from God?

(pause 5-8 seconds)

Imagine now that God finds you. He is not angry—but he is very sad.

God brings you both close to him and hugs you. He looks at you and reminds you that eating from the tree of the knowledge of good and evil was a choice that cannot be undone.

God reminds you that the consequence of this is that you cannot live forever, as he intended.

What does it feel like knowing that if you hadn't eaten from that tree that you would have lived forever?

(pause 8-10 seconds)

God explains to you now what it means that you will someday die. For the first time ever you understand what death is.

Imagine God takes you now to the edge of the Garden and tells you to leave.

You walk out of the Garden and look back, and you notice that God has built a large gate in front of the entrance of the Garden and has set guards there—you will never enter the Garden again. You will not live forever, and God's presence is no longer with you.

Jesus is the King who came to undo the power of death.

Question: What did Jesus the King come to do?
Answer: Jesus is the King who came to undo the power of death.

 How do you experience this scene where God discovers that Adam and Eve have chosen against his will? Do you imagine that God is angry, or do you imagine that God is heartbroken? This question

reveals much about our own life with God. It may also reveal something about ourselves and our parenting. We all get angry with our children. But how often do we feel heartbroken? How often do we take the same posture that God took with Adam and Eve? He covered their nakedness and shame with clothes. He issued consequences (the pain of childbirth and the curse on the ground) not as punitive measures but as an effort toward restoration. Even God's banishment of Adam and Eve from the Garden was God's first step toward restoration. God's effort has always been toward restoration. Revoking the privilege of eternal life is the first step toward restoring Adam and Eve, because what Adam and Eve needed most at that moment was to be reminded of their limits—the proper order of creation and their place in it. Our first lesson in experiencing a relationship with God is to remember not only that we are created and God is our Creator, but that our very breath is his own breath. Our breath is something we wouldn't have if he had not given it. Jesus' victory over death is not a random victory. Jesus conquered something that, up until the resurrection, had a certain finality about it. Death is the ultimate separation. Conquering death demonstrates that God's ability is limitless; he even has sway over something so final and universal as the end of life. Thus, through God's conquering of death we are re-membered; that is, we become members again of a rightly ordered creation. Do you see God's banishment from the Garden as anger keeping you away, or do you see a heartbroken God who is waiting for your return? How might this relate to the ebb and flow of your child's obedience and disobedience? Are the instances of disobedience moments of disconnection in your home? Or can they become opportunities for deeper connection?

- Spend some time this week at bedtime helping your child review the day. Pretend that you are the snake slithering up next to your child, and begin to reenact the scene in Genesis 3. Pretending to be the snake is a great way of opening up conversation. Say (in a slithering voice), "Is it true, that God has said to you that you may not eat of any of the fruit in the Garden?" This provides a bit of playfulness while helping to remind your child of the lesson during the middle of the week.

- Spend some time reflecting with your child on the sense of separateness we often feel from God.

○ Explore ways in your home that cause separateness or disconnection from each other. What kind of behaviors cause disconnection? Are there similar behaviors in our life that can cause disconnection with God? Ask, "Are there times when we all feel connected?" "What is going on when we feel like this?" And similarly, "Are there times when we are disconnected as a family?" "Why do you think this happens?"

○ Read, once again, the story found in Genesis 3. Talk about the separateness that we see in this story:

  ○ the conflict and blame that happens with Adam and Eve

  ○ Adam and Eve's hiding and the sense of shame that enters

  ○ the disconnection from God and his gift of the Garden

  ○ the ultimate separateness found in death

○ Help your child understand that Jesus came to reverse all separateness and to create connection, both to God and to each other.

FOR THE JOURNAL Set aside about fifteen minutes and ask your child to remember the imaginative prayer from this week. Have your child think again about the scene in the Garden. Ask your child to think about and imagine what it would be like to live forever, once all things are restored. Have your child pretend that today is the day before the day that all of humanity gets to enter into the Garden once again. Ask your child to write a letter to God describing what they hope to see when the unity of the Garden is restored.

20

Jesus is the King who came to defeat the power of sin

 **CONNECTION AND FORMATION** This week's imaginative prayer is meant to introduce your child to more specific categories of sin and the powers they exhibit. Much of the work of spiritual formation is learning to recognize the patterns of our own sinful behavior. "Classically, spiritual writers have often broken our moral struggles down into a battle with a number of innate propensities that they called the seven deadly sins."[1] The seven deadly sins have a rich tradition in the church as being the source of all other sin.

This week's prayer will help your child experience the pull of temptation—into a cave with murky water and thick, foul air—and the reality and normalcy of that pull in our lives. However, the real work of this week's imaginative prayer is the conversation that you will have with your child. I have been purposeful in placing this material here. With long stretches of God's love, grace, and forgiveness having already been explored, it's time to cultivate some language for your child to grow more familiar with their own patterns and compulsions.

Again, a healthy self-disclosure from you as a parent can go a long way. I have found that as I share with my children (for example, my long-time struggle with hurry and impatience), they too have started to notice their own patterns. Recently, I have considered getting the word *patience* tattooed on my forearm for me and all the world to see. As I shared this bit of news with one of my daughters and described the pull of impatience on me, without any prompting from me she responded, "I'd want to get a tattoo that said *trust*." With just a few questions and some reflection she was able to name her tendency toward *fear*, connecting it to a deeper desire to trust God more. Spiritual formation isn't the management of sin or making efforts to eradicate these compulsions. But once we are aware of them, we're able to bring this awareness before God in conversation and trust that through the Holy Spirit's work in our lives, these compulsions will be met with the healing power of Jesus.

Question: What did Jesus the King come to do?
Answer: Jesus is the King who came to defeat the power of sin.

Close your eyes and let's take a few deep breaths together.

God, I pray that you will release our imagination and help us to hear you speak to us during this time together. We open our hands to you. We open our ears to you.

(pause 8-10 seconds)

Come, Holy Spirit.

Imagine with me that you are in the middle of a deep forest and you are surrounded by trees. And you are standing in front of giant cave.

(pause 8-10 seconds)

The entrance to the cave is right in front of you. It's a large cave. Perhaps one in which a dragon or a great beast might live inside. The cave seems dark. But you are curious about what lies beyond the entrance of the cave. Is it a deep cave? Is there, in fact, something living inside?

(pause 5 seconds)

You decide you want to find out what is inside. You take courage and move to the front of the cave. Imagine that you have some rocks in your hand, and you throw the rocks into the darkness of the cave, and you hear a faint echo call back to you. This is a deep and dark cave. And the darkness feels almost like a thickness in the air. A bad smell is coming from the cave, and as you make your way deeper inside the cave, the smell gets worse; it becomes difficult to breathe.

(pause 5-8 seconds)

Imagine walking down a dark trail that curves around and around, heading deeper into the cave.

There is a great power inside this cave. There is something like gravity or a great magnet pulling you deeper into the cave. It is almost like quicksand, except you aren't sinking into the ground, you are being pulled deeper and deeper into the cave. And the smell is getting worse. It is becoming more and more difficult to breathe.

(pause for 5-8 seconds)

You try to turn around and walk the other way, but you can't. The force is too strong. The power is too great. You feel powerless to escape the cave. You feel trapped.

How does it feel to be inside this cave? Are you scared? Are you angry? Are you sad?

Imagine now that you reach the center of the cave. You see that there is a giant wall at the end of the cave. And on this wall hang seven faucets, like the faucet at your kitchen or bathroom sink, or the faucet that you connect your garden hose to when you want to run through the sprinkler or water the garden. This giant wall with giant faucets is a strange sight, indeed. Each faucet is the size of a car. Imagine looking at the seven giant faucets mounted on the wall of the cave.

(pause 8-10 seconds)

Pouring out of each faucet is thick, colored liquid. Each faucet has a different color coming out of it. But it isn't just a trickle flowing out of these faucets, it's like a rushing waterfall. Imagine colored water rushing out of each faucet. These are powerful faucets, and the water rushes together into a giant pool. The stink is coming from this pool. As the liquid mixes together, there is a mist—a gas that fills the air around you. It rises up like steam rises when you take a warm bath or shower. Imagine looking into the pool and seeing all the colors mix together. The pool is dark and murky and smelly.

(pause 5-8 seconds)

As you look closer at each faucet, you now notice that each faucet has a label. A large wooden sign hangs on each faucet, and a word is written on each sign. It's too dark in here to read them, but you re-member the flashlight in your pocket. Take the flashlight out of your pocket and shine the light on the signs.

The first one says Lust.

Lust is a word that describes when our desire for something is stronger than it should be. Sometimes we lust after things when we want them a little too much. When we desire something so much that it feels like there is power drawing us to that thing, this is called lust.

The second one says Gluttony.

Gluttony is a word that means taking too much. Sometimes we have too much of something—too much food, too much TV, or too much activity. We have gluttony when we are wasteful.

The third faucet says Greed.

You know what *greed* means. It is like lust and gluttony, but greed is when you keep wanting more. Greed is when you want more and more and more, all for yourself.

You move on to the fourth faucet, which says Sloth.

Sloth means laziness. It's a funny word that describes what it is like to not want to do anything. Experiencing sloth is like having important work to do and instead deciding to just lie down and ignore the work.

You shine your light on the fifth faucet. It says Wrath.

Wrath means excessive and violent anger. Wrath is what makes people fight and kill each other. Wrath is anger that won't go away.

The sixth faucet's sign says Envy.

Envy is when you are discontent with what you have. We envy when we look at what someone else has and want it for ourselves. Envy is feeling sad when someone else has something better than us.

And the sign on the final faucet, with colored water pouring out of it, says Pride.

Pride is when you feel so good about yourself and your accomplishments that you compare yourself to others. It is the opposite of humility. We have pride when we rely too much on ourselves and not enough on God's grace.

(pause 8 seconds)

You step back from the faucets and watch the powerful waterfalls pouring into the pool below. You feel icky and the air is smelly, and it is becoming more difficult to breathe.

Imagine that there is a giant wheel in the center of the cave. You wonder if this is the way to turn off these faucets. All of these faucets have bad things pouring out of them. Bad and powerful things. Imagine trying to turn the giant wheel (which looks like the wheel that a captain of a large ship might use to turn the boat). It's too heavy, and you aren't able to turn it.

Now imagine Jesus is there. He is standing right behind you. Imagine stepping back from the wheel to make room for Jesus to try to turn off the faucets. Jesus turns the wheel, and the faucets shut off.

Immediately.

Completely.

The cave fills with light and fresh air. And there is a sweet smell.

Jesus is the King who came to undo the power of death.

This is Jesus the King, who came to defeat the power of sin.

Question: What did Jesus the King come to do?

Answer: Jesus is the King who came to defeat the power of sin.

 FOR THE PARENT OR MENTOR Sin is powerful. It draws us in, doesn't it? One of the most difficult practices is to pay attention to our sin and its effect on us, without falling into shame or condemnation. We pay attention so that we are aware of the way sin has its way with us. We pay attention so that we can come to God and confess it. "If we confess our sins," writes John, "he is faithful and just and will forgive us" (1 Jn 1:9).

When is the last time you considered the specific ways sin draws you in? What does your current conversation with God look like? What does it feel like to talk to God about sin?

One of the helpful things about the seven deadly sins is the way they get at the heart of our behaviors that aren't yet aligned with God. Lust isn't just sexual, it's wanting things in such a way that we are inordinately attached to the thing we want. We want it with such a great desire that it pushes out the desire for God. We can lust over anything. In the same way, greed isn't merely about money. It can be about our time, our energy, our words, and even our own spiritual growth. Spend some time in conversation with God this week reflecting on each of the seven deadly sins. As you get more insight about your sin, bring it before God and receive forgiveness—you'll be amazed by how this opens up grace-filled conversations with your child about their own pull toward sin. When we experience the grace of God (which we can't do unless we are confessing our sin), we are more likely to extend grace to others.

O Spend some time this week at bedtime helping your child review the day. Talk about power and compulsion. Talk about the way we can sometimes be pushed or pulled into making choices that go against God's desire for our lives.

O Be on the lookout for opportunities to appropriately share with your child how you were pulled into a bad choice this week.

   O If you find that you were impatient with your child this week, let them know you noticed it and talked to God about it.

- ○ "Did you notice how I got pulled into being impatient with you this morning? I'm so sorry about that. Please forgive me."

- ○ Demonstrate gratefulness for God's grace. "I'm so glad that I can ask for God's help when I start feeling impatient."

- ○ If, in your child's presence, you sin against someone, let your child see you ask for forgiveness.

○ Help your child see ways that they may also be pulled into sin. Be careful not to shame your child. Simply notice it out loud with them and offer grace. Invite your child to consider their actions.

- ○ "Are you having trouble sharing right now? Well, let's ask God to help you. Remember, Jesus turned off the faucet of greed. Let's share."

- ○ The more open you are with noticing your own sin, the easier it might be to ask your child if they notice any of these in their life.

- ○ Don't point it out for them. Simply ask good questions. If they aren't ready for this kind of noticing and self-reflection, don't press it.

○ Spend some time this week talking through each of the seven deadly sins. Perhaps spend five minutes each day talking about one sin. Try to make it lighthearted. These are hard concepts. Try to bring things up without any sense of condemnation.

 **FOR THE JOURNAL** Set aside about fifteen minutes and ask your child to remember the imaginative prayer from this week. Encourage your child to sit quietly for a few moments and ask God to help them see where sin may be tugging at them this week. If you've been able to talk through each of the seven deadly sins, ask your child to list these in a journal and pray, "God, which of these is pulling on me this week?" Remind your child that God helps us see our sin, and then he always extends his grace to us. (Remind them of the lesson on God's love.)

21

Jesus is the King who came to defeat the power of the Accuser

 **CONNECTION AND FORMATION** This imaginative exercise is the last in a three-part series unpacking a classical view of Christ's work: defeating the power of sin, death, and the devil.[1] Here, we are trying to help your child understand that the Accuser, sometimes known as Satan or the devil, once had a great deal of power. This power was defeated by Jesus on the cross as he took onto himself the accusations that were outstanding against the whole human race. This is one of the main themes of each of the Gospel writers in telling the stories of Jesus as he worked toward defeating the power of the enemy by inaugurating his kingdom, the kingdom of God. The enemy is being defeated, and the work and life of Jesus are just the beginning.

The Accuser is actively opposed to the goodness of God in your child's life. And yet we often fail to take seriously this kind of activity. Within many streams of Christian tradition (Orthodox, Catholic, evangelical, charismatic) we find teaching on the importance of what is often referred to as the "discernment of spirits."[2] We learned in lesson thirteen that we often experience disconnection from God—a feeling of separation. Sometimes this separation has to do with things going on inside our own heart; other times the disruption comes from outside circumstances; and sometimes these disruptions stem from the Accuser.

Again, we learn some practical tips from Ignatius of Loyola, who wrote a guide for how to discern what forces are at work in our inner lives: we simply must be willing to consider the influence of the devil. This all may seem like a steep climb. You may be wondering how this can be incorpo-rated into your child's spiritual formation. The truth is that this level of discernment requires a degree of self-awareness that is likely a bit down the road from where most children are developmentally. So please don't ask your child to consider whether their view of the kingdom or habits of life are being unduly influenced by the Accuser. As this conversation is opened up, we hope that your child will become at least *aware* that forces are actively working against the purposes of God. These forces are at work internally and externally. And these forces have been stripped of their real power through the work of Jesus. As with so much of what we're doing here, we are laying a foundation for work at a later developmental stage.

Question: What did Jesus the King come to do?

Answer: Jesus came to defeat the power of the Accuser.

IMAGINATIVE PRAYER

Close your eyes and let's take a few deep breaths together.

God, I pray that you will release our imagination and help us to hear you speak to us during this time together. We open our hands to you. We open our ears to you.

(pause 8-10 seconds)

Come, Holy Spirit.

Imagine with me that there is a great power in the world. This great power comes from the one who is called the Accuser.

(pause 5 seconds)

The Accuser is a villain who likes to destroy. He likes to tell lies and cheat and steal. But most of all, he likes to accuse people and make them feel bad. This is his power. He likes to remind people of all their mistakes and all the ways that they aren't perfect.

(pause 5-10 seconds)

The Accuser is the one who showed up in the Garden and introduced temptation.

(pause 5-10 seconds)

The Accuser got his power long ago. He has used his power to bring disobedience and sin into the world.

From last week, picture again the deep, dark cave with all of the faucets. Remember the signs hanging from each faucet.

Remember the powerful flow of each sin: *lust, gluttony, greed, sloth, wrath, envy,* and *pride*?

The Accuser is looking throughout the world for these sins. And when he finds them, he accuses people as though they have committed a crime. If he finds a little bit of greed in someone, he brings a complaint against that person. He reminds them of their greed.

Think with me about your life. Have you ever done something wrong or made a mistake? Have you ever been disobedient? Have you ever been mean or unkind to someone?

Did you ever feel bad about yourself after you made a mistake? Did you ever feel like someone was accusing you, or whispering bad things in your ear? This is the Accuser. His evil villain power is to accuse us of sin and to try to make us feel ashamed.

(pause 8 seconds)

Now imagine Jesus with me. Remember the stories of Jesus' welcome to the great party. Remember Jesus' kindness to Zacchaeus. Remember with me how gentle and loving and forgiving Jesus is. He has never done anything wrong, and yet when King Jesus comes into the world, the Accuser begins to accuse him.

(pause 8-10 seconds)

Imagine with me that the Accuser has a large jar, and inside this jar are tokens or coins. These tokens are part of his power. When he accuses someone, he has to spend one of these tokens like at an arcade or in a vending machine. Every time the Accuser points out a sin in someone, he has to spend a token.

Imagine with me that Jesus is the King and is standing before the Accuser.

Imagine the Accuser begins to accuse Jesus of wrongdoing. He accuses Jesus of lust and greed. He accuses Jesus of envy and wrath. And every time he accuses Jesus the King, a token in his jar disappears. Imagine that the jar is as big as the world, and it seems like it is filled with millions and millions of tokens. Millions and millions of accusations and lies.

The Accuser has so much deception and so much power in that giant jar. There are so many lies.

Jesus the King is standing in front of the Accuser, and one by one all the tokens from the jar disappear. Every accusation and lie and deception that the Accuser has stored up in his jar is slowly emptied out onto Jesus the King.

Jesus takes on all those accusations and lies—he takes them all on—all at once.

Imagine with me now that the Accuser, this evil supervillain, reaches into his giant jar of power and finds it is empty. He spent all his power and all his accusations on Jesus. Imagine looking at the giant, empty jar and now look at the Accuser. He is powerless.

In fact, he is chained up, and his power is all gone.

(pause 5-10 seconds)

What the Accuser forgot, what he didn't realize, is that all his power was taken away by Jesus the King because none of the Accuser's lies and accusations about Jesus were true. Jesus is the King who stood innocent before the Accuser and made all the tokens disappear.

The Accuser has no power.

Jesus is the King who came to undo the power of death.

Jesus is the King who came to defeat the power of sin.

Jesus is the King who came to defeat the power of the Accuser.

Question: What did Jesus the King come to do?

Answer: Jesus came to defeat the power of the Accuser.

 The apostle Peter wrote a letter warning people that the devil is like a lion who prowls around waiting and looking to devour someone. One of the greatest realities of parenting is that you are consistently making mistakes. It's true. Read all the books you want about parenting and you'll still make mistakes. Most parents become so used to the nagging thoughts of inadequacy that it's hardly even noticed. As parents, we live with a constant reminder that we aren't able to be everything and give everything to our children that we wish we could. The little voice that reminds us of this is the Accuser.

When was the last time you noticed the little voice making accusations against you, telling you a story about what is happening around you that isn't true? When was the last time you confronted that little voice? The Accuser is the "father of all lies." He lies all of the time. Spend some time this week noticing when that little voice shows up. Are there certain areas of your life where the Accuser shows up more often? Are there areas of your life where you constantly feel inadequate or shame? Perhaps you can even start making a list of the lies you hear in your head throughout the week. Set aside some time for prayer in which you can bring all of these lies before Jesus. Imagine that Jesus is present to you every time you notice that the Accuser is prowling around you. When the Accuser shows up and begins his lies, Jesus shows up too. What would Jesus say to combat the specific lie that the accuser is whispering?

- Spend some time this week at bedtime helping your child review the day. Perhaps bedtime isn't the best time to talk about the evil one, but it's a great time to ask questions about your child's day. Ask them if they experienced any thoughts today or this week that felt like someone accusing them.

- Read the temptation story with Adam and Eve from the Garden of Eden (Gen 3). Help point out the deception involved in the Satan's tactics.

O Read Matthew 4:1-11 together with your child. What is the Accuser tempting Jesus with?

  O "Bread" = temptation for self-preservation, not trusting in God's provision.

  O "Temple" = temptation to show-off in front of people. The temple was a public place. If Jesus were to "throw himself down" only to be rescued by angels, the effect would be immediate attention from the onlookers. The temptation here is to quickly draw attention to himself, rather than the long servant's journey to the cross.

  O "Kingdom" = temptation for power and influence.[3]

O Help point out the accusations behind each temptation.

  O "If you are truly God's son . . ." The accusation is that if you don't do this thing, you are not God's Son.

  O How else is Satan accusing or deceptive in this scene?

O Read Colossians 2:13-15. Help your child imagine "the powers and authorities" (and here, these are referring to the powers of darkness) being "disarmed."

O Watch *The Lion, the Witch and the Wardrobe* and discuss the "deep magic" and the scene where Queen Jadis demands blood because Edmund is a traitor. Notice together how she demonstrates many of the features of the Accuser. C. S. Lewis wrote this part of the story to help illustrate a "deeper magic"—the deeper magic of self-sacrificial love and forgiveness.

FOR THE JOURNAL Set aside about fifteen minutes and ask your child to remember the imaginative prayer from this week. Have your child think again about the big jar of tokens that the Accuser spent on Jesus. Encourage your child to write a prayer of thankfulness, expressing gratitude to Jesus for standing before the Accuser.

22

Jesus is a faithful King,
even when his people
are without faith

 **CONNECTION AND FORMATION** This week's imaginative prayer is meant to lead your child into an experience of being in a covenant. Covenant is an important theme throughout Scripture. God made a covenant—a promise—with his people Israel. Israel promised to follow God and not worship other gods, and God promised to be Israel's King, to provide a place for them to live, and to protect them from their enemies. The people, however, were not faithful to their side of the promise. The *good news* of God is that even in spite of this, God has always been faithful to uphold his end of the deal. The *righteousness of God* is the phrase that the apostle Paul uses to refer to God's faithfulness to his promise. God's faithfulness to his chosen people is demonstrated in the incarnation. In Jesus, God put on flesh to fulfill his promise to make things right.

Here we are trying to give your child the experience of being part of a group that entirely dismisses the promise of God. It's often difficult for children to grasp the thrust of God's covenant with Israel and how the arrival of Jesus is connected to it. But it boils down to a promise and to God's *faithfulness* to that promise. Our life in Jesus makes us a people of the "renewed promise," which we pick up later in this book in the section on "The Good News of God." This imaginative prayer sets us up for the next lesson, where we will discover that God fulfills his promise to his people through the *faithfulness of Jesus*.

What does this have to do with spiritual formation? Trust. Trust is at the core of surrender. And "surrender is at the core of spirituality."[1] In his book

Surrender to Love, David Benner argues persuasively that "surrender can only be offered to Perfect Love. Only God deserves absolute surrender, because only God can offer absolutely dependable love."[2] God's consistent faithfulness is what allows us, and your child, to trust. His love and commitment to us are dependable.

Question: What happens when we struggle to have faith in God?

Answer: God is a faithful King, even when his people are without faith.

Close your eyes and let's take a few deep breaths together.

God, I pray that you will release our imagination and help us to hear you speak to us during this time together. We open our hands to you. We open our ears to you.

(pause 8-10 seconds)

Come, Holy Spirit.

Imagine that you have a special friend.

Your friend is the leader of a club. But it's not an exclusive club.

It's not a club where some people are allowed into the club and others are not allowed into the club. This is a club where everyone is supposed to be friends, and everyone is supposed to invite others.

If you had a club like this, who are some people you might invite?

(pause 8-10 seconds)

Your special friend has made a promise. Everyone in the club will one day get to live in a beautiful forest filled with treehouses that your special friend is going to build.

Imagine a beautiful forest where everyone is safe and has food to eat, and everyone lives in an awesome treehouse with a rope ladder for getting into the treehouse, and a firefighter's pole for sliding down.

The leader of the club has promised a treehouse to every member. Everyone will live together in the forest. Each person will have a treehouse made just for them.

Can you imagine what your treehouse might look like?

(pause 8 seconds)

And imagine that right now all members of the club live scattered in different places.

So this club has just a few rules. Every club has rules, and the rules of the club are decided by the leader. The leader of this club is your friend.

If you follow these rules, the treehouse project will turn out just fine.

These rules are part of the promise. As you join the club, you agree that you will follow the rules of the club, and the leader of the club will build you a treehouse in the forest along with all the other treehouses.

This is how the promise works.

Here are the rules of the club:

> 1. Everyone in the club wears a green scarf. This is a green-scarf club. Everyone wears a green scarf so that you always know who is in the club.

Imagine joining this club and receiving your green scarf.

(pause 5 seconds)

Put the green scarf around your neck. Imagine that you are with other people in the club, and they are all wearing a green scarf.

And the second rule is

> 2. Everyone shares. This is a sharing club.

Imagine if you were in a club where everyone in the club shared.

(pause 5 seconds)

This is a fun club. Everyone is wearing green scarves: And everyone is sharing.

The leader of the club reminds everyone of the forest and the treehouses. The leader is making plans to build the treehouses. He's chosen the perfect forest for those treehouses. He's picking out just the right trees and getting everything ready.

(pause 5 seconds)

Everything is going fine until some of the people in the club decide that they don't want to wear the green scarves. Something is happening. The club leader keeps reminding everyone about the promise, but many people are ignoring the promise.

They aren't sharing either.

First, it's just a few people. A few people take off their green scarves and put those scarves in the trash can. You come to a club meeting to play games and have a picnic, and soon a lot of the people aren't wearing a scarf. There are some people who don't have food at the picnic, and others don't have games to play.

How could some people not have food if everyone is supposed to share?

How could some people not have games to play if everyone is supposed to share?

It feels like the club is falling apart.

And the leader of the club, your special friend, doesn't come to the club meetings very much.

Before long, there is no one wearing a green scarf. And nobody is sharing.

(pause 5-8 seconds)

You also have taken off your green scarf. You've hidden your green scarf under your bed. You also are not sharing with others.

The club is not fun anymore.

(pause 8-10 seconds)

And then one day the leader of the club comes around. He notices that no one is wearing their scarf. He notices that no one is sharing. No one has kept their promise to keep the rules.

How do you think he'll respond? Will he be angry? Will he cancel the plans for the forest and the treehouses?

(pause 5 seconds)

The leader now begins to walk away. But he motions for everyone to follow him, and so you follow the leader. He walks through the park and leads you into a beautiful forest. The trees are high, the leaves are beautiful, and there are rope swings dangling from beautiful treehouses.

The forest is full of treehouses. There is a treehouse for every member of the club.

The leader has kept his promise, even when no one else kept their promise.

The leader has kept his promise to you, even when you didn't keep your promise.

He has prepared the place he promised.

(pause 5 seconds)

Now with your eyes still closed, listen to the meaning of this story.

Jesus is a faithful King, even when we don't have faith.

Long ago, God made a promise to his people. He named his people Israel and called them the chosen ones. It was like God had a special club. He was the leader, and he promised to always be their King and to lead them into a land where they would live in safety from all their enemies. God asked his people to keep some promises. He gave them some rules to follow, but they didn't follow the rules. They were not faithful to the promise.

God kept his promise to his people, even when his people didn't keep their promise.

Jesus is the King who came to undo the power of death.

Jesus is the King who came to defeat the power of sin.

Jesus is the King who came to defeat the power of the Accuser.

Jesus is a faithful King, even when we don't have faith.

Question: What happens when we struggle to have faith in God?

Answer: God is a faithful King, even when his people are without faith.

FOR THE PARENT OR MENTOR Sometimes we make promises to our children that we are tempted to break. It can seem like nothing at the time—a baseball game missed in order to work late at the office, or a bedtime story skipped because we've lost track of time. Promises are important to children. When we keep our promises to our kids, it helps them develop a sense of trust. Over time, building their trust in the promises you make to them will go a long way in helping them build trust in God.

Certainly there are times that we promise things to our children that just don't pan out. The goal is not perfection but consistency. Take some time this week to think about the role that promises play in how you parent. What are some of your own memories from childhood regarding promises your own parents made? How do you feel about the sentence *Jesus is a faithful King, even when we are without faith*? Spend some time this week talking with God about your own experience of his faithfulness. When we as parents have a deep belief in the faithfulness of God, our children will pick up on it. They'll notice it in the way we speak about our lives, our future, and the daily disappointments that come at us. How might your experience of faithfulness be impacting your trust in God?

○ Spend some time this week at bedtime helping your child review the day. Talk about *faithfulness*—what does it look like when people keep their promises? Ask, "Can you think of a time when someone kept their promise to you?" "What about a time when someone didn't keep their promise?"

○ Talk with your child about what it means that God is faithful. Ask if your child can remember Mom or Dad breaking a promise. For example, Dad says, "Do you remember that time when Daddy promised to take you on a bike ride, and I broke my promise?" Help them remember the little promises that you may have broken recently. Ask for forgiveness.

○ Have a conversation with your child about broken promises. Remind them that one of the best things about God is that he doesn't break promises.

○ Together, read Psalm 86:15 several times this week.

○ Tell the story of the Israelites crossing the Jordan River (Josh 3–4), focusing on Joshua 4:20-24. Ask, "What are some ways that God has been faithful to our family? To you? What are some promises that you can count on God keeping?"

○ As you tuck your child into bed, ask, "Do you know that God is a faithful King, even when we don't have faith?" Say it over and over.

 **FOR THE JOURNAL** Set aside about fifteen minutes and ask your child to remember the imaginative prayer from this week, as well as the story of the Israelites crossing into the Promised Land. Ask your child to imagine being among those who finally made it into the Promised Land. Encourage your child to write a pretend entry into their diary about the crossing of the Jordan River. For reference, have them read Joshua 3–4.

23

We have life with God
through the faithfulness
of Jesus the King

CONNECTION AND FORMATION This week's imaginative prayer is full of little bits of the story of Scripture. Things like being clothed with a white robe and sitting at a feast—all pictures of God's kingdom. These are true of our experience of God when we are presented before God clothed in white and are invited to a feast in God's new creation. Additionally, Jesus tells a story of a man who invites people to a feast, and they are too busy to make preparations to come, instead, they all make excuses. We used this scene above in part two on "Loving Others." In this imaginative prayer we experience the free gift of God's grace. Entrance into the feast (God's kingdom) demands certain requirements. All of these requirements are things that Jesus the King does for us. Through Jesus' faithful work, the door to God's kingdom is opened for us.

So many merit-based systems form and shape our children. Between school and sports and doing chores for allowance, our children are formed into believing that what comes to them is based on what they deserve, what they earn, and how they perform. And in many ways this is how the world works. There is very little unmerited favor in the world. But not so with Jesus. All of it is grace. It's all a free gift. The journey of spiritual formation is resting in God's unconditional love and grace. Our ability to see the kingdom of God around us is itself a grace of God.

Question: How do we have life with God?
Answer: We have life with God through the faithfulness of Jesus the King.

Close your eyes and let's take a few deep breaths together.

God, I pray that you will release our imagination and help us to hear you speak to us during this time together. We open our hands to you. We open our ears to you.

(pause 8-10 seconds)

Come, Holy Spirit.

Imagine you have been invited to a very special meal.

The king has invited you to dine with him. He is throwing a big feast, and you have received an invitation.

You have never been to a feast before. And you have never met the king.

How do you feel knowing that you are about to meet the king?

Are you excited? Nervous? Maybe a little scared?

(pause 5-8 seconds)

Enclosed in the invitation is a list of things you need to think about as you prepare for the feast. You have been asked to bring a dish to share with everyone. You have been asked to wear a special robe to the feast. That's right. All the people, boys and girls, men and women, will be wearing a robe to this feast. And, finally, you have been asked to give a speech at the beginning of the meal.

There is just one problem.

You don't know how to cook.

You only own a few items of clothing, none of which is a fancy robe for a fancy meal.

And you have never prepared a speech before.

Everything that is required of you to attend the feast are things you simply cannot do.

How does this make you feel?

(pause 8-10 seconds)

You certainly don't want to miss the feast with the king, but you are unsure how you will make all the preparations to attend the feast.

You go to sleep hoping you will figure out how to cook, what to wear, and how to give a speech at the beginning of the feast.

The next morning, you hear a knock on the door. A man has come to visit you. He is very kind. You know his face and have seen him before.

Imagine going on a walk with this kind man. Explain the feast to him, and the robe, and the speech, and the dish you are supposed to bring to the feast.

Imagine now that he is here to help you.

You walk with the man to find fabric at the store. The man chooses a beautiful piece of white fabric. This is the fabric he has chosen for your robe.

You watch as the man takes measurements of your arms and legs and around your waist. This robe is going to fit perfectly.

You watch as the man begins to cut the fabric along the lines he has drawn. And with thread and a needle, he begins to sew a robe for you. He slowly works on each stitch.

All day and into the night, the man is sewing and hemming, and with each stitch the robe begins to come together.

You doze off while the man is still working. When you wake up, the robe is hanging on a hook ready for you to try on.

It fits perfectly.

Imagine trying on the robe.

(pause 8-10 seconds)

Next, the man is in the kitchen, chopping vegetables and preparing a dish for you to take to the feast. There are pots and pans on the stove, and the smell of the food is wonderful. He hands you a bowl of stuff to stir, and you slowly stir the food that is in the bowl.

You both are laughing and smiling and having fun preparing the food.

You are working together, side by side, getting ready for the feast.

You put the food in the oven to cook, and the man leaves. He tells you that he too is going to the feast. He has to leave now and help prepare some other things for the feast. You say goodbye.

Imagine how thankful you would be if someone came and helped you prepare for a feast with the king—making you a custom-fit robe, and teaching you how to cook a wonderful dish to share with others.

(pause 8-10 seconds)

Let your heart feel thankfulness right now as you imagine yourself all dressed up in a fancy robe, with a pot of food in your hands.

You are ready to go to the feast.

Imagine now that you walk into the place where the feast is held and place your dish of food on the table. There are others there, and they too are dressed in white robes. Everyone is sitting around a giant table, dressed in white robes, laughing and talking and sharing stories before the meal begins.

There is a chair at the head of the table. That chair is for the king.

Just now you remember that there was something else you were supposed to prepare for the feast. *Your speech!* You forgot about the speech you were supposed to give before the meal.

Imagine that someone makes an announcement. "We will now hear a speech, to be given before the meal begins."

And then a man stands up and begins to speak. It is the same man who made your robe and prepared the dish you brought for others to share.

He gives a beautiful speech before the meal.

And then he takes his seat at the head of the table.

This is the king.

The man who sewed your robe is the king.

The man who helped you prepare your food is the king.

The man who gave your speech is the king.

And his name is Jesus.

Everything you were supposed to do for the feast, he did with you and for you.

Jesus is the King who came to undo the power of death.

Jesus is the King who came to defeat the power of sin.

Jesus is the King who came to defeat the power of the Accuser.

Jesus is a faithful King, even when we don't have faith.

We have life with God through the faithfulness of Jesus the King.

 Question: How do we have life with God?
Answer: We have life with God through the faithfulness of Jesus the King.

 One of the greatest temptations in following Jesus and participating in the kingdom of God is thinking that the work of God's kingdom rests on our shoulders. While it's true that God has invited us to join him in his work in the world, it's helpful to remind ourselves of how we got into God's story in the first place—it's all grace. God did it. He is the one who came. He took on flesh, lived among us, and became the representative of what the new creation would become. He became the "new Adam" and walked the path of God's will; he came

as a king who was faithful to do for us what we could never accomplish on our own.

John Wimber used to say "The way in is the way on."[1] The way we came into the kingdom is the same way we keep going. It's all grace. The faithful King is the one doing the work; our job is to join him in it. What is your recent experience of the faithfulness of Jesus? What burdens do you feel that perhaps you can ask Jesus to take from you? What would it be like for you to approach the next thing on your agenda and find that the work you needed to do had already been completed? Spend some time this week in prayer asking for God to demonstrate his faithfulness to you by removing the experience of being burdened.

○ Spend some time this week at bedtime helping your child review the day. Talk about faithfulness as it relates to accomplishing a task. Ask, "How did Jesus help you today?"

○ Talk with your child about what it means that Jesus was faithful.

○ Get creative this week! Act out the imaginative prayer with your child. Your child may be hesitant at first to engage in the playfulness of it, but playfully urge them to go along with it.

  ○ Invite your child to a feast and give them a written invitation with all the instructions about the robe, and the dish, and the speech.

  ○ Surprise them with a special robe (made from a white sheet you buy at the thrift store). There's no need to get fancy; just cut a hole in the sheet, slip it over your child's head, and let the sheet flow freely. Tie a belt around your child's waist. They'll get the point.

  ○ Make a special dish for the feast.

  ○ Prepare a three-minute speech. Really ham it up. Pretend that you are the king (or queen).

  ○ Lavish your child with kindness. Tell them how great you think they are. Remind them of how much you love them.

○ Read the parable of the two sons out loud (Mt 21:28-32). Feel free to modify the story a bit if your child isn't ready to hear about prostitutes (v. 32).

○ This is what it looks like to say you are going to do something and then don't do it. It's actually a story of judgment on the Jewish people. Their purpose was to be a light to the world, to be the salt of the earth, but when Jesus was telling the story, they were failing.

○ Jesus follows up with a declaration that the tax collectors and prostitutes are entering the kingdom of God ahead of these others.

○ Try to engage your child in some conversation about how it was possible that sinners, people who were doing bad things, were entering the kingdom ahead of the religious people. It's about Jesus paving the way for them, not what they can do for themselves.

 **FOR THE JOURNAL** Set aside about fifteen minutes and ask your child to remember the imaginative prayer from this week. Encourage your child to think about the reality that everything required for us to join in God's story was accomplished by God through the faithful life of Jesus. Help your child write a prayer to God, thanking God for his love and faithfulness.

24

Love and forgiveness: this is how God became King

 **CONNECTION AND FORMATION** This imaginative prayer contrasts two different kinds of kings. One is dressed for battle, full of power, riding on a mighty horse, and surrounded by everything that communicates power and prestige. The second rides into town on a donkey (an allusion to Jesus' riding into Jerusalem on a donkey), full of humility and kindness. The imaginative prayer is also obliquely referencing the story of the good Samaritan, which is about someone—the Samaritan—who becomes a hero against our expectations. Jesus tells the story to Jewish law keepers and Pharisees. They expect a hero who looks like them, and Jesus uses the racial tensions of the day to show they are wrong. He is challenging them in their ethics (they should care for everyone they come across) and in their expectations regarding who will inherit eternal life.

We're trying to give your child an experience of Jesus as one who embodies love and forgiveness, paired with a story of Jesus riding on a donkey and taking his throne. God does not become King through the typical venues of power, but through humility and mercy, which is demonstrated by the Samaritan.

Humility is a central theme in spiritual formation. There is a well-worn path in the contemplative stream, particularly in the monastic tradition, of the journey toward the kind of humility that Jesus demonstrates when he rides into town on a donkey, and the kind of humility demonstrated in the Samaritan's decision to take care of the man on the side of the road. Love and forgiveness both require humility. And somewhere in adolescence your child's world begins to revolve around their own self, and humility and empathy can seem nonexistent. This is a normal part of growing up, and, understood as a natural part of separation, you can stay connected to your child during this time and continue to give them a picture of Jesus, the King who chose to go low rather than use power. We live in a culture of power, which is the opposite of how God became King.

 Question: How did God become King?
Answer: Love and forgiveness: this is how God became King.

 **IMAGINATIVE PRAYER**

Close your eyes and let's take a few deep breaths together.

God, I pray that you will release our imagination and help us to hear you speak to us during this time together. We open our hands to you. We open our ears to you.

(pause 8-10 seconds)

Come, Holy Spirit.

Imagine that you live in a village in a distant country. This is not a time when people played video games or drove in cars, but when people rode horses and children played barefoot on dusty streets.

I want you to imagine this is a time when soldiers dressed in armor and carried swords and shields. It is a time when lands were ruled by kings and queens, and war often occurred.

In fact, the land that you live in, and the village that you live in, has just had a war.

Imagine what it would be like to be a boy or a girl during a war.

(pause 8-10 seconds)

There is some big news in the town square today. Everyone is gathered in the center of your village to hear the announcement that the war is over.

But your king has died in battle.

(pause 5 seconds)

You remember the king well. You remember when he left your village on a giant horse.

He was dressed in fine clothing and wore a purple scarf.

He carried a sword for battle.

He carried a shield.

He rode on his horse followed by lots of men, and he seemed very strong.

He was covered in armor.

Picture this king in your mind.

Try to remember what it was like to see him leave the village with the other men to go into battle.

(pause 8-10 seconds)

People are saddened that this king will not be coming back.

They announce that a new king will be coming sometime soon, but nobody knows when this will be.

Everyone leaves the center of town and goes about their business.

Everyone is happy that the war is over, but everyone seems a little anxious to meet the new king.

What would it be like to wait to meet the new king?

What will he be like?

Will he be kind?

Will he be gentle?

Will he be strong?

Will he be generous?

Or will he be mean?

And harsh?

Will he treat others poorly?

(pause 5-8 seconds)

Imagine now that you are walking along a road outside of the town.

There aren't a lot of people who travel this road. It's very quiet.

You notice from a distance that there is a man on the side of the road and he has been badly beaten. Someone has hit him on the head and stolen his money. He is badly hurt.

You are a little bit afraid to get too close because your mom and dad have told you to not talk to strangers. This is a stranger, and he does not look well.

You notice that some other men see this man lying on the side of the road. But they do nothing. They cross to the other side of the road so they don't have to see the beaten man up close.

No one has stopped to help this man.

(pause 5-8 seconds)

You begin to wonder what you should do.

Should you run for help?

Should you try to help the man yourself?

(pause 5 seconds)

And then you notice that another man is coming down the road.

He is traveling all by himself and is riding a donkey.

Most men ride on horses—a man riding on a donkey looks a little bit funny to you.

You wonder what sort of man would ride to town on a donkey.

The man on the donkey notices the man who has been beaten on the side of the road.

You watch him as he gets off of his donkey and kneels beside the beaten man.

He takes water from his backpack and rinses the man's wounds.

He gives the man something to drink and something to eat.

He takes a towel from his backpack and gently wipes the man's face. Then he uses the towel as a pillow, placing it under his head.

You watch the man go back to his donkey, and you wonder if he is leaving.

Don't leave, you think to yourself.

And he doesn't leave. He found a bandage in another bag.

You watch as the man gently bandages the hurt man's wounds.

He is so kind.

And he's strong. He lifts the man from the ground and carries him to his donkey.

You watch the man as he walks with the beaten man on the donkey to the nearest motel. You follow him and see that he pays for a room and food and medicine for the beaten man.

And then he leaves, riding the donkey into town.

You follow him there too, wondering who this kind man is.

As you head into town, you see the man who was riding on a donkey and kindly and gently caring for the man on the side of the road now sitting on the king's throne, with a crown on his head.

This is your king.

They say his name is Jesus.

Jesus is the King who came to undo the power of death.

Jesus is the King who came to defeat the power of sin.

Jesus is the King who came to defeat the power of the Accuser.

Jesus is a faithful King, even when we don't have faith.

We have life with God through the faithfulness of Jesus the King.

Love and forgiveness: this is how God became King.

Question: How did God become King?

Answer: Love and forgiveness: this is how God became King.

 **FOR THE PARENT OR MENTOR** Power is an interesting thing in our lives as parents. We often have all the power, and sometimes we exert this power unnecessarily. One of the greatest mysteries of following Jesus is the model he gave for us to follow requires giving up power. God did not become King through conquering but through submitting himself to the powers of this world, ultimately showing how little power they actually held.

How parents use power is important. We don't need to give up our authority, however. Power and authority are not the same thing. Our parental authority is a God-given gift. Our children need us to exercise authority. The role of the parent is to exercise authority, to mold and shape our children. Our job is to train them up in the proper way they should go. But authority doesn't always mean power. Jesus always had the authority and exercised it powerfully, but most often he refused to exert power over others. His path toward the throne of the kingdom was through humility, which is mostly characterized by love and forgiveness. Where can you model this to your child this week? Are there ways you hang onto power in your home? Do you exert your own will simply because you can? Or do you consider your child's desire to be empowered? Ask God to show you how you might be able to follow Jesus in the way of humility with your child.

○ Spend some time this week at bedtime helping your child review the day. Pay particular attention to helping your child notice what humility looks like in others. Be on the lookout for people who serve others. This is hard to see on a day-to-day basis, but if you look for it, you'll find it. Ask, "Did you notice how that man held the door for us today?" "Did you see anyone loving and serving today?" "Did anyone go out of their way to love?"

○ Talk through the story of the good Samaritan from different angles. Ask, "What kinds of things did Jesus do that look similar to what we see the good Samaritan doing?"

○ Ask your child, "How did God become King?" Explain that the answer is "Love and forgiveness: this is how God became King." Make this into a game this week. Ask the question often, pretending that you forgot the answer.

○ Read Luke 10:25-37 out loud to your child this week. Have them close their eyes and imagine the story once again.

○ Read Philippians 2:5-11. Help your child see the way of humility modeled in the life of Jesus. Humility is key to love and forgiveness.

FOR THE JOURNAL Set aside about fifteen minutes and ask your child to remember the imaginative prayer from this week. Ask your child to imagine watching the scene from Luke 10:25-37 unfold before them. Ask your child to describe what they see in the story that grabs their attention. "What really stands out to you about this story? What really surprises you here?" Encourage your child to take some time to imagine themselves as the person on the side of the road, and Jesus as the one who provides comfort and care.

Jesus is the King who came to undo the power of death.
Jesus is the King who came to defeat the power of sin.
Jesus is the King who came to defeat the power of the Accuser.
Jesus is a faithful King, even when we don't have faith.
We have life with God through the faithfulness of Jesus the King.
Love and forgiveness: this is how God became King.

CREEDAL QUESTIONS AND ANSWERS

Question: What did Jesus the King come to do?
Answer: Jesus is the King who came to undo the power of death.

Question: What did Jesus the King come to do?
Answer: Jesus is the King who came to defeat the power of sin.

Question: What did Jesus the King come to do?
Answer: Jesus is the King who came to defeat the power of the Accuser.

Question: How do we have life with God?
Answer: We have life with God through the faithfulness of Jesus the King.

Question: What happens when we struggle to have faith in God?
Answer: God is a faithful King, even when his people are without faith.

Question: How did God become King?
Answer: Love and forgiveness: this is how God became King.

QUESTIONS AND ACTIVITIES

- Spend time this week reviewing each of the past six weeks.
- Ask good questions or make some suggestions that might stimulate reflection. For example:
    - What do you think about a King who is so loving?

- How does it make you feel knowing that God will always be faithful to you?

- What are some ways you see Jesus being faithful as you read stories about his life? How is he being faithful in our lives right now?

- Can you see any of the seven deadly sins in the world? Are we struggling with any of these in our life as a family?

- Read the newspaper together this week and be on the lookout for the seven deadly sins at work in the world.

- What are some things we can pray about?

- Have you felt any whispering in your ear from the Accuser this week? (If your child responds with a yes, ask some follow-up questions.) "Tell me more about it."

- What would it look like if we lived in the Garden of Eden? How do you think it will feel to see people resurrected?

- What do you think it would be like to live as though we had eternal life right now?

- Review the portion of the creedal poem that corresponds with part four, "Jesus Is the King." Help your child memorize these next six lines. Review the creedal poem from parts one through three. See if you can recite them all together with your child. Make it fun!

PART 5

The Good News of God

God made a new promise and it comes to us through Jesus

CONNECTION AND FORMATION This imaginative exercise is meant to help your child understand that a new promise comes from God in the person of Jesus. We're trying to foster a sense of anticipation for seeing the promises of God come through the life of Jesus. Some of our focus in this session intentionally revisits themes from chapter twenty-two. This chapter looks at God's new promise (covenant) through Jesus. This promise fulfills Deuteronomy 30. The promise of God to Abraham comes to its climax in Jesus (see Gal 3:1-15), and ushers in a new promise (covenant) with a wide-open invitation for people to come into the family of God (see Heb 8:10-11).[1] The coming of Jesus as King was what everyone had been waiting for (see Zechariah's song in Lk 1:67-79), and the promise of God, the good news of God, spilled out of the life of Jesus (which will be the focus of this chapter).

Where will your child look to see their longings fulfilled? Longing and desire are key elements of formation. If we teach our children to long for and hope for things to be made right in the world, our children will long for the coming of God's kingdom on earth as it is in heaven. God promises the fulfillment of those longings. He can and will make it all happen. The birth of Jesus is the most hope-filled event in history. It serves as a symbol and focal point of our desires for the world. What if the Christmas morning incarnation became the centering imagine of hope and expectation? What if your child associated the baby in the manger with promises spilling out of the hands of God? And what if our children understood the story for what it demonstrates—that God's kingdom doesn't come from high and lofty places, but from the margins? Jesus was born outside of the city, in the lowliest of places. Again, we touch on the theme of the humility of God to be born into the world he created, in a way that "he had no beauty or majesty to attract us to him, nothing in his appearance that we should desire him" (Is 53:2). While the humble state of God's entry into the world will not be our direct focus in this imaginative prayer, the scene depicting Jesus' birth in a stable makes for a nice connection to the way the kingdom comes.

The kingdom comes from the least expected places.

 Question: How did God's new promise come into the world? *Answer*: God made a new promise, and it comes to us through Jesus.

Close your eyes and let's take a few deep breaths together.

God, I pray that you will release our imagination and help us to hear you speak to us during this time together. We open our hands to you. We open our ears to you.

(pause 8-10 seconds)

Come, Holy Spirit.

Imagine with me that God is holding a great number of promises in his hands. Imagine God has large and gentle hands, and his hands are full of promises.

(pause 5 seconds)

God is full of promises. And he wants to give those promises to the whole world. God's promises aren't written on paper or in a book. They aren't promises he gives to his people on stone tablets. God's promises can be given only in person.

God has promised to make all things right in the world, and he wants to give that promise.

He has promised to remember those who are poor and suffering, and he wants to give that promise to the poor and the suffering.

He has promised to fill the hungry with good things.

He has promised to free slaves from the hands of their enemies.

He has promised to put his Spirit into the hearts of men and women. He will put his Spirit into the hearts of boys and girls.

(pause 5-8 seconds)

Imagine with me, what it looks like for God to remember the poor,

to feed the hungry,

to free slaves,

to put his Spirit into people.

Imagine with me that God makes everything in the world right again.

God brings good news to people.

God makes promises and keeps them.

So imagine God has armfuls of promises to deliver.

And then he comes to be with his people so he can deliver those promises.

God put his Spirit and his life in a man named Jesus. God became a human.

He started as a little baby who was born in a barn in a small city.

We read in the Bible that a messenger from God visited a girl named Mary. The messenger told Mary that she was going to have a baby, and that the baby's name was to be Jesus, which means "God saves."

This Jesus would become King and rule over an everlasting kingdom.

He will forgive sins.

He will guide people into the way of peace.

He will bring light to the world.

He will bring God's mercy.

He will bring the promises of God.

This baby will be God with a human body, and we will watch the promises of God come to the world through the life and words of Jesus.

Imagine that you are in the story.

Picture with me that you are in the middle of a field, surrounded by sheep in the middle of the night.

Suddenly, a bright light shines right in front of you. You are terrified by this.

And then a man appears from the bright light and quickly reassures you:

> Don't be afraid. I'm here to announce a great and joyful event that is meant for everybody, worldwide: A Savior has just been born in David's town, a Savior who is Messiah and Master. This is what you're to look for: a baby wrapped in a blanket and lying in a manger. (Lk 2:11-12 *The Message*)

Imagine now that as the man is speaking you hear a choir of one thousand voices singing from the sky. And the voices fill the whole field and valley with God's peace.

Take a moment and imagine what those voices might sound like. Imagine that as the voices sing, the sound is both loud and beautiful. You've never heard a song like this before. And all the sheep are at peace. And resting on your knee, surrounded by the sheep, you too feel a great sense of peace come over you.

(pause 8 seconds)

The stars are shining bright and the sky is clear. And you are completely at peace. You know you have just experienced something great. What does it feel like to have just heard those voices singing the most beautiful song you have ever heard?

(pause 5 seconds)

Imagine now that you decide to join the other shepherds on a journey to the town where this little baby, the one who is to be the King, has just been born.

You travel all through the night, still tending your flock of sheep as you go over the hills and through the valleys. And you arrive on the edge of the city where you see some animals feeding outside a small barn.

Imagine that you come to the barn where this baby, Jesus, has just been born.

What does it feel like to see this baby who will bring all the promises of God?

(pause 5-8 seconds)

Do you remember seeing God's hands full of promises?

Every wrong thing in the world will be made right—and it will happen through this baby.

With your eyes still closed, imagine you walk over to the place where this baby is lying. Pick up the baby Jesus.

Hold in your arms the promise of God for the world.

Hold this baby close to your chest. Feel this baby squirm, his breath, and even his cry.

Imagine holding the baby Jesus in your arms.

This little baby is the hope for all the world's troubles.

And whatever you long for in the deepest place in your heart can only be met in the life of this little baby.

God made a new promise, and it comes to us through Jesus.

Question: How did God's new promise come into the world?
Answer: God made a new promise, and it comes to us through Jesus.

 **FOR THE PARENT OR MENTOR** What comes to your mind when you think about a promise God has made? Has God ever made a promise to you? Can you think of a moment when God touched your heart and promised to fill it up? Can you remember the last time this happened? And if you can't, how does that make you feel?

God makes promises, and then he keeps them: to David, to Abraham, to the children of Israel, to Sarah, to Jonathan, to Paul, to Peter, and to you and me. How often do you think about the promises God has made to you? How much do you, in the midst of difficult circumstances, lean on what God has said he would do?

What do you think about when you consider what you long for? What has been your experience of bringing that longing to God in prayer? All of God's promises are fulfilled in Jesus. And all of our longings, when they are aligned with the picture of God's kingdom that we see unfold in the Gospels, can be met with this promise of God that comes to us in Jesus.

Spend some time this week jotting down things that you long for. Perhaps it's been a while since you've considered this. Spend all week asking God to help you pay attention to your longings. And then sit with those longings and do what Mary did: she "treasured up all these things and pondered them in her heart" (Lk 2:19).

O Spend some time this week at bedtime helping your child review the day. Talk about the promises. Help your child think through the promises God has made throughout Scripture. Try to name one promise each evening or each morning at breakfast.

O Read Deuteronomy 30 together. This is God's promise to his people, Israel. Talk to your child about how this promise begins to unfold when Jesus comes to earth. Jesus, in his life, his words, his death, and his resurrection, fulfills perfectly what this promise requires of Israel. The promise has two sides (also called a "covenant"). Help your child understand that Jesus is the substitute for God's people. Jesus holds up the end of the bargain that was meant to be fulfilled by the people of Israel, and everyone gets blessed because of his faithfulness.

○ Read Galatians 3:15-20. This is God's promise to Abraham. Through the seed of Abraham, the whole world gets the promises of God.

○ Talk with your child about the things they are longing for. Children have a lot of desires and a lot of wants. Help your child understand the difference between *want* and *longing*. When we want something deeply that is good, this is a longing. Your child may not be able to name something offhand. Try this question: "After all the things you have heard in this book and all the things you have imagined in the past few months, is there anything you've heard about God, or what he feels about the world, that you really want to see happen?"

 **FOR THE JOURNAL** Set aside about fifteen minutes and ask your child to remember the imaginative prayer from this week. Encourage your child to sit quietly for a few moments. Ask your child to think through their answer to the question, "What about the world right now do you most want God to fix?" Encourage them to spend some time writing to God about the issue that comes up as an answer to that question. Ask, "What would you hope God would promise about this?"

26

The good news of God
comes to us through
the *words* of Jesus

CONNECTION AND FORMATION This imaginative exercise is meant to give your child an experience of hearing the words of Jesus and expecting that life comes from his mouth. This week is heavy on Scripture. In fact, almost the entire imaginative prayer involves listening to words Jesus speaks. Everything that comes out of Jesus' mouth is good news for the world. He is the messenger of God's good news and new promise to the world. This week's lesson is on the words of Jesus. In the next few lessons we'll explore Jesus' *life*, his *death*, and his *resurrection* as also bringing God's new promise to the world.

Hearing Jesus' words to us personally and individually is a lifelong journey. It's a lifetime of increasingly attuning our eyes and ears to noticing and listening for the work and words of God to us. We nurture connection to Jesus so that we become familiar with the sound of his voice. Spiritual transformation into Christlikeness involves learning to pay attention to our conversational relationship with God. Jesus' relationships with people were nurtured through time spent together, talking and listening, inviting and responding. These same rhythms of hearing and responding lead us toward a formational life.

What is the most prevalent voice in your child's life? Is it a voice from pop culture? A friend's voice? A teacher's? A school bully's? Or yours? We're training our children to listen to us, because as parents we, all of us, are trying our best to steward the gift—both to us and to the world—that our child is. We are asking our child to listen to our voice, praying that our voice will echo the words of Jesus.

 Question: How does the good news of God come to us? *Answer*: The good news of God comes to us through the words of Jesus.

Close your eyes and let's take a few deep breaths together.

God, I pray that you will release our imagination and help us to hear you speak to us during this time together. We open our hands to you. We open our ears to you.

(pause 8-10 seconds)

Come, Holy Spirit.

Imagine with me that you are standing next to Jesus.

That you get to travel with Jesus. That you are one of his followers.

And imagine that you are really listening to Jesus.

Listen to his words.

You are with Jesus and he is speaking to a crowd of people.

You are in the crowd. In fact, you are standing right next to Jesus.

(pause 5-8 seconds)

Listen as Jesus says the following words:

I am the world's Light. No one who follows me stumbles around in the darkness. I provide plenty of light to live in. (Jn 8:12 *The Message*)

(pause 5-8 seconds)

Imagine you are in a dark room. Imagine Jesus walks into the dark room, and when he walks in, the room is filled with light.

(pause 5-8 seconds)

I am the Bread of Life. The person who aligns with me hungers no more and thirsts no more, ever. (Jn 6:35 *The Message*)

(pause 5-8 seconds)

Picture in your mind now that you are hungry and thirsty—like you haven't eaten all day. And you are so thirsty that you are weak. Imagine Jesus coming up to you. He gives you a hug, and you are immediately filled up; your thirst is quenched.

(pause 5-8 seconds)

You are in a room now, and Jesus gets up in front of everyone to read from a book written by a man named Isaiah. Isaiah was a man who loved God and spoke God's words to his people many years before Jesus. Imagine now that Jesus opens the book, looks out into the crowd, and begins to read out loud:

God's Spirit is on me;
    he's chosen me to preach the Message of good news to the
        poor,
Sent me to announce pardon to prisoners and
    recovery of sight to the blind,
To set the burdened and battered free,
    to announce, "This is God's year to act!" (Lk 4:18-20 *The Message*)

(pause 5-8 seconds)

Jesus is telling everyone that all of this is about to happen, and it is going to happen through him.

What does it feel like to hear Jesus say these words?

How do you feel about Jesus as you learn that he is going to give good news to the poor?

(pause 5-8 seconds)

How do you feel as you hear that Jesus is going to give new sight to the blind?

(pause 5-8 seconds)

How do you feel knowing that Jesus is going to set free those who are burdened and beaten?

(pause 5-8 seconds)

Listen to these words of Jesus:

> God's Spirit is on me;
>> he's chosen me to preach the Message of good news to the
>> poor,
> Sent me to announce pardon to prisoners and
>> recovery of sight to the blind,
> To set the burdened and battered free,
>> to announce, "This is God's year to act!" (Lk 4:18-20 *The Message*)

One day Jesus saw crowds gathering and he went to the mountainside and sat down. Imagine following Jesus out of the city to the mountainside. Everyone is trying to find a place close to Jesus.

Imagine you, being smaller than most of the adults, make your way right up to the front. You sit down, and Jesus looks right at you. He smiles at you and says,

(read slowly and thoughtfully)

> God blesses those who are poor and realize their need for him,
>> for the Kingdom of Heaven is theirs.

Have you ever experienced poverty? Or have you ever been close to someone in poverty?

How might the kingdom of heaven be particularly close to the poor?

(pause 5 seconds)

> God blesses those who mourn,
>> for they will be comforted.

Have you ever mourned for something? Have you ever been in grief over something that has happened?

What comfort did you feel?

(pause 5 seconds)

> God blesses those who are humble,
>   for they will inherit the whole earth.

When have you felt a complete reliance on God rather than on yourself? Or who do you know who seems to rely on God?

What would it be like to be someone who will inherit the whole earth?

(pause 5 seconds)

> God blesses those who hunger and thirst for justice,
>   for they will be satisfied.

Have you ever wanted something wrong in the world to be made right?

Justice is when wrongs are made right.

Imagine what it will be like when all the wrongs are made right.

(pause 5 seconds)

> God blesses those who are merciful,
>   for they will be shown mercy.

(pause 5 seconds)

> God blesses those whose hearts are pure,
>   for they will see God.

(pause 5 seconds)

> God blesses those who work for peace,
>   for they will be called the children of God.

Have you ever worked to bring peace between two people?

(pause 5 seconds)

> God blesses those who are persecuted for doing right,
>   for the Kingdom of Heaven is theirs.

God blesses you when people mock you and persecute you and lie about you and say all sorts of evil things against you because you are my followers. Be happy about it! Be very glad! For a great reward awaits you in heaven. And remember, the ancient prophets were persecuted in the same way.

You are the salt of the earth. But what good is salt if it has lost its flavor? Can you make it salty again? It will be thrown out and trampled underfoot as worthless.

You are the light of the world—like a city on a hilltop that cannot be hidden. No one lights a lamp and then puts it under a basket. Instead, a lamp is placed on a stand, where it gives light to everyone in the house. In the same way, let your good deeds shine out for all to see, so that everyone will praise your heavenly Father. (Mt 5:3-16 NLT)

And later, Jesus says this:

Anyone who listens to my teaching and follows it is wise, like a person who builds a house on solid rock. Though the rain comes in torrents and the floodwaters rise and the winds beat against that house, it won't collapse because it is built on bedrock. But anyone who hears my teaching and doesn't obey it is foolish, like a person who builds a house on sand. When the rains and floods come and the winds beat against that house, it will collapse with a mighty crash. (Mt 7:24-27 NLT)

(pause 5 seconds)

Imagine hearing these words spoken:

"Listen to my *words*," Jesus says. "Follow my *words*—this is wisdom!"

God made a new promise and it comes to us through Jesus.

The good news of God comes to us through the words of Jesus.

Question: How does the good news of God come to us?
Answer: The good news of God comes to us through the words of Jesus.

FOR THE PARENT OR MENTOR What is the most significant thing to you as you read what Jesus speaks to the people around him? Some Bibles have the words of Jesus in red so we can easily find them. The words of Jesus have been very significant to people. They are so important that in controversial issues people sometimes say, "Well, Jesus never said anything specific about this issue." The words of Jesus are weighty, aren't they? But the weightiest words of all, the ones that feel most significant, are the words he says to you. Your life. Your context. Your hopes and dreams and desires. And your pain too.

When was the last time you heard Jesus speak to you? What was it about? What did he say to you? What good news has he brought to you recently in prayer or through worship or reading Scripture? Are there any words from Jesus you are clinging to right now? Jesus said, "I am the bread of life" (Jn 6:48). How is he bread to you? He said, "Take my yoke upon you for my yoke is easy and my burden is light" (Mt 11:29-30). What does the yoke (or way) of Jesus feel like to you right now? This week, spend some time thinking about the same passage that you'll be walking your child through (Jn 6:60-68) later this week. What words of Jesus throughout the Gospel feel like eternal life to you? Share these words with your child. Hearing you reflect on the words of Jesus will help your child have an imagination for doing the same.

- Spend some time this week at bedtime helping your child review the day.

- Spend some time talking to your child about how people were desperate to hear Jesus.

- Ask, "Is there anything Jesus says that is meaningful to you?"

- Spend some time this week looking through the Gospel accounts for words of Jesus that feel like eternal life to you. Make this like a scavenger hunt with your child. Look for words of Jesus that make you want to live a full life in him. What words stand out to you as "words of eternal life"? Make a list of these on the refrigerator. When you find words of Jesus that stand out to you, explain to your child why those words feel special to you.

○ Read John 6:60-68. Give some background to the story here: Jesus just delivered a tough teaching, and a lot of people stopped following him because of it. Walk your child through the story. Help your child see Peter's response in verse 68. "To whom shall we go? You have the words of eternal life!" Help your child notice how the words of Jesus either drew people toward him or pushed them away. Help your child see that some people couldn't get enough of Jesus' words, while others felt offended by him.

○ With your child, memorize John 5:24.

○ Together, read Matthew 7:24. Explore together what this metaphor might mean.

○ For bedtime: Have your child close their eyes and imagine they are with Jesus. Give them some time and space to get quiet, and then ask, "If you could have Jesus say one thing to you tonight, what would you want him to say?"

 **FOR THE JOURNAL** Set aside about fifteen minutes and ask your child to remember the imaginative prayer from this week. Encourage your child to sit quietly for a few moments. Ask your child to think through their answer to the question, "If you could have Jesus say one thing to you tonight, what would you want him to say?" Encourage them to spend some time writing to God about what words they would want Jesus to speak. Try to help your child get to the question or longing behind this desire to hear Jesus speak something specific to their life.

27

The good news of God comes to us through the *life* of Jesus

CONNECTION AND FORMATION This imaginative prayer leads to the experience of Jesus' life filled with good news for the people around him. His life drew people toward him, and then they left changed. People experienced Jesus like they experienced no one else. People want to be close to Jesus because great things happen all around him. This week's imaginative prayer takes your child through a number of scenes in the life of Jesus. The Gospel writer Luke strings together a series of stories and scenes from Jesus' life in which people get healed, blessed, and walk away having experienced something wonderful.

C. S. Lewis writes that "the Church exists for nothing else but to draw men into Christ, to make them little Christs."[1] The work of the church is making disciples, followers of Jesus. This is the work of spiritual formation. His life demonstrates what our lives can be. He is the "firstfruits" of the new creation, the one who first demonstrated what a life devoted to God can be. We learn from Jesus what kingdom living is all about. Dallas Willard asks, "How would Jesus live my life, if he were I?"[2] Our formational journey moves us toward imagining how Jesus would live our life. Your child's journey is the formation of their imagination for how Jesus would respond in their everyday situations. Your child's formational journey moves them to be curious about how Jesus would live their life, were he the one living it.

Question: How does the good news of God come to us?

Answer: The good news of God comes to us through the life of Jesus.

Close your eyes and let's take a few deep breaths together.

God, I pray that you will release our imagination and help us to hear you speak to us during this time together. We open our hands to you. We open our ears to you.

(pause 8-10 seconds)

Come, Holy Spirit.

Close your eyes and imagine with me that you can visit all the places where Jesus loved and healed people. Imagine not only visiting those places, but being there at the moment Jesus is there. You can hear him speak words to people. You can see him touch people.

(pause 5-8 seconds)

Imagine you can watch every moment of Jesus' life, and as I describe these scenes for you, let them play like a movie in your mind.

Picture this in your mind: Jesus has just finished reading the scroll in the synagogue when he says he has come to announce God's year of good news. Remember, Jesus said that he is going to set free those who are held captive, that he is going to give sight to the blind, and that he will open the ears of those who can't hear. Imagine that Jesus has just finished telling people about all the good news he is going to bring from God, and as he is leaving, an angry man runs up to him. The angry man is accusing Jesus of doing wrong. This man is listening to the Accuser (the devil) and is doing and saying what the Accuser tells him to do and say (see Lk 4:31-37).

(pause 5 seconds)

Jesus looks at the man, quiets him, and tells the Accuser to go away and leave them alone.

After this, Jesus leaves and goes into the home of his friend Simon. Simon's mother-in-law is sick with a fever. She is lying in bed. She feels awful. Imagine Jesus comes into her room and tells the fever to go away. Simon's mom immediately feels better, and she gets up to make some hot tea. Jesus has made her well (Lk 4:38-39).

Now imagine you are with Jesus as he is walking next to a lake. Jesus sees two boats next to the lake and some fishermen who are washing their fishing nets. They're all done fishing for the day, and they are disappointed because they didn't catch any fish, and so they don't have anything to eat or to sell at the market. Jesus climbs into the boat and asks the fisherman to go a little way into the lake and lower their nets over the side of the boat. They pull up the nets full of fish. Everyone is excited. There is plenty of food to eat. Plenty to share. And plenty to sell in the market. Everyone is laughing and smiling (Lk 5:1-11).

(pause 8-10 seconds)

And now picture in your mind that you are walking with Jesus and all of a sudden a man comes to Jesus and falls at his feet. This man is sick. He has a skin disease. There are sores and infections covering his entire body. Imagine this man is crying, and he says to Jesus, "Lord, if you are willing, you can make me well." Everyone is watching. Everyone is looking at Jesus. Imagine Jesus looks at the man, hugs him, and says, "Of course I am willing. Be well." The sores and infections on the man disappear. Jesus has healed him (Lk 5:12-16).

(pause 8-10 seconds)

On another day, Jesus is just about to head into a small town with his disciples. As they approach the town, they see that a man who had died is being carried out of the town. He was the only son of his mother. She had no husband and no other children. Imagine Jesus sees the woman. She is crying. She is tired. She is headed to bury her son. She is sad. Watch Jesus as he has compassion on the woman.

(pause 5 seconds)

He goes to her. He looks at her and says, "Do not cry, dear woman." He puts his hands on her son, who is dead, and says, "Young man, I say to you, get up!" And the dead man sits up and begins to speak. Jesus takes the young man into his arms and carries him to his mother (Lk 7:11-17).

(pause 8-10 seconds)

Now, imagine Jesus is surrounded by a crowd of people. Everyone is pressing in close to him. Everyone wants to get close to Jesus because he has been healing people and loving people. He's been saying such wonderful things to people. And now an important man comes to Jesus and says that his daughter is sick at home. His daughter is about twelve years old. Imagine she is about your age, and she's dying. Everyone is stopping to watch how Jesus will respond. The father of this daughter is very worried about her. Imagine this girl is one of your friends. She is someone you have playdates with or see at school or on the playground.

And then, before Jesus has a chance to say anything to the man, he stops. Someone has grabbed his coat. Someone from the crowd has reached out and grabbed ahold of Jesus' coat, and he stops. "Who was it that touched me?" Jesus asked. Imagine Jesus looking around. Looking at each person. Actually, everyone was touching Jesus. Everyone was pressing in on him. Meanwhile, the father of the dying girl is still standing there. Everyone is waiting for Jesus to say something. Waiting to see what he will do next. "Someone touched me," he said again.

A woman came out from the crowd and raised her hand; she was trembling. "I touched you," she said.

(pause 5-8 seconds)

Imagine now that everyone is looking at the woman who had touched Jesus. She is trembling, but you can tell that she is happy. In fact, she is so happy that she can barely speak. Everyone is now waiting for the woman to speak. She can hardly talk because she is so excited. She starts to tell her story. And she tells a story about how sick she has been. She has been bleeding for over twelve years now. She has been very sick and has seen every doctor in town. She tells everyone that she has spent all her money on seeing doctors and trying to be made well. She has been depressed because of her sickness, and the moment that she touched Jesus, she stopped bleeding. Immediately she was made well. Jesus smiles at her and says, "Daughter, your faith has made you well; go in peace."

But what about the man whose daughter is at home, sick? He is still standing there. In all the excitement of hearing about the woman being healed, everyone has forgotten about the man's daughter.

(pause 5 seconds)

And then someone comes into the crowd and says to the man, "Your daughter is dead—there is no need to trouble Jesus any longer." But Jesus heard this and quickly says to the man, "Don't be afraid—only believe, and she will be well."

Picture with me now that you are walking with Jesus as he follows the man to his house to check on his daughter. Do you think she will be well?

Imagine arriving at the house and everyone is crying. You see Jesus move toward them, and he says to them, "Don't weep, for the child is not dead." Watch as Jesus takes the girl by the hand and says to her, "Child, get up!" The little girl got up at once. Her spirit returned to her. She is alive. (Lk 8:40-56).

God made a new promise, and it comes to us through Jesus.

The good news of God comes to us through the *words* of Jesus.

The good news of God comes to us through the life *of Jesus.*

 Question: How does the good news of God come to us? *Answer*: The good news of God comes to us through the life of Jesus.

 FOR THE PARENT OR MENTOR Jesus lived a model life. His life is what a good life looks like: full of purpose, joy, friendships, mission, parties, and laughter.

And yet there were also challenges, confusion, sorrow, betrayal, doubt, funerals, and weeping. What is your life full of? Spend some time today taking a look at your life. What do you see? Where does your life look like the life of Jesus? I'm not talking about the miracles. I'm talking about the family gatherings where conflict erupted, the weddings and celebrations, the death of loved ones, and eating dinner with people in the neighborhood. We often consider Jesus' life to be extraordinary. And of course it was. But nearly everything Jesus did took place in the context of an ordinary life. Ordinary days and nights lived with a particular attention paid to noticing what his Father was doing, and joining him in that work.

What is Jesus inviting you into during the ordinary events of your life? Where can you see the good news of God to you in the everyday life of following the way of Jesus? Church events are great. Church outreach and ministries that you may be involved in are one of the ways our lives can be shaped toward the mission and life of Jesus. But the normal everyday events like going to the grocery store, stopping to engage someone on the street who is hungry, offering to pray for someone on the bus or train— these are the everyday events that make a life. These are the events in which your child needs to see the good news come through. As you spend some time taking stock of the normal events of your life this week, consider how Jesus might live your life if he were the one living it. How might this shape your imagination for how your life might change and bend toward the life of Jesus?

- Spend some time this week at bedtime helping your child review the day. Look together for highs and lows throughout the day. Thank God for the joys, and pray for the pains.

- Spend some time in the Gospels looking for some of the stories of Jesus' life. What scenes stick out to you?

- Take about twenty or thirty minutes and read Mark 5–8 out loud together.

- Ask your child, "What's your favorite story about Jesus?" Ask this question a few times this week. "Tell me more about that story you love about Jesus. What do you like about it?"

- Engage your child this week with the following questions: "How is our life as a family bringing good news to others?" "What can we do to celebrate this?" "What else do you think God might be inviting our family to do to bring God's good news to others?"

O With your child, brainstorm how more of the good news of Jesus can affect the way you live together as a family.

 **FOR THE JOURNAL** Set aside about fifteen minutes and ask your child to remember the imaginative prayer from this week. Encourage your child to sit quietly for a few moments. Ask your child to think through their answer to the question, "What is your favorite story about Jesus?" Encourage them to spend some time writing about what makes this story their favorite. Help your child think about how their own life might contain an everyday event similar to this story.

28

The good news of God comes to us through the *death* of Jesus

 **CONNECTION AND FORMATION** Why did Jesus die? This is a complex question. In short, he gave his life for us. But how does that work? And more importantly, how can we best develop a child's thinking on the work of Jesus' death without glossing over the tensions that exist when we try to answer questions about how his death does something for us? This week's imaginative prayer takes us to the scene where Jesus says the most about what his death means: the last meal he had with his followers, which was a Passover feast. The goal for our imaginative prayer is to highlight the same thing that Jesus highlights—that his body and blood do the work of making a new promise (covenant) with God's people. The new promise is the fulfillment of the old one (remember the exodus), that God would deliver his people from exile, which came about because of their sins.

One of the most powerful ways to form the imagination of our children is to take every opportunity to imbue the celebration of the meal Jesus gave us (that is, the Eucharist, Communion, the Lord's Supper) with as much meaning and significance as we can.[1] Regular participation in this event will nourish your child's imagination. "The form of historic, Christian worship is cruciform: it is worship that rehearses the life, death, resurrection and ascension of Jesus as the Messiah of Israel. It is in Jesus alone that we learn to be human."[2]

But the Lord's Supper isn't only an event of remembering or learning. Somehow, Jesus is present with a unique offering of grace and nourishment to the soul. This imaginative prayer is meant to help foster deeper conversation about what Jesus was doing in reimagining the Passover meal around the events of his own life, particularly his crucifixion. We often fail to take the time to articulate the mystery of Jesus' death and what makes our salvation possible as a result of it. My hope is that this imaginative prayer might deepen your child's experience of the Lord's Supper within the context of your faith community. Communion can only happen with other people. This shared meal makes the story of Jesus tangible. We, with our bodies, take in the story, chew it, swallow it, and trust that God's presence will help us digest its meaning.

One quick note about this imaginative prayer. I've kept the authentic details of the story intact. Jesus and his disciples would have been drinking wine. During this imaginative prayer, there is a moment when your child is encouraged to imagine taking a sip. Use your discretion here as a parent and substitute grape juice for wine if that seems best for your context.

 Question: How does the good news of God come to us?
Answer: The good news of God comes to us through the death of Jesus.

 **IMAGINATIVE PRAYER**

Close your eyes and let's take a few deep breaths together.

God, I pray that you will release our imagination and help us to hear you speak to us during this time together. We open our hands to you. We open our ears to you.

(pause 8-10 seconds)

Come, Holy Spirit.

Imagine with me that you are sitting at a table with Jesus. It's dark outside, but the room is lit by lamps and candlelight. You are about to begin a feast that has been set before you. Others who have been following Jesus too are there with you.

There is warm bread on the table. And everyone is waiting for Jesus to start the meal.

(pause 5-8 seconds)

This is a special meal. This is the meal you celebrate each year to help you remember when God freed his people from slavery. This meal is called the Passover meal. It helps you remember the promise of God.

Imagine that Jesus stands up and looks around the room. Everyone is quiet. Everyone is looking at Jesus. And then he says,

> I have been looking forward to sharing this meal with you. Thank you for being here. This is the last time that we will eat together before I will begin to suffer some of the things I have been telling you about.

Everyone knows Jesus is talking about his death. He has been telling his followers for a while now that people are going to take him away and kill him.

What does it feel like to know that this is the last meal you will share with Jesus?

(pause 5 seconds)

What does it feel like to know that Jesus is very shortly going to be killed?

(pause 5 seconds)

Jesus speaks again: "God's kingdom is coming."

He then picks up a cup of wine and he gives thanks for it with a prayer.

> Here, take this cup of wine and share it. Each of you, take some and drink it.

Imagine watching as the cup of wine is passed around the table. This cup of wine feels special. Others are taking a sip of wine. Everyone knows that there is something special about this night.

Imagine now that the cup comes to you. Imagine raising the cup up to your lips. Take a big sip of the wine (or grape juice).

As you lower the cup, look at Jesus. He's about to say something.

He says, "This cup represents a new promise from God. The new promise is found in my blood, which I am about to shed."

You are reminded again that Jesus is about to be taken and be led to his death.

(pause 8-10 seconds)

How do you feel about this new promise of God?

(pause 5 seconds)

And now, Jesus is holding some bread in his hands. Watch Jesus as he takes the bread and breaks it. He says, "This bread is my body, which is broken for you. As often as you eat this bread and drink this cup, remember me."

Everyone now reaches for the bread and eats it.

What does it mean to you that you are eating the body of Jesus? What does it mean that Jesus said that his body is broken for you?

(pause 8-10 seconds)

Try to remember some of the scenes in the life of Jesus. Remember his love and friendship with people. Remember how gentle he was and how much fun he was. Remember how everyone wanted to be close to him and to hear him speak.

Imagine some of the words Jesus has spoken.

Remember these words:

> I am the light of the world.
> I am the bread of life.

What would it feel like to know that Jesus was about to die?

(pause 8-10 seconds)

What does it feel like to know that the death of Jesus is somehow going to mean freedom for you?

(pause 5 seconds)

Take a moment now and imagine yourself speaking to Jesus after you have sipped the wine and eaten the bread. What would you say to Jesus?

(pause 8-10 seconds)

Imagine Jesus leans over and whispers in your ear. Remember, these are his last words to you before he dies. He has just told you that his body and his blood are about to be shed so that God's kingdom can come.

What would you want Jesus' last words to be to you before he dies?

(pause 8-10 seconds)

God made a new promise and it comes to us through Jesus.

The good news of God comes to us through the *words* of Jesus.

The good news of God comes to us through the *life* of Jesus.

The good news of God comes to us through the death *of Jesus.*

Question: How does the good news of God come to us?
Answer: The good news of God comes to us through the death of Jesus.

 What has been your experience of God through pondering the death of Jesus? The traditional church calendar suggests that we spend the season of Lent contemplating the death and suffering of Jesus. Many who immerse themselves in the Lenten journey find that their understanding of Christ's death and suffering grows deeper, not through rehearsing doctrinal statements about the nature of Jesus' death, but by immersing themselves into the experience of Jesus' forty days of fasting, his final weeks as he heads toward Jerusalem, his journey toward the cross, and the climactic scene at Golgotha.

As you interact with your child on the topic of God's good news coming to us through Jesus' death, help your child embrace the mystery. If they ask a question that you don't quite understand, do your best to answer, and yet be honest about your own questions. Your child needs to know that in following Jesus some things are indeed a mystery. Nearly every child in their teenage years and beyond, particularly in the college years, begins to wrestle with the story of Jesus in some pretty significant ways. Children at this age are most likely learning in school that everything is black and white, right and wrong. Your child could benefit from watching you embrace mystery, to not know all the answers and yet still have faith while doing the hard work of holding those questions before God in prayer. Ask God to give you wisdom to invite your child into some of the mystery and tension. If you teach your child now about the mystery of Christ, of faith, of the resurrection, they are less likely to be frightened by it later when some of the certainty that we tend to cling to begins to fade. If you introduce your child to the dimly lit glass at a young age (when they are not yet afraid of it), their eyes will be more accustomed to seeing through it when life begins to feel more complex.

- Spend some time this week at bedtime helping your child review the day. Look together for highs and lows throughout the day. Thank God for the joys, and pray for the pains.

- Spend some time this week talking about the death of Jesus. We have been intentional in allowing you as a parent or mentor to carve out some time to visit the crucifixion scene in the way you think is best for you and your child.

- Spend some time talking about the events between the Last Supper and the crucifixion.

- Read John 11:45-53. Help your child understand that the Jewish leaders were wanting to kill Jesus because they thought he was a false prophet and didn't like what he was teaching. Help your child understand that because Jesus was talking about being the "Son of Man" and because people were calling him the "Son of David" (both of which would mean that Jesus is the long-awaited Messiah), the Romans wanted to keep any would-be Jewish king in check. The Romans killed

Jesus, ultimately, because they feared an uprising of followers of the Jewish Messiah.

○ Read Matthew 27:32-56 with your child. Try to help them imagine what it would be like to walk with Jesus up the hill toward the cross.

○ Visit a Catholic church when there isn't a service. Walk through the Stations of the Cross with your child and explain what each scene means. Ask, "Which one of these scenes is your favorite?"

○ Try to memorize this passage of Scripture:

> Whoever wants to be first among you must be your slave. That is what the Son of Man has done: He came to serve, not be served—and then to give away his life in exchange for the many who are held hostage. (Mt 20:27-28 *The Message*)

FOR THE JOURNAL Set aside about fifteen minutes and ask your child to remember the imaginative prayer from this week and perhaps something else related to Jesus' death that came up in conversation. Encourage your child to sit quietly for a few moments. Ask your child to write a brief journal entry about what the death of Jesus means. Encourage your child to ask questions about Jesus' death. Help your child understand that there is some mystery in *how* the death of Jesus accomplishes our freedom. Encourage your child to ask questions directly of God. Help your child understand that these are great questions to talk about with God. Sometimes, God will even grant some insight or wisdom to the questions we ask. And sometimes no matter how much we try to understand, some things remain a bit of a mystery.

29

The good news of God comes to us through the *resurrection* of Jesus

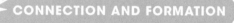 **CONNECTION AND FORMATION** This week's imaginative prayer puts your child in the place of the travelers on the Road to Emmaus (Lk 24:13-29). So often the resurrection seems like a fairy tale—but this is a story of doubt, confusion, and then direct experience with the risen Jesus. The death of Jesus brought a real experience of disappointment, doubt, and surprise, which quickly turned to excitement and even confusion at the resurrection. The resurrection is not just a theological happening; it's something that happened in front of real people whose lives were radically shifted as a result. People believed in the resurrection because they saw Jesus. This imaginative prayer, like many others, is trying to nurture an experience of Jesus who is alive and empowering us for the work of the kingdom of God. It's not just a fairy tale.

What is the formational work of focusing on the resurrection? When Christ was raised from the dead, "his gains become the whole world's story."[1] We are part of the same story as that couple walking on the road to Emmaus. We can relate to their walk. Your child can see that disappointment and missed expectation are normal parts of the story we are living in. And yet those disappointments are the short-term perspective. All things will rise.

 Question: How did God's new promise come into the world?
Answer: The good news of God comes to us through the resurrection of Jesus.

 **IMAGINATIVE PRAYER**

Close your eyes and let's take a few deep breaths together.

God, I pray that you will release our imagination and help us to hear you speak to us during this time together. We open our hands to you. We open our ears to you.

(pause 8-10 seconds)

Come, Holy Spirit.

Imagine with me that you are walking along the road with a friend. Close your eyes and imagine you have a long walk back to your hometown. You are leaving Jerusalem, where just a few days ago Jesus was killed, and his body was placed in a tomb.

(pause 5 seconds)

Imagine you have been following Jesus. Picture again the miracles you have witnessed throughout the towns and villages over the past several years. You've seen Jesus feed thousands of people at the Sea of Galilee. You've watched him heal people in the streets, and you have seen him make dead people get up from their death bed. And people who couldn't walk pick up their mat and run with joy.

A few days ago, you watched as Jesus was executed—crucified on a cross. And then just this morning you heard reports that the tomb Jesus had been placed in is empty.

They can't find his body, and now all of his closest friends are hiding.

What would it feel like to you if this had happened to you?

(pause 5-8 seconds)

What are some words you would use to describe how you feel?

(pause 5 seconds)

Would you feel sad? Afraid? Confused?

(pause 5 seconds)

You and your friend are walking along the road, asking each other questions, and talking about all the things that had happened over the past few days.

Imagine as you are talking with your friend, a man comes up, joins you on your walk, and begins asking you questions about the things you are discussing.

"What's this you're discussing so intently as you walk along?" he asks.

This question makes you sad. How could you possibly explain to this stranger all that has happened?

Your friend asks him, "Are you the only one in Jerusalem who hasn't heard what's happened during the last few days?"

"What's been going on?" the man asks you. "What has happened?"

You answer:

> The things that happened to Jesus the Nazarene. He was a man of God, a prophet, dynamic in work and word, blessed by both God and all the people. Then our high priests and leaders betrayed him, got him sentenced to death, and crucified him. And we had our hopes up that he was the One, the One about to deliver Israel. And it is now the third day since it happened. But now some of our women have completely confused us. Early this morning they were at the tomb and couldn't find his body. They came back with the story that they had seen a vision of angels who said he was alive. Some of our friends went off to the tomb to check and found it empty just as the women said, but they didn't see Jesus. (Lk 24:19-26 *The Message*)

Imagine now that the man is smiling at you. He says, "It seems you are having a difficult time understanding everything about the Messiah. Didn't the Messiah have to suffer and die in order for God's kingdom to come?"

This makes you think. Why does God's kingdom come when his Messiah gives up his life?

(pause 5 seconds)

And then the man who has been walking with you begins to tell you more about God's kingdom.

He starts with Moses and tells the story of all the prophets God has sent from the beginning.

"What has it all been about?" you ask.

The man goes on to tell you all the things about God's plan to begin something new in the world.

(pause 5-8 seconds)

Imagine now that the man continues to walk along the road ahead of you as you arrive at your house.

You ask him to come into your home and to stay for dinner.

You are sitting with him at dinner when he takes bread and breaks it, and gives thanks.

And then your eyes are opened. You see that the man is Jesus himself, who is with you. He has been talking with you all this time, and you didn't even recognize him.

And then he is gone.

You get up and run back into the city and find Simon and John and the other disciples.

Imagine that you arrive at the home of one of the disciples, and they greet you and let you know that the resurrected Jesus has appeared to Simon. "It's true! Jesus has risen from the dead."

And then you tell your story. Imagine telling others about how Jesus had walked with you out of the city and into the next town, telling you the whole story of why he was put to death, and what it means that God has raised him from the dead.

What would it feel like to be surrounded by people who believe you? They all believe Jesus really did rise from the dead. They believe you when you tell them that you were with him, that he shared a meal with you and broke bread with you.

(pause 5-8 seconds)

While you are still talking, you notice that Jesus is standing with you. He's with you right now in the room.

"Peace be with you," he says.

Imagine feeling a little afraid. Everyone around you believes Jesus has risen from the dead, and yet, as he is standing right in front of you, it feels as though you are looking at a ghost.

"Why are you troubled?" you hear Jesus ask. "Why are there doubts rising up in you?"

(pause 5-8 seconds)

"Look at my hands and feet! It's me. It's me, Jesus."

(pause 5-8 seconds)

"Touch me and see; a ghost does not have flesh and bones. Touch my flesh; feel my body."

Watch as Jesus holds out his hands for you to touch.

And then listen to these words that Jesus says:

"Everything I told you while I was with you comes to this: All the things written about me in the Law of Moses, in the Prophets, and in the Psalms have to be fulfilled."

He went on to open their understanding of the Word of God, showing them how to read their Bibles this way. He said, "You can see now how it is written that the Messiah suffers, rises from the dead on the third day, and then a total life-change through the forgiveness of sins is proclaimed in his name to all nations—starting from here, from Jerusalem! You're the first to hear and see it. You're the witnesses. What comes next is very important: I am sending what my Father promised to you, so stay here in the city until he arrives, until you're equipped with power from on high." (Lk 24:44-49 *The Message*)

God made a new promise, and it comes to us through Jesus.

The good news of God comes to us through the *words* of Jesus.

The good news of God comes to us through the *life* of Jesus.

The good news of God comes to us through the *death* of Jesus.

The good news of God comes to us through the resurrection *of Jesus!*

 Question: How did God's new promise come into the world? *Answer*: The good news of God comes to us through the resurrection of Jesus.

 **FOR THE PARENT OR MENTOR** As I read this passage I often ask myself, "Would I recognize Jesus if he showed up in the middle of my day?" How attentive are you throughout the day to the person of Jesus showing up? Jesus tells us in Matthew 25 that when we are present to the poor, when we give someone else something to eat or drink, we are in fact giving those things to him. We are quenching his thirst. We are satisfying his hunger. What are some ways you are expecting Jesus to show up in your life and in the life of your family? Are you in a season of attentiveness? Or do you find that it's rather difficult to see Jesus? Spend some time this week reading through Luke 24:44-49, known as the Road to Emmaus. Spend some time thinking about where Jesus might be walking with you, even when you don't notice him.

Consider what it means that Jesus is alive, that he has a resurrected body. One of the things we often neglect is our own body. And yet the embodiment of God is so important. Not only did the Son enter into a body through the incarnation, but the resurrection means that God continues to be embodied in the person of Jesus. How do you feel about your body right now? How often do you think about your body with a sense of joy and gladness, for it is a gift from God? Spend some time this week praying that God would speak to you about your current body, his desire for your body, and what he might want to speak to you about your own bodily resurrection when the fullness of Christ's kingdom is revealed.[2]

○ Spend some time this week at bedtime helping your child review the day. Look together for highs and lows throughout the day. Thank God for the joys, and pray for the pains.

○ Spend some time talking about the resurrection. Read Luke 24:13-52 together. Focus on verse 41 and the *joy* and *amazement* of the experience. What job did Jesus give his followers after the resurrection? Why do you think resurrection means forgiveness?

○ Ask, "Are there times when you don't feel like Jesus is walking with you? When do you notice that he's really there with you?" Share with your child a time when you failed to notice Jesus was near to a particular situation. Share a time when you did notice. What was that like for you to feel the presence of Jesus?

○ Go back and read the resurrection account in John 20.

○ Listen to the song "All Things Rise" (www.youtube.com/watch ?v=hLttio7yWCo). Talk about how "his gains become the whole world's story."

○ Read Ezekiel 37:1-14. This is one of the first clues in Scripture of the hope for resurrection (written almost 2,500 years ago). This story is about Israel's exile and restoration. This story about dry bones coming to life is what restoration looks like. Help your child understand that Jesus was living in a time when the people of Israel were still waiting for the long-expected restoration of their relationship with God. The resurrection meant that life with God was beginning again. He was offering them return from exile, which meant that their sins would be forgiven.

FOR THE JOURNAL Set aside about fifteen minutes and ask your child to remember the imaginative prayer from this week. Read Luke 24:13-52 again with your child. Encourage your child to think about how they might respond to Jesus should he suddenly appear. Encourage your child to write a scene where they are walking with Jesus. "If you had an opportunity to take a walk with Jesus, what would you want to say to him?" "What would you want him to say to you?"

30

We receive the promises of
God when we choose
to follow Jesus

 This week's imaginative
prayer places your child
in a situation where Jesus is extending the invitation "Follow me." We're
trying to help your child experience the reality that a choice needs to be
made to follow Jesus, and that all the promises we've been talking about, all
the good news of God, come to us when we choose to follow Jesus. What
does this choice look like? A written invitation from Jesus. We allude to
several passages in this imaginative exercise that we hope will jog your child's
memory of scenes in the Gospels when Jesus was with his disciples. By
placing your child in the role of a potential disciple, the invitation here is the
same invitation given to Peter, James, and all the other disciples: "Follow me!"

The spiritual formation journey is one of continued invitation from Jesus.
One of the reasons kids lose interest in their faith is that it begins to feel
static. We often forget to invite children to consider what God might be up
to right now, and how he is inviting them to join him in his work (which is
the focus of part six, "The Mission of God").

"What is Jesus inviting you into?" This question can open up a great deal
of conversation. The typical response from a child is, "I don't know." To
which I have often replied, "Well, what would you *want* to be invited into?"
or "What kind of *assignment* would you like in the work of the kingdom?"
The formational journey is a response to God's invitation from Jesus by the
Spirit. We want to nurture in your child a personal invitation to follow Jesus
on an ongoing basis, not merely as a conversion experience.

Question: How do we receive the promises of God?
Answer: We receive the promises of God when we choose to follow Jesus.

 **IMAGINATIVE PRAYER**

Close your eyes and let's take a few deep breaths together.

God, I pray that you will release our imagination and help us to hear you speak to us during this time together. We open our hands to you. We open our ears to you.

(pause 8-10 seconds)

Come, Holy Spirit.

Imagine with me that you are sitting at a table in front of a giant wooden door. This door is like the giant doors on the front of castles. It's an old door. It's beautiful and big. You are sitting at a table that is set for a feast, though you are the only person at the table right now. You are waiting for others to arrive.

(pause 5-8 seconds)

Suddenly, there is a knock at the door. Imagine getting up from your seat at the table and walking to the door. You turn the handle and hear the door creak a bit as it opens. It opens slowly. You can see someone standing in front of you, and once the door opens all the way, you can see that it is Jesus. He's smiling.

(pause 5-8 seconds)

Imagine you are looking up at his face. He's much taller than you, of course. But then he crouches down so that his face is right in front of yours. He's still smiling, and then he gently says to you, "Hey there, can I come in?"

Invite Jesus into the room right now, and let me know when he's there. Let me know when you can picture him with you.

(pause 5-8 seconds)

Next, Jesus invites you to sit in a chair in the corner of the room. There is a pitcher of water and a basin sitting next to the chair. You watch as Jesus takes off his robe and picks up a towel. He kneels in front of you, and it looks like he is about to wash your feet. Imagine looking down at your feet. You realize that you don't have any shoes on. You've played all day in the dirt and ran around without shoes. If there was a contest for who had the dirtiest feet, you would most certainly win!

Then, Jesus reaches down and takes your feet into his hands. He holds your feet over the bowl and pours water over your feet. You are reminded of the story when he washed the disciples' feet at the Last Supper.

What does it feel like to let Jesus wash your feet?

(pause 5-8 seconds)

He takes soap and gets those feet really clean. And then he dries them off and invites you to join him at the table. Jesus reaches for his robe and puts it back on. And then he sits right next to you at the table. You wonder if others will be joining you. This seems like quite the feast.

What does it feel like to be at a table all alone with Jesus?

(pause 5 seconds)

Imagine now that Jesus begins pouring juice in some of the glasses around the table. He looks at you and says, "Others will be joining us soon, but there is something I would like to ask you before they get here."

Next, Jesus takes some bread from the table and breaks it into smaller pieces. You watch him as he places a small piece of bread on each plate on the table.

You are reminded of the Last Supper when Jesus broke the bread and gave thanks for the wine. You remember that the bread was to remind you of his body, and that the cup with wine was to remind you of his blood.

This feels like a very special moment.

(pause 5 seconds)

Jesus hands you a plain, white envelope. On the front of the envelope are written two words. It says, "An Invitation."

(pause 5 seconds)

You hold the envelope in your hands and wonder what Jesus could be inviting you to.

"Go ahead and open it," he says.

Jesus looks on with a smile. You are excited. It kind of feels like your birthday.

You open the envelope and see a card inside.

You open the card and see two words. It simply says, "Follow me."

You look at Jesus. And then there is a moment of silence.

(pause 10 seconds)

Imagine as Jesus reaches out and takes your hands. And then he says,

(*slowly*) I'd like for you to follow me.
I'd like to show you what a good life looks like.
I'd like to invite you into helping me bring good news to the whole world.

What does this invitation feel like?

(pause 5 seconds)

You look down at the card again: "Follow me."

You are reminded of when Jesus said these words to Peter one morning when he was fishing. He said these words to Matthew the tax collector, and he said the same words to that little man Zacchaeus, who climbed up into a tree to get a better view as Jesus was passing by.

"Do you have faith in me?" Jesus asked.

"Do you believe that I am the King?"

"Do you trust that I will take care of you?"

"Do you know that I love you?"

"Do you believe that I speak the words of God?"

"Do you believe that I died and rose again?"

(pause 5-8 seconds)

What do you say to all of this? Do you trust Jesus? Do you want to follow him?

You look at Jesus again, and you look at the feast before you.

You look again at the invitation from Jesus.

"Follow me," it reads.

"Follow me," says Jesus.

God made a new promise and it comes to us through Jesus.

The good news of God comes to us through the *words* of Jesus.

The good news of God comes to us through the *life* of Jesus.

The good news of God comes to us through the *death* of Jesus.

The good news of God comes to us through the *resurrection* of Jesus.

We receive the promises of God when we choose to follow Jesus.

 Question: How do we receive the promises of God?
Answer: We receive the promises of God when we choose to follow Jesus.

 When was the last time you heard Jesus invite you into something? What did it feel like for you the last time you made a conscious choice to follow him? I think we sometimes forget what it is like to experience a firsthand, personal invitation. And yet there is always an invitation to more. One of the important ways we can model spiritual

formation for our children is to say yes to Jesus again and again. Your child needs to watch you struggle through the process of saying yes to Jesus. Saying yes is part of our formation. It's more difficult at first, but then it gets a little easier. As we say yes—not out of an unhealthy compulsion but as a response to the love of God—we form a habit in our heart of saying yes. Your child needs to watch what it looks like to receive the love and grace of Jesus, and then to say yes to whatever else is written inside that envelope marked "Invitation."

Jesus' invitation to us, all of us, is the same invitation he gave to his disciples: "Watch me serve and love, and then go and do likewise." Spend some time this week asking God this question: What are you inviting me into next? Notice even the small ways that God is tugging on you. God's invitation is most often in the small things. An invitation to speak more gently, to be more patient, to slow down, to rest. As we are faithful with the small things, God often trusts us with bigger projects and larger acts of faith.

Share with your child some of your process in this. Be vulnerable with your child and let them know where you sense God is asking you to take a risk in following Jesus. What are your hesitations? What seems hard here? Speak those things out loud and let your child in on your own process of faith. You don't need to protect them from your struggles, your questions, and your fears. For them to grow, they need to know that you have these struggles.[1]

- ○ Spend some time this week at bedtime helping your child review the day. Look together for highs and lows throughout the day. Thank God for the joys, and pray for the pains.

- ○ If this material is being used in your child's Sunday school class or in a small group environment, open up some conversation this week by saying to your child, "Tell me about your lesson at church this past Sunday." Give your child time to explain what was in their imagination. Be patient with the process. If they say, "I don't remember," help their memory a little by saying something like, "I hear there was a story where Jesus knocked on a door?"

- ○ Read Revelation 3:20 together. Explain that this is from a letter written by John to future churches. The Holy Spirit is using John's imagination (with John's prayerful willingness) to teach future churches about God's heart for them. Jesus is knocking on the doors of the people in this church because he wants to have a feast with them, but they aren't very focused on Jesus. They aren't following him with their *yes*.

- ○ Try to create some space this week to share with your child about when you made the decision to follow Jesus. Say, "Can I tell you about when I made a decision to follow Jesus?"

- ○ After you share your story, say something like, "You know, we're a family that tries to follow Jesus. This is a decision that Mommy and Daddy have made [or just you if you are in a household where just one of you has made a decision to follow Jesus], but someday you'll have to make that decision for yourself."

- ○ Read Ephesians 3:12 together sometime this week. Talk to your child about how faith in Jesus (that he is King, that he loves us, that he forgives us) enables us to come to God with confidence and freedom.

- ○ Tell some stories about the ongoing choices you have made that align your life with the life of Jesus.

FOR THE JOURNAL Set aside about fifteen minutes and ask your child to remember the imaginative prayer from this week. Encourage your child to think about the image of Jesus standing at a door and knocking. Ask, "What do you think Jesus is inviting you into?" or "How is Jesus asking you to follow him this week?" Sit with your child, talk this through, and encourage them to write down some of those things.

God made a new promise, and it comes to us through Jesus.
The good news of God comes to us through the *words* of Jesus.
The good news of God comes to us through the *life* of Jesus.
The good news of God comes to us through the *death* of Jesus.
The good news of God comes to us through the *resurrection* of Jesus.
We receive the promises of God when we choose to follow Jesus.

CREEDAL QUESTIONS AND ANSWERS

Question: How did God's new promise come into the world?
Answer: God made a new promise, and it comes to us through Jesus.

Question: How does the good news of God come to us?
Answer: The good news of God comes to us through the words of Jesus.

Question: How does the good news of God come to us?"
Answer: The good news of God comes to us through the life of Jesus.

Question: How does the good news of God come to us?
Answer: The good news of God comes to us through the death of Jesus.

Question: How did God's new promise come into the world?
Answer: The good news of God comes to us through the resurrection of Jesus.

Question: How do we receive the promises of God?
Answer: We receive the promises of God when we choose to follow Jesus.

QUESTIONS AND ACTIVITIES

O Spend time this week reviewing each of the past six weeks.

O Ask some good questions or make some suggestions that might stimulate reflection. For example:

  o What do you think about the good news of God's promises?

○ What are some of your favorite words of Jesus? (Parent or mentor: share your favorites here as well.)

○ What are some of your favorite stories of Jesus' life?

○ How do you feel about that scene where Jesus shares a meal with his disciples?

○ Is there anything about this story that seems confusing? If so, what?

○ Regarding resurrection: perhaps read some other stories of Jesus' interaction with his followers after his bodily resurrection.

○ What has it been like for you as you have learned about Jesus?

○ What do you think Jesus' invitation for you would be today if he handed you another envelope?

○ What are some ways you could follow Jesus this week?

○ Review the portion of the creedal poem that corresponds with part five, "The Good News of God." Help your child memorize these next six lines. Review the creedal poem from parts one through four. Together with your child, see if you can recite them all.

PART 6

The Mission of God

31

When we follow Jesus, we join the mission
of God to bring his love into the world.

32

The mission of God is to make everything in the world good again,

33

to bring all things under the reign of King Jesus,

34

to bring peace and reconciliation to everything.

35

The mission of God is to take away the veil
that covers up the presence of God.

36

God is at work all around us: open your eyes
and join God in his mission to the world.

When we follow Jesus, we join the mission of God to bring his love into the world

CONNECTION AND FORMATION This week's imaginative prayer will introduce your child to the mission of God, often referred to as the *missio Dei*. God's mission to the world is his movement toward people. God's mission is his love connection to people. His instrument of that mission and connection is the church. As one scholar has articulated, "There is church because there is mission, not vice versa."[1]

This week we will introduce the idea and experience that we are part of the epic story of God's love coming into the world. We are the continuation of the story we see in Scripture. Our role is to faithfully improvise as we carry out God's mission in the world based on the storyline of the New Testament. You are inviting your child into this adventure.[2]

This is where we help your child to understand that these ancient stories, which often feel so far away from our present context, are the beginning chapters of a much longer story stretching to the present day. Spiritual formation eventually leads to mission. When we nurture closeness to God's heart, we'll naturally find ways to join God in loving the things close to his heart: mercy, justice, orphans, widows, and strangers (to name a few). When your child gets close to the heart of God, your child's heart will break for what breaks God's heart, and rejoice in what makes God rejoice. The love of Christ compels us (2 Cor 5:14).

Question: What happens to us when we follow Jesus?
Answer: When we follow Jesus, we join the mission of God to bring his love into the world.

Close your eyes and let's take a few deep breaths together.

God, I pray that you will release our imagination and help us to hear you speak to us during this time together. We open our hands to you. We open our ears to you.

(pause 8-10 seconds)

Come, Holy Spirit.

Imagine with me that you are standing in front of a giant book. The greatest story ever told is in this book. In this book are poems and stories. There are songs about war, about love, and about loneliness. There is dancing and crying in this book. There is peace and conflict. There is beauty and destruction. Imagine the book is in front of you, and it is closed. In this book is the greatest story.

(pause 5-8 seconds)

Do you want to open the book?

Imagine you open the book to the first few pages. Suddenly, a soft wind is blowing in the room where you are standing. The wind gets stronger, and you look toward the book and find something magical is happening here. It is almost as though you are seeing into another world or another time. You see the planets and stars being formed. The wind is blowing and you feel a great sense of peace and calm, and then you see the oceans forming; you watch as the land emerges from the sea. The wind is still blowing. You watch as animals come to life and begin to run and fly and swim. You watch as the soil slowly turns into a person, and then there is another person. They have life together, and there is great peace.

God is in this story. You can see him. This is his great story.

(pause 5 seconds)

As you turn the pages you watch as God loves the world he has created. You watch as God talks to people and invites them to take care of the world.

He invites them to take care of each other.

Imagine looking at this giant book and you can see, almost like a movie, all the action of this book coming to life. There are wars and floods. Babies are born and families grow up. There are kings and queens in this great story. Some kings are good and some are bad. There are men and women who follow God, and there are men and women who don't follow God.

You watch as God reaches out his hand to help people. God provides for people. He shows them a new land safe from their enemies. And then those people forget about God. They forget their promise to him.

God makes promises to his people, and he is faithful to those promises.

Imagine there are great scenes in this story where God does special things to show his love and care. He sends people to speak on his behalf. Prophets, like Isaiah, and Amos, and John the Baptist, whose lives are mysterious.

And because God loves the world so much, God comes himself in the body of a baby named Jesus to show the world what it looks like to really live. He comes to show the world what it looks like to love and serve and give. This is the mission of God.

(pause 8-10 seconds)

You turn the page in this story and watch as God comes into the world that he made, and again you feel the wind blowing around you. You watch as God is born into the world to Mary and Joseph. You watch as this baby grows into a boy and then into a man.

You listen to the words he speaks and watch him as he speaks to great and powerful kings, and to little girls and boys. And big girls and boys your age.

(pause 5 seconds)

You watch as he lives his life and loves people. He touches them, and they are healed. He puts his arms around them, and they are made well. He laughs with them and eats with them.

(pause 8-10 seconds)

This is the greatest story ever told.

You watch as God shows the world what it looks like to love. He looks and acts like a servant, even though he is a King. He gives up his life and is handed over to death.

(pause 5 seconds)

And you watch as God shows the world what it looks like to have real and lasting power—power to overcome even death. You watch as Jesus rises from the grave and shares a meal of fish and bread with his friends at the seaside. You watch as he walks and talks with friends.

You look now at this story and see that this story is the story of God's mission to the world. Then you turn the page in this great book before you, and you find your name written at the top of the next page. Picture your name there. The next chapter in this book of great adventure is the chapter about your life.

And suddenly you feel your feet begin to lift. Imagine you begin to float, and as you approach the page of this book you grow smaller and smaller, until you are the size of that page.

The wind is blowing, and you magically step inside the pages of this book.

You are now part of this story.

(pause 5-8 seconds)

What would it look like for you to tell part of this story?

What parts of your life fit inside the story God is telling?

If you could do anything in the world to join in God's mission to bring his love and kindness into the world, what would you do?

You are now part of this story.

When we follow Jesus, we join the mission of God to bring his love into the world.

Question: What happens to us when we follow Jesus?
Answer: When we follow Jesus, we join the mission of God to bring his love into the world.

 FOR THE PARENT OR MENTOR   When is the last time you thought about the role you are playing in the larger story of God? What parts of your life feel like they are part of what God is doing in the world? Where do you see restoration happening in the world through the work of your hands? What would you want to ask God about the next chapter of your life? Spend some time this week imagining your life story as a chapter in the larger story God is telling. What do you feel God is inviting you into? Is he inviting you into a quiet and humble life? Is there adventure on the horizon for you? When was the last time you asked the Lord about the longings of your heart? Your child will catch the mission of God as they see you living and leaning into the mission of God in your own life.

Thomas Aquinas was asked if life was better spent in an active or contemplative manner. He answered yes. There is a unique balance to strike between nurturing your inner life—getting filled with the love of God—and then taking it into the world. Some of this will be dictated by the season of life you are in, how much time you have to sit quietly in God's presence, how much energy you have to nurture this spirit in your family, and how much discipline you can wield to slow your life down enough to ask some of these questions. That's okay. This will always be a struggle. There will be seasons of life when you overextend into mission, only to realize that you need to pull back a bit rather than doubling down. There will be other seasons in life when you'll recognize a bit of sloth at work. It's okay. God's invitation is always present.

Help your child see the process you are in, both in pursuing a life full of sabbath and rest and long periods of quiet restoration, as well as periods of fervor, passion, and laboring with every last bit of energy God provides for you. Talk about the balance. Name it. And introduce your child into the exciting story found on the pages of your own life.

- ○ Talk with your child this week about big stories: "Tell me about one of your favorite books you are reading. What are some of your favorite scenes in that book? Tell me more about why you like it."

- ○ See if you can get your child to do a bit of role playing. Make it completely unrelated to talking about church or Jesus, for now. For example: "Let's pretend we travel to outer space. Here, climb under this sheet and let's make this our space shuttle." Let this play out a bit. Imagine going to Mars or jumping on an asteroid. Then, introduce something into your story that doesn't quite fit. Like, "Hey, let's milk that cow over there." This should create a little dissonance. A cow wouldn't be in outer space. You know your child best and can create the best scenario, but the point is to put something into your story that shouldn't be there. Say, "That would feel odd in the story wouldn't it?"

- ○ This is how it works in our life with God. We have this story we are part of, and we are trying to live in line with the same story of love, grace, and forgiveness that we see demonstrated in Jesus. Helping the poor and loving our neighbors fits into the story. Being mean or disrespectful to people, or being unkind or impatient, doesn't fit with the story of God's love coming into the world.

- ○ The goal is to help your child experience the reality that they have a role to play in this great story that God is telling—the story of his love coming into the world.

 **FOR THE JOURNAL** Set aside twenty minutes once this week to sit with your child while they take a stab at writing or drawing in their journal. Ask them to spend just a few minutes thinking, writing, or drawing an answer to these questions: "What is something in your life happening right now that feels like part of God's story? Why do you think this feels like it's part of God's mission in the world?"

The mission of God is to make everything in the world good again

CONNECTION AND FORMATION This week's imaginative prayer builds on the *missio Dei* concept to help your child imagine all things in the world being made good and right again. Here too we continue to introduce in subtle ways the power of the Holy Spirit (pay attention to the wind). We pair the work of God with the movement of God's Spirit—foreshadowing further conversation on God's special power that comes at Pentecost. God accomplishes his work in the world through the power of his Spirit, who is alive in his people and in the church. God's mission to make all things good again comes from the new creation story found in Revelation 21:1-5. This apocalyptic language is itself an imaginative prophetic prayer and longing for all things being made right again. John, the writer of Revelation, is imagining (through the inspiration of the Holy Spirit) what a renewed and restored creation would be like.

Faith is forward looking. It isn't merely believing in something that happened long ago. Faith is an assurance that what we hope will happen is going to happen (Heb 11:1). This is the kind of faith that pulls us out of focusing on our own life and draws us into imagining more adventure and more pages to fill the story of God's mission to the world. Formation for your child will develop along lines of what they hope for. We have to give our children an enhanced vision for what they hope for. We need to expand their hopes beyond making the team next fall, getting into college, and finding a job. We need to help create in them hope and longing for things outside their immediate context, as well as hope and longing for the things close to them.

Question: What is the mission of God?

Answer: The mission of God is to make everything in the world good again.

 **IMAGINATIVE PRAYER**

Close your eyes and let's take a few deep breaths together.

God, I pray that you will release our imagination and help us to hear you speak to us during this time together. We open our hands to you. We open our ears to you.

(pause 8-10 seconds)

Come, Holy Spirit.

Imagine with me that you are surrounded by all sorts of things and all kinds of people.

Imagine you are in a wide open field of grass, and this field is filled with things and people. Some of the things belong to you, and some are things you have never seen before. They must belong to someone else.

(pause 8-10 seconds)

And you know some of the people who are in the field, but others are people you do not know. They are strangers, and many of them are speaking a different language. It seems as though they are from all sorts of places in the world.

Imagine that you are walking through the field and you notice that many of your toys and books are there. You can see some of your toys there that no longer work; they are broken. What are some of your toys you see there? Is there a doll you used to play with that is missing an arm? Or a robot that used to walk and no longer works? Imagine looking all around and noticing all the broken toys and damaged books.

Now imagine you see houses with broken windows. Imagine walking up to a house to get a closer look, and you notice that the paint is chipping and the steps are falling off the front porch. The house is old and in disrepair. It has been neglected. Imagine now that this is your house. What would it feel like to see your very own house or your apartment in this condition?

(pause 8-10 seconds)

Again you notice the people. There are people scattered throughout this field. There are people there who cannot walk or cannot see. There are people there who are clearly poor and hungry. And there is fighting. You see a father who is angry at his son, and brothers and sisters throwing stones at each other. People are arguing and angry. People are hurt. Some people are lonely.

(pause 8-10 seconds)

Now imagine that you continue to walk through the field. The grass beneath your feet turns brown as you get closer to the edge of the field. The trees there are barren, and you notice that there is rotten fruit on the ground near the trees. You take a deep breath of air, and it seems polluted. The sky is green where it should be blue, the water is brown where it should be clear, the ground and soil are hard and shallow where they should be deep and rich.

(pause 8-10 seconds)

Take a moment to look back over the entire field. The broken toys, the torn books, the neglected houses. Look at the people in the field. Watch as two brothers fight one another and two sisters yell at each other. Some people are lonely. Some are poor. But others right beside them are sitting down to a great feast. There are blind people and sick people. Some people are crying; others are homeless. Notice that there are children without parents, and mothers and fathers without children. And again you notice the trees and the sky and the pollution that surrounds you.

(pause 8-10 seconds)

What would it look like if everything in this field could be made right again? If everything could be made good again?

(pause 8 seconds)

Imagine now that a breeze begins to pick up. Feel the wind press against you at your back. It's not a cool but a warm breeze. It warms you up unlike any breeze you have felt. The wind begins to warm your heart and fill you with joy.

Imagine too that as the breeze arrives, the sun comes out and begins to shine light on the field. The breeze is strong and full of life. And it is just like the breeze you felt when you stood in front of the giant storybook that describes God's great story.

Close your eyes and remember that this breeze is the Holy Spirit. That's right! God's Spirit has shown up to this field. And when this happens, everything begins to slowly change. Even all the small things: the doll that had no arms grows new arms; the robot that couldn't walk begins to walk.

Imagine that you feel compelled to get involved. You pick up a paint brush and begin to give the house a new coat of paint.

(pause 5 seconds)

You clean the windows and grab a hammer and some nails to repair the front porch.

And then the really important things start to change.

You see fathers embrace their sons and daughters with great big hugs. These same fathers who were angry and impatient are full of love and grace.

You see mothers and daughters speaking kind words to each other. Brothers and sisters are hugging too. The Spirit of God blew through and snatched up all the conflict and carried it away on the strong breeze that went through.

Who do you want to reach out to? Are there any broken friendships you would want to see mended here in this field? In your life?

(pause 5 seconds)

Watch as families are reunited with each other.

Watch as new, healthy babies are born to women who couldn't have babies.

Watch as the breeze blows and these women are healed.

You reach your hand out to pray for someone who is blind, and their eyes are opened. You touch the legs of those who can't walk, and they are lifted onto their feet by the strong wind that blows through once again.

Watch as the sun shines brighter and brighter all over the field, and the Spirit of God rushes through like a strong wind.

Watch as the rich who dine at fancy feasts kneel before the poor and invite them to the table. You too are invited to the table, and you serve giant platters of food to people who haven't eaten in days.

Watch the poor and needy feast at the table with the rich: their glasses full, their plates full.

Watch as the trees sprout new fruit, and the grass and soil are restored. They are full of life and rich with nutrients and minerals.

Watch as leaves grow on trees, the sky turns bright blue, and the water becomes clear.

Watch as animals show up to the field full of playfulness and beauty.

(pause 8-10 seconds)

Before your eyes the Spirit of God came through first like a warm breeze and then like a rushing wind, and everything before you was made right. Everything that your eyes can see and your ears can hear, everything that you smell and sense has been made good again.

When we follow Jesus we join the mission of God to bring his love into the world.

The mission of God is to make everything in the world good again.

 Question: What is the mission of God?
Answer: The mission of God is to make everything in the world good again.

 **FOR THE PARENT OR MENTOR** How in tune are you with God's plan to make everything in the world good again? When you see brokenness and pain in the world, what is your level of hope for renewal? Hope is one of the most contagious characteristics of people with faith. As a parent, your belief that God is at work in all those hard and desperate places will impact your child's ability to have hope. Spend some time this week sitting with these questions: Where am I struggling right now to believe in the goodness of God's mission to the world? Where do I feel engaged in the mission of God to make everything in the world good again?

Ask the Lord to draw you into his mission. If you could see God make something in the world good again, what would it be?

- Spend some time this week at bedtime helping your child review the day. Look together for highs and lows throughout the day. Thank God for the joys, and pray for the pains.

- Engage your child in conversation this week about God's mission in the world:

  - to fill the world with his love (see chap. 31)

  - to make everything in the world good again

- Spend some time noticing (with your child) things that need to be made good again. We're not trying to merely notice broken things, we're trying to see them and reimagine what they could look like if God made them good again. If you see a homeless person, for example, say something like, "Look, this is something that God wants to make right. How can we help in God's plan right now? What could we do right now to participate in God's mission?"

- Spend some time in the evening reminding your child of their response to the preceding questions: "Do you remember a few nights ago when we talked about . . . ?" Pray with your child for God to have his way on the earth in that area.

- Read Revelation 21:1-5 together. Explain that this is a vision God gives John as an imaginative metaphor for what God is up to in the world.

○ Read Luke 1:46-55. How is Mary's hope related to the mission of God in the world and this week's imaginative prayer?

○ Ask your child to do some research (at church, on the Internet, in a newspaper) about ways you as a family could get involved in works of mercy or justice around your city. Talk and pray about this together as a family.

FOR THE JOURNAL Set aside fifteen to twenty minutes once this week to sit with your child in a focused way with their journal in hand. Remind them of the imaginative prayer from this week and ask them to think about something that happened this week (at home, at school, etc.) that God would want to make good again. Help your child put into words a prayer for this particular situation. Write the prayer in the journal.

The mission of God is to bring all things under the reign of king Jesus

 **CONNECTION AND FORMATION** This week's imaginative prayer continues our unit on the *missio Dei*. The mission of God in the world is clearly laid out in Ephesians 1:7-10:

> Because of the sacrifice of the Messiah, his blood poured out on the altar of the Cross, we're a free people—free of penalties and punishments chalked up by all our misdeeds. And not just barely free, either. *Abundantly* free! He thought of everything, provided for everything we could possibly need, letting us in on the plans he took such delight in making. He set it all out before us in Christ, a long-range plan in which everything would be brought together and summed up in him, everything in deepest heaven, everything on planet earth. (*The Message*)

All things summed up in him. Other translations say that all things will come "under" him. The lesson last week was about God's mission to make all things in the world good again. This week is about imagining all those good things responding in obedience to Jesus the King. All things connected to the will of the Father.

This chapter's imaginative prayer allows your child to see the uniqueness of God's creation fully attuned to his Word. Submission to a good and loving King is the invitation of spiritual formation. Obedience to Christ is the measure of how much we have allowed Christ to be formed in us (Gal 4:19). But notice that the image and experience we are cultivating is not obedience that is difficult; it is meant to feel joyful and easy. We are not talking about obedience rooted in legalism, focused only on actions and outcomes. The vision of obedience that Jesus gives us is one of participation as learners. We learn from him as we take his way (his yoke) upon us. David Benner observes,

> Christ is the epitome of life lived with willingness. "Your will be done," he prayed in what we call the Lord's Prayer (Matthew 6:10). And more than just in prayer, he lived this posture of preferring God's will to his own. Christian spirituality is following Christ in this self-abandonment. It is following his example of willing surrender.
>
> Obedience that is grudging fruit of willful determination does not give God any more pleasure than it gives a parent. Nor does it bring us the vitality and fulfillment for which we long. . . . Obedience that flows from a surrendered heart is totally different. Rather than willpower and resolve, love is the motive for what we will and what we do. This is the pattern of genuine Christian spiritual transformation.[1]

God is bringing all things under the willful obedience of King Jesus. He does it with love.

Question: What is the mission of God?
Answer: The mission of God is to bring all things under the reign of King Jesus.

Close your eyes and let's take a few deep breaths together.

God, I pray that you will release our imagination and help us to hear you speak to us during this time together. We open our hands to you. We open our ears to you.

(pause 8-10 seconds)

Come, Holy Spirit.

Imagine you are standing once again in front of Jesus. King Jesus.

Now, I'm going to ask you some questions that you don't need to answer out loud. Just think about the answers in your head.

Do you remember how God became King?

Do you remember the story of the King coming into town and offering help to the man injured on the side of the road?

(pause 5-8 seconds)

God became King through love and forgiveness. Do you remember the story of the faithful king who built you a treehouse in the forest, even when no one obeyed the rules of the special club you were a part of?

Do you remember the dark cave with the big faucets inside?

Remember, as you look at Jesus, that this is the faithful King you saw defeat the power of sin in a deep, dark cave. Remember watching as the faithful King turned off the stinky faucets of lust, gluttony, greed, sloth, wrath, envy, and pride.

Do you remember how the Accuser whispers accusations in your ear? Do you remember the lies that the evil one tells? Do you remember also that the Accuser used up all his lies and spent all his power on Jesus?

This is the King who came to defeat the power of the Accuser.

Imagine standing before him now.

(pause 5 seconds)

Do you remember imagining that you were in the Garden of Eden, watching as the Accuser led Adam and Eve toward death and away from God? This is Jesus, the good and kind King, who you stand before.

Remember, this is the King who came to free us from the power of death.

What does it feel like to stand in front of King Jesus?

(pause 5-8 seconds)

Imagine now that you aren't the only one standing in front of King Jesus. Your friends are there too. In fact everyone is there. People from every village and tribe and nation on the earth are standing before King Jesus. Imagine you are in a wide open space, and Jesus is sitting in the middle of a beautiful place, with mountains surrounding you and streams and hills behind you. Jesus is sitting on a throne. Every person is standing in front of Jesus, and he sees each person. He looks at each one and calls each person by their own special name. Imagine that all the animals are there too. Every animal that you can imagine is right here. Everything is here.

Everything on land and everything in the sea. The ocean is right next to you and there are fish and sea creatures jumping out of the water and into the air just to get a glimpse of Jesus. And the birds are flying back and forth overhead, each bird singing its song and calling its call.

And then all the people start to sing, and they lift their hands toward Jesus, singing praises to him. Sometimes they shout with joy, and sometimes they stand quietly with arms stretched out to feel on their hands the great love of God. Imagine you too are singing, and that your arms are stretched out toward Jesus.

The whole earth is filled with a great party for King Jesus.

And then everything is silent. Everyone is quiet, for Jesus is about to speak.

Imagine you are quietly standing in front of Jesus.

There is quietness all around you, and you are with King Jesus.

(pause 5-8 minutes)

And then he speaks with the authority of a King. He speaks with boldness, and yet his voice is kind and gentle. You watch as each person comes before Jesus, and he gives each person a task. Each person Jesus talks to bows when Jesus is finished speaking—and then each person goes away to do the thing that King Jesus requested.

Watch as Jesus speaks to the earth below your feet. He speaks to the mountains and to the trees and to all the plants that grow in the fields. He speaks to the birds and all the animals. It's as though Jesus were conducting a symphony from his throne—he gives a command, and it is done with great joy. The birds go and do and be the birds that King

Jesus created them to be. The plants grow perfectly in response to the voice of Jesus. The animals help complete all sorts of tasks, each according to the way they were made—big animals doing big things and small animals doing small things.

Everything on earth is following the way of Jesus. Everything is under the reign of King Jesus, who is a good and kind King.

When we follow Jesus, we join the mission of God to bring his love into the world.

The mission of God is to make everything in the world good again.

The mission of God is to bring all things under the reign of King Jesus.

 Question: What is the mission of God?
Answer: The mission of God is to bring all things under the reign of King Jesus.

 FOR THE PARENT OR MENTOR   What has God entrusted to you right now? What do you reign over? Are you in charge of anything? Are you the boss at work, or do you manage the budget at home? One way God brings things under the reign of Jesus is by entrusting small portions of his created world to us. He empowers us to govern and make choices about things in our domain. The question is whether we are leading and governing in the same way he would do it. One of the most important questions we can ask as parents is, Am I leading the way God leads? Am I reigning over what God has given me in the spirit of Jesus? Spend some time this week thinking through all the areas of life under your governance. Reflect in prayer and imagine how Jesus would lead these areas of your life if he were living your life. How would you articulate the differences you see? How would you name the way Jesus reigns? What words would you use to describe it?

- Spend some time this week at bedtime helping your child review the day. Look together for highs and lows throughout the day. Thank God for the joys, and pray for the pains.

○ Engage your child in conversation about God's mission in the world (1) to fill the world with his love, (2) to make everything in the world good again, and (3) to bring all things under the rule and reign of King Jesus.

○ Sometime this week read Ephesians 1:7-10 together with your child.

○ Talk about the long-range plan of God. Talk about how all the stuff we see in the world is moving toward the picture in our imaginative prayer—everything in obedience to the good and kind King Jesus. This is how it ends up.

○ Read Revelation 5:10-14 together. Remind your child that things in the world are not all yet in alignment with God's plan, but we're working on it.

○ Talk to your child about Jesus as King. Ask, "Is there anything you sense that Jesus might be asking you to do? Is there any special project he is inviting you into?"

○ Encourage your child to wonder how God has made them. What personality does your child seem to be leaning toward? What natural gifts and talents does your child have? Help them see the way they are made. Help your child be curious and wonder about how God might want to use their gifts in his mission.

○ Share with your child where you feel God leading you. Talk to them about your own conversations with God. What do you want to see come under Jesus' rule and reign? Share this. You and your child are in this project together!

 **FOR THE JOURNAL** Set aside fifteen to twenty minutes just once this week to sit with your child in a focused way with their journal in hand. Remind them of the imaginative prayer from this week, and invite them to journal about how they want to be involved in God's work. What special project has God invited your child into? Ask your child to brainstorm ways to get involved in God's invitation.

34

The mission of God is to bring peace and reconciliation to everything

 **CONNECTION AND FORMATION** This week's imaginative prayer continues our lesson on the mission of God (*missio Dei*). We are trying to bring together many of the experiences from the past few months and connect some dots for your child. The apostle Paul tells us that God is reconciling *all things* to himself in Christ (Col 1:19-20). This speaks to the Old Testament concept of *shalom*—all things being at *peace* with God and in relation to one another. The *missio Dei* is for the whole world and everything in it. We play a role in participating with God in moving the project of *peace* and *reconciliation* forward. This week's lesson foreshadows our concluding lesson on God's mission, when we talk about looking around the world for what God is doing and joining him in that work.

The peace of Christ is meant to rule in our hearts (Col 3:15). Paul's exhortation is for us to be *reconciled* to God (2 Cor 5:20) and to each other (Eph 2:11-22). Our ability to bring peace will in many ways depend on the peace we carry. Spiritual formation for your child will include a healthy dose of conflict and reconciliation. Every home has conflict. There will be no lack of opportunities for you and your child to pursue peace and reconciliation. These are opportunities to connect and go deeper in your understanding of each other.

Question: What is the mission of God in the world?
Answer. The mission of God is to bring peace and reconciliation to *everything*.

Close your eyes and let's take a few deep breaths together.

God, I pray that you will release our imagination and help us to hear
you speak to us during this time together. We open our hands to you.
We open our ears to you.

(pause 8-10 seconds)

Come, Holy Spirit.

Imagine you are at the beginning of the story God has been telling.
Imagine you are there at creation when God forms all the things we
see in the earth. Listen as you hear God call everything good. Watch as
he breathes his breath on the man and woman, and makes them in his
image, his likeness. He fills them with his Spirit. Put yourself there in the
Garden, enjoying the pleasure of just being with God and his creation.
Put yourself there, together with God, experiencing peace.

(pause 8-10 seconds)

Where, in your body, do you experience God's peace?

(pause 5 seconds)

This peace is what the Bible calls *shalom*. This is a special peace. This
peace means that everything is good. Relationships are good. Creation
is good and full of love.

And then remember that this peace, this *shalom*, is lost through
disobedience. Remember the story about how Adam and Eve hid from
God? In their disobedience they hid from God, and the peace, the
shalom, ended. It disappeared.

Imagine the word *peace* in your mind right now. Imagine the letters
being formed in your mind: P-E-A-C-E. Peace.

Imagine this word is written on a blank page in big, black letters.

Do you have a picture of the word in your mind?

(pause 5 seconds)

And now it disappears. The page is blank. The peace is gone.

(pause 8-10 seconds)

Imagine you are forced to leave the place where God is. Imagine there is a great distance between your life and God's life. What does it feel like to be separated from God?

(pause 8-10 seconds)

You notice that others too are separated from God. Even the earth seems to groan and complain that the peace it once knew has disappeared.

Imagine everything is hostile to God. Something has gone terribly wrong.

How can we have peace with God again?

(pause 5 seconds)

What we need is called "reconciliation."

Reconciliation is when people who are in conflict come together and find peace.

Reconciliation is when things that don't seem to fit together start fitting together.

The mission of God is to bring peace and reconciliation to everything.

God's mission is to reconcile all things to himself. To see to it that every conflict is worked out and that all things that lack peace with God come to have peace with God.

(pause 5-8 seconds)

Picture something, or maybe someone, right now in your mind that is not at peace with God.

What is it? What comes to your mind when you think about things that are not reconciled to God?

(pause 5-8 seconds)

Imagine now that you see Jesus.

Imagine you see Jesus and the cross.

Imagine Jesus is opening his mouth to speak. He opens his mouth and big, black letters come out of his mouth: P-E-A-C-E. Peace.

Listen to Jesus say the word *peace*.

The way Jesus would have said it would have sounded like this: *shalom*.

Next, he says the word *reconciliation*.

Listen as he says these words to you:

> I came to bring peace with God. I came to bring reconciliation of all things.

The mission of God is to bring peace and reconciliation to everything!

(pause 5 seconds)

Look again at the cross where Jesus is.

You now notice that there is something at the bottom of the cross. It looks like a present. A gift that is wrapped up. Walk closer to the gift.

Imagine you see your name on the gift, like on Christmas morning, this gift is resting under the cross like a present under the Christmas tree.

Imagine walking closer to the gift, which is wrapped in brown paper.

Open the gift.

(pause 5-8 seconds)

Inside, you find two stacks of cards. Each stack is the size of a deck of playing cards like *Uno* or *Skip-Bo*. The cards are white and sticky, like Sticky Notes.

On each card of one of the stacks is written the word *peace*.

The other stack of cards has the word *reconciliation* written on each card.

Peace and reconciliation.

Take these cards and put them in your pockets. In your left pocket you have a stack of cards that say "peace." And in your right pocket you have a stack of cards that say "reconciliation." These stacks of cards are gifts to you from Jesus. And imagine Jesus gives you instructions.

He says, "Give away *peace* and *reconciliation* in the world! Go, give it away."

Imagine this is like a board game or a video game. The goal of the game is to walk around the world with peace and reconciliation in your pockets. Picture in your mind, again, something that is not at peace with God. What comes to mind right now that is not reconciled to God?

(pause 5-8 seconds)

Imagine now that you see something in the world where peace needs to be restored. Maybe you are aware of a conflict at school, or perhaps you have a friend whose parents are separated or divorced. Take a card from your pocket that has the word *peace* written on it, and like a Sticky Note, stick one of those cards on all those people. Each Sticky Note has the word *peace* written on it. Imagine that the *peace of God* comes to whatever touches a card that has *peace* written on it.

(pause 5 seconds)

Now imagine you see something in your life or in the world around you that is not yet reconciled to God. Can you think of a person in your life who doesn't yet know God? Take a card from your pocket that has the word *reconciliation* written on it. Give the reconciliation card away to someone who is not reconciled to God.

(pause 5-8 seconds)

When we follow Jesus, we join the mission of God to bring his love into the world.

The mission of God is to make everything in the world good again.

The mission of God is to bring all things under the rule and reign of Jesus.

The mission of God is to bring peace and reconciliation to everything!

Question: What is the mission of God in the world?
Answer: The mission of God is to bring peace and reconciliation to *everything*.

 FOR THE PARENT OR MENTOR   Are you experiencing the *shalom* of God? Peace is not just the absence of conflict; peace (*shalom*) is the presence of true reconciliation, true restoration. Peace and reconciliation are where things are headed in the world, according to God's stated mission. And yet sometimes we experience the lack of peace and reconciliation in our own home, with those whom we love the most. How are you doing with reconciliation in your home? Spend some time reflecting this week on where peace and reconciliation might be lacking in your own world. Are there any relationships in your home lacking peace? Is there anything in your own life that is not reconciled to God? Ask God to highlight some of these areas, and let them be the focus of your prayers this week. In a way that is reassuring, share with your child what God is showing you.

This week's imaginative prayer requires some engagement and conversation to move it from a fairly abstract experience to your child's real life. You may be aware of some difficult situations in your child's school, your city, or even your own family. This imaginative experience was intentionally open-ended, which allowed your child to experience things without too much prompting. Help your child pay attention to the things that came to mind. We're allowing God to speak to us through bringing a specific person or situation to mind.

○ Spend some time this week at bedtime helping your child review the day. Look together for highs and lows throughout the day. Thank God for the joys, and pray for the pains.

○ Engage your child in conversation about God's mission in the world to bring peace and reconciliation to all things.

○ Spend some time this week noticing (with your child) things that could use more peace and reconciliation. As you notice, ask your child, "What would it look like for this situation to be reconciled to God?" or "What would peace look like in this situation?" Remind your child of the concept of the peace and reconciliation cards.

○ Review with your child what we've looked at so far regarding the mission of God:

   ○ to fill the world with his love

   ○ to make everything in the world good again

   ○ to bring all things under the rule and reign of King Jesus

   ○ to bring peace and reconciliation to everything

○ This week read and discuss with your child one or more of the following passages:

   ○ Romans 5:1-2

   ○ 2 Corinthians 5:17-20

   ○ Colossians 1:15-23 (replace the word *gospel* in v. 23 with "good news")

 **FOR THE JOURNAL**   Set aside fifteen to twenty minutes once this week to sit with your child in a focused way with their journal in hand. Remind them of the imaginative prayer from this week and ask them to think about something they noticed this week that needs peace and reconciliation with God. Help your child put into words a prayer for this particular situation. Write the prayer in the journal.

35

The mission of God
is to take away the veil
that covers up the
presence of God

 **CONNECTION AND FORMATION** This week's imaginative prayer tries to create an experience for your child that is hard to put into words—the experience of God's glory. The Bible says that it is hidden. It's veiled. We carry in our bodies the glory of God as in jars of clay so that we don't think the glory we see in ourselves (and in others) originates with us. Though we may be creative and full of life, the glory is God's alone. The apostle Paul teaches that we are on our way toward having our likeness (our image) transformed into the likeness of Christ. Our reflection of God's presence will one day be like that of Jesus.

In their voice, body, and life our children carry the very presence of God. A great deal of spiritual formation requires seeing our own self as someone worth loving. We are worthy of being loved because God has put his very imprint and nature upon us. We often focus on teaching our children more about their sin and depravity than we do about the reality that they are breathing the very breath of God and that the Spirit of God has decided to make their body and soul his home. Jesus says, "Apart from me you can do nothing" (Jn 15:5). It is possible to be transformed inwardly such that the glory and image of God begins to shine through. Inward transformation is the work we are nurturing here. With this imaginative prayer we are specifically introducing the possibility for the glory of God, the *presence of God*, to shine through the veil.

And when it does shine through, we call this worship. When we express our love for God through music, through silence, through kindness to those in need, and through welcoming a refugee, all of this is worship. It's allowing God's image—as one who loves—to shine through. It's allowing God's presence to be revealed. When we worship God we give and reflect back to God what he first gave to us, an imprint of himself. And if this is true, then worship itself is an act of spiritual formation. When we worship God we help facilitate the growth of our capacity to reflect God's image and glory. When we worship, we are engaged in veil removal.

Question: What is the mission of God in the world?
Answer: The mission of God is to take away the veil that covers up the presence of God.

Close your eyes and let's take a few deep breaths together.

God, I pray that you will release our imagination and help us to hear you speak to us during this time together. We open our hands to you. We open our ears to you.

(pause 8-10 seconds)

Come, Holy Spirit.

Imagine with me that you wake up in the morning and begin to get ready for your day. Picture climbing out of bed and heading to the place where you get dressed in the morning. You pick out your clothes and put them on. You straighten your dress or tuck in your shirt or roll up your jeans. Imagine brushing your hair.

Stand in front of the mirror. Take a good look at yourself. What do you see?

(pause 5-8 seconds)

Smile at yourself in the mirror. Take a deep breath and feel your chest rise and then fall. Take a good look at yourself. Look at the color in your eyes. You are God's creation; you are his beautiful creation.

God's glory, his presence, is in there. It's in your eyes. It's in your body. It's in your voice when you sing. It's in your heart as it pumps. It's in your breath as you breathe.

The presence of God—his glory—is just beneath what you can see with your own eyes. Look closer in the mirror.

(pause 5 seconds)

Can you see God's glory?

Imagine God's presence—his glory—is like a light that shines from your face. Picture your face glowing with the light and the presence and the glory of God. Look in the mirror and see God's presence.

(pause 5 seconds)

Imagine now that you pull a cloth from your pocket. This cloth is a veil. A veil is a cloth used to cover something up or to block light from coming in the window. A veil is like a window shade.

Take this piece of cloth and put it over your face. It's a thin piece of cloth that you can see through, but the light that was coming from your face is now covered up.

Imagine now that you go about your day and you notice that others too have faces that are veiled. At the breakfast table your brother or sister is wearing a veil. Your mom and dad are in the kitchen making breakfast, and they too are wearing veils.

What does it feel like to look at the people you love through a veil?

What does it feel like to know that there is a smile underneath the veil, but you can't see it? That the very presence of God—God's glory—is shining from their faces but you can't see it? The veil is covering God's presence.

Imagine going about your day, and everyone you meet has a veil covering their face. Every face is covered. Every voice sounds muffled. When people sing, it sounds so soft. When people dance, it's as though they are barely moving. The veil is covering the presence and the glory of God.

And with your eyes closed, imagine now that Jesus enters into your day. Where are you when Jesus comes in? Are you at home? At school? At the playground?

Jesus is the only one without a veil. He is the only face you can see. His voice is strong because it is not covered. His laughter is bright and loud because there is no veil. And when Jesus sings, his song is loud and beautiful.

Imagine Jesus invites you to follow him, and you begin walking toward a person near you. Imagine you are standing in front of someone you know. Your face is veiled, and their face is also veiled. You are facing one another, and Jesus invites you to share something with this other person. Who is the person across from you? Is it a parent? A brother? A sister? A friend? Picture someone you know. What is something you can share with that person? How can you be kind to them? How can you give love to them? Imagine Jesus is inviting you to share that specific love and kindness with that person.

(pause 5-8 seconds)

Now imagine doing it! Share and watch as your veil and the other person's veil is lifted just enough for you to catch the presence of God shining out from where the veil was lifted. Look closely at the other person and see them for a brief moment without the veil covering their face. Look at the beauty of God in the face of Jesus. Look at the same beauty in the face of the person standing near you.

This is what love does to people. This is what grace and forgiveness do to people. This is what peace and reconciliation do to people. They lift the veil that covers the glory and the presence of God. They let the beauty of God's creation shine through in everything. Jesus is the King with an unveiled face shining and reflecting the presence of God into the world.

(pause 5-8 seconds)

Imagine now that Jesus begins to sing. And as he sings his face shines more brightly.

Jesus is singing your favorite worship song or hymn. What is your favorite song you sing at church? Let that song come into your ears right now.

(pause 5 seconds)

And now Jesus invites you to sing. His face is shining with God's presence.

And as you begin to sing with Jesus, as you begin to worship God with music and song, Jesus reaches down and removes your veil completely, and your face also shines and glows with the presence of God.

You are a worshiper.

Imagine that you laugh together with Jesus. You are filled with joy as you stand in front of Jesus experiencing the presence of God, singing, and dancing, and laughing as your face glows bright, and all the people around you are also singing and dancing and worshiping God, and their faces too are glowing bright with God's presence.

(pause 8 seconds)

And now look in the mirror again. Imagine looking in the mirror again and seeing yourself. But this time you see something else. Your face is shining and reflecting the presence of God. Something about your face in the mirror looks more like Jesus' presence than before.

You are a worshiper.

When we follow Jesus, we join the mission of God to bring his love into the world.

The mission of God is to make everything in the world good again.

The mission of God is to bring all things under the rule and reign of Jesus.

The mission of God is to bring peace and reconciliation to everything.

The mission of God is to take away the veil that covers up the presence of God.

 Question: What is the mission of God in the world? *Answer*. The mission of God is to take away the veil that covers up the presence of God.

FOR THE PARENT OR MENTOR When or where are you most likely to be aware of God's presence? When or where are you least aware of God's presence? What would it look like for you to intentionally be on the lookout for God's presence throughout your day? Spend some time this week imagining what people around you would be like if the veil that covers God's glory was removed. Try to look at people this week, particularly your own child, as though they have had the veil removed. Where in your workplace is the presence of God covered right now? How might you participate in uncovering God's presence there? What about at home? Make a list this week of what events about your day help you see God's presence in your family.

- Spend some time this week at bedtime helping your child review the day. Look together for highs and lows throughout the day. Thank God for the joys, and pray for the pains.

- Talk to your child this week about God's presence.

- Spend some time this week worshiping together with your child. Put on music and dance. Find your favorite songs and make a playlist to listen to together.

- Read Exodus 34:29-34. Start a dialogue with your child: "Why do you think Moses put the veil over his face?"

- On another day, read 2 Corinthians 3:3-18, Paul's second letter to the church in Corinth. Consider these points:

  - Paul is talking here about the difference between the kind of ministry Moses had, which was delivering the law, and the kind of ministry Paul and others were engaged in—delivering the grace of God.

  - Remind your kids about the new promise of God (the new covenant) that came to us in Jesus.

  - Talk about how the law brought a sense of failure because people couldn't live up to it, but the Spirit brings life and freedom.

  - Starting in verse 13, Paul is again making a distinction between the new covenant in Jesus, and the old covenant in Moses: Moses put a veil over his face because he was afraid people would see the glory of God in his face eventually fade away. Paul says, essentially, "In Jesus, the veil is removed! We don't need to be afraid of when our face doesn't radiate God's presence. We are hopeful, we have freedom, and we believe that we are being transformed in a way that will allow all the presence of God to be revealed."

○ Ask, "Where do you see the glory of God in our lives? Where do you see his presence?"

○ Consider memorizing together 2 Corinthians 4:6 and Habakkuk 2:14.

 **FOR THE JOURNAL** Set aside fifteen to twenty minutes once this week to sit with your child in a focused way with their journal in hand. Remind them of the imaginative prayer from this week and ask them to reenter the imaginative space. This may be a week to simply reread the imaginative prayer out loud to your child and ask them to write where they see God's presence coming through in their life.

36

God is at work all
around us: open your
eyes and join God in his
mission to the world

CONNECTION AND FORMATION This last imaginative
prayer invites your child
to *watch* and *listen* for what God is doing in his mission to the world around
us. We've built a lot of silence into this week's prayer. Looking and listening
for what God is up to takes time. We get a picture of how to engage in this
kind of observational work by watching Jesus. We are able to discover what
God was up to simply because Jesus opened his eyes and ears to see what
the Father was doing—and he joined him in it. Jesus' actions in his everyday
life made public what God was doing all along. God is at work all around
us. We are trying to cultivate intentional listening and watching for what
God might invite us to do alongside of him. Or, as Jesus might say, "He who
has ears to hear, let him hear."

Much of our life of following Jesus, and the formation of Jesus in us,
hinges on our intentions. Formation simply cannot happen where there is
no intention to be inwardly formed. The seeds of the kingdom are scattered
throughout our lives, but without our attention to them the worries of this
world choke out the life that the kingdom can bring. The enemy will snatch
up the seeds and steal them away if we aren't paying close attention (Mt
13:1-23). Where there is no intention to join in the work of God in the
world, the story we're invited into will feel like a dream, and we'll miss it.
"Open your eyes," says Jesus. "Look out into the field. Do you see how ripe
that grain is for harvest?" Indeed, it's ripe. In your life and in your child's.

We end the same way Jesus ended. Go into all the world. Pray for eyes to see and ears to hear the work of God's kingdom among you.

 Question: Where do we see the mission of God?
Answer: God is at work all around us: open your eyes and join God in his mission to the world.

Close your eyes and let's take a few deep breaths together.

God, I pray that you will release our imagination and help us to hear you speak to us during this time together. We open our hands to you. We open our ears to you.

(pause 8-10 seconds)

Come, Holy Spirit.

Imagine you have special eyes to see things and special ears to hear things.

What would your eyes look like if they had special powers? Would they be big? Would they rest behind large glasses, or maybe you would need special spyglasses to see the special things? Picture in your mind how you would imagine yourself if you had eyes to see special things.

And your ears—what would they look like if they could hear special things? Would they be big ears?

Imagine that you can see special things and hear special things without needing to have different eyes or ears. What kinds of things would you want to see and hear? What do you think would be the most important things in the world to pay attention to?

(pause 5-8 seconds)

Imagine you could see everything in the world that God was doing, and you didn't need big eyes or special glasses. Imagine you could hear God's voice when he speaks—that you could hear when God was saying something about the work he was doing all around you—and you didn't need big ears or any special spy equipment. What would it feel like to have those kind of eyes and ears? What would it feel like to be able to pay attention to the things God was doing in the world?

(pause 5 seconds)

Imagine going to your school or to the grocery store with you parents. Imagine looking around you and hearing God's voice tell you about what he is doing in the lives of some of the people you see. This girl is feeling lonely. That boy needs a friend. That woman is sick and needs prayer. That man has just lost someone he loves; he needs comforted.

(pause 5 seconds)

Imagine if you had eyes to see the new creation that God is involved in. What if you could see God's love flow from one person to someone else? What if you could see what people needed—even before they asked? What if you could hear exactly how God wanted you to participate in his work of bringing love and peace and reconciliation to the world?

Imagine if you could see the veil that covers God's glory and hear the invitation of King Jesus to lift up that veil and uncover the presence of God.

What would you do with these kind of eyes? What kind of person would you be if you had these kind of ears?

(pause for 5 seconds)

What would your life look like if you could see and hear what God was doing around you?

(pause for 5 seconds)

Take a moment and think about your family. What do you see God doing in your family? Where do you see him at work?

(pause for 10 seconds)

And what about at school or at the playground or with your friends?

Where do you see God's mission? Who are the people God is inviting you to love? Who are the people you can see that need God's love?

(pause for 10 seconds)

What do you see in the world that needs to be made good? Where do you go throughout your week where something needs the goodness of God?

(pause for 10 seconds)

Is there anyone you know who does not have life with God? Is there anyone that comes to mind who isn't experiencing peace with God? Is there anyone who maybe isn't reconciled to God?

(pause for 10 seconds)

Who is God bringing to mind?

Take a few moments and pray for that person right now.

(pause for 10 seconds)

Imagine now that you are standing with Jesus the King. Imagine you are looking out into the world with special eyes. You are looking at every-thing in the world that God wants to make good again. You are looking at all the things God wants to bring under the reign of King Jesus. All the people—all of creation, in fact—that God wants to bring peace and reconciliation to. Imagine standing next to Jesus, and you ask him this: "Jesus, is there anything specific that you want me to help you with?"

Listen to Jesus with those special ears and hear him speak to you.

What is God saying to you right now about what he is doing around you?

(pause for 20 seconds)

When we follow Jesus, we join the mission of God to bring his love into the world.

The mission of God is to make everything in the world good again.

The mission of God is to bring all things under the rule and reign of Jesus.

The mission of God is to bring peace and reconciliation to everything.

The mission of God is to take away the veil that covers up the presence of God.

God is at work all around us: open your eyes and join God in his mission to the world.

 Question: Where do we see the mission of God?
Answer: God is at work all around us: open your eyes and join God in his mission to the world.

 FOR THE PARENT OR MENTOR Jesus lived with a rhythm of watching. People caught his eye. He moved toward them. He entered into their lives. What thoughts have come to mind as you lead your child through this imaginative prayer? Have any questions caught your attention? What special power of seeing and hearing would you like to ask Jesus for? We parents are sometimes blind to the work God is already doing in our child's life. It's often easier to see the shortcomings and difficulties of our children than it is to notice the graces. Spend some time this week making a list of areas of your child's life where you see the Father at work. How is your child growing? How have they grown this past year in their awareness of God's presence? How have you grown? Ask God to give you eyes to see and ears to hear his present work in you.

- Spend some time this week at bedtime helping your child review the day. Look together for highs and lows throughout the day. Thank God for the joys, and pray for the pains.

- Talk to your child this week about God's work all around us. Ask, "What do you see God doing in our family?" and "Do you see God's mission at work anywhere at your school? In your friends' lives? On the playground?"

- Together, make a list of where you see God at work around you.

- Read John 5:1-20 together. What did people see? What were they focused on? What did Jesus see? What did Jesus say? Talk about verses 19-20—Jesus *seeing* what his Father was doing.

○ Have a conversation with your child about the role of an apprentice. Share a story about something you have taught your child to do while they were standing next to you, learning at your side (baking bread, building a fire, etc.). We learn to see and hear what the Father is doing by watching how Jesus did it.

○ Remind your child of the passage where Jesus invited people to take his yoke—his way and teaching—upon them.

○ Ask your child where God is at work in their life right now: "What is God inviting you into?"

○ Next time you are at the grocery store, ask your child, "Do you think God is up to anything here? Is there anything we can join him in?" Take a risk. Stop someone in the produce section and ask if you can pray for them. Be willing to listen to hear what God might be speaking to that person through you.

 **FOR THE JOURNAL** Set aside fifteen to twenty minutes once this week to sit with your child in a focused way with their journal in hand. Remind your child of the imaginative prayer from this week, and ask them to think of places where they can be intentional about looking and listening for what God might be up to. Specific places: the bus stop, the school lunch room, the playground. Ask your child to name some place where they can commit to opening their eyes and ears, and wondering what God is doing there.

When we follow Jesus, we join the mission of God to bring his love into
the world.

The mission of God is to make everything in the world good again,
to bring all things under the reign of King Jesus,
to bring peace and reconciliation to everything.

The mission of God is to take away the veil that covers up the presence of God.

God is at work all around us: open your eyes and join God in his mission to
the world.

CREEDAL QUESTIONS AND ANSWERS

Question: What happens to us when we follow Jesus?
Answer: When we follow Jesus, we join the mission of God to bring his love
into the world.

Question: What is the mission of God?
Answer: The mission of God is to make everything in the world good again.

Question: What is the mission of God?
Answer: The mission of God is to bring all things under the reign of King Jesus.

Question: What is the mission of God?
Answer: The mission of God is to bring peace and reconciliation to everything.

Question: What is the mission of God?
Answer: The mission of God is to take away the veil that covers up the
presence of God.

Question: Where do we see the mission of God?
Answer: God is at work all around us: open your eyes and join God in his
mission to the world.

QUESTIONS AND ACTIVITIES

○ Spend time this week reviewing each of the past six weeks.

○ Ask some good questions. For example:

  ○ What are some things you'd like to see God working on in the world? Is there something about the way the world works that bothers you? What?

  ○ Who do you feel God is inviting you to love this week?

  ○ What has patience and kindness looked like for you this week? What has been hard?

  ○ Who did you notice was left out this week?

  ○ Is there anything you see going on in the world that makes you feel sad? If so, what is it?

  ○ Tell me about how God has spoken to you recently.

  ○ Have you had any interesting dreams that God might be speaking to you through? Would you share them with me?

  ○ What are some of the things you are praying about right now?

  ○ What are you talking to God about?

  ○ What are you asking from God?

  ○ Where do you want God to do something?

○ Review the portion of the creedal poem that corresponds with part six, "The Mission of God." Help your child memorize these next six lines. Review the creedal poem from parts one through five. Spend the next few weeks trying to memorize the entire creedal poem.

···

Epilogue

THIS BOOK HAS BEEN AS MUCH about your own formation as a parent as it has been about the spiritual formation of your child. It's been the same for me as I wrote it. My capacity to connect with my children has continued to grow as my own connection with God deepens. Our capacity to connect with our children and to nurture their spiritual life in real and vulnerable ways is directly related to our own connection with God. When we take time to nurture frequent conversation with God, our awareness of God is heightened in our own lives, and we seem to be able to see more clearly his work and grace in others.

As I put some finishing touches on this manuscript I notice in me a renewed desire to lead my children on the path of spiritual formation, alongside the contemplative stream. I continue to see the fruit of these conversations in the life of our family. My nine-year-old often asks me how my day was, and "What was your favorite part?" My eleven-year-old asked me to pray for her recently because she sensed that God wanted to give her a gift. And there have been seasons over the past three years of working on this book when one of my children has suffered a disease that continues to impact her life—and all of our lives. She has a deep hunger for God in the midst of it. She longs to see the kingdom. Another daughter has had long stretches of time when she feels as though God is not listening, not present, and not answering. She's been confused about why there is so much pain and suffering in the world. She has trouble hearing from God (don't we all) and doesn't see the purpose of prayer. We experience consolations and desolations under the same roof.

Since I first began thinking about ways to nurture a contemplative spirit in my family, the inner dialogue in my spirit about the reality of those consolations and desolations has changed. In the early stages of this book I hoped to create a path of formation that would lead my children to nurture and welcome the experience of God (consolation). While I may be successful in this, I know now that even when my children remain unhealed or struggle to sense God's presence (desolation), God is, in fact, still present. He is present to my children in ways I will never see or know, and in ways they may never be able to articulate. He is present because he is loving. And while my heart as a father is that my children would flourish, his heart as the Father is the same.

The anxiety I once carried is absent. And I wonder what kind of anxiety you may carry as a parent regarding the faith and formation of your children. Parenting is no small task. Sometimes it's all we can do to see that our children's teeth are clean and they have eaten something healthy today. Tending, at the same time, to the inner life of your child and to your own inner world feels like a giant task. I'm learning that it's all grace. We have intentions, we exert our will to make things happen, and then we find that someone flushed a washcloth down the toilet and the lawn mower is broken. Increasingly, these moments are becoming God's secret answers to my prayer to love well, to hurry less, and to be present to the real life around me.

In the final few months of completing this book, I was traveling and teaching in several cities, planting a new faith community in a new neighborhood, buying a house and doing renovations, and traveling to East Africa. My family tends to live at a fairly good and slow rhythm, which makes possible some of the deep and lasting conversations that have grown out of my work on this material. And yet the past six months have made it clear that it is yet again time to realign, slow down, and settle into good and spacious rhythms like morning hugs in my reading chair and evening meals around the table.

As you close this book, what do you notice about your own life? What has God been inviting you into over the past six or twelve months through a deepening connection with him and with your child? What are some ways you can continue the kind of conversations with your child that you may have gleaned through this experience?

As your children grow up, they will eventually outgrow the playful imaginative prayers in this book. You may already be seeing some waning interest. But like every other memory, they will carry it with them. You may find that you can continue to ask the questions found in this book.

"What's the most important part of the story?"

Acknowledgments

I AM SO GRATEFUL TO so many people who make my life rich and full.

Some of those people have contributed directly to the vision and formation of this book. First, I'd like to thank my editor, Al Hsu, and the folks at InterVarsity Press for taking a risk on something (and someone) new. Al's insights and suggestions for framing this book have been tremendously helpful. I'm grateful for Jay Pathak's introduction to my agent, Greg Johnson. Thank you, Greg, for also taking a risk and for your persistence and vision for this project.

I am grateful for Central Vineyard Church, and specifically my friend Jeff Cannell, who saw a vision for this material from the very beginning. Thank you, Jeff, for always being willing to experiment. You are still one of the best pastors I know. Karl and Jessie Boettcher were of great encouragement, both as colleagues and friends, in the early stage of writing this material for use at Central Vineyard Church. Jessie was a helpful reader and editor of many of these imaginative prayer sessions in their earliest stage. John McCollum, your hospitality and welcome have impacted me in very practical ways, such that much of what I do would be more difficult without it.

I'm also grateful to Becky Waugeman and Mike and Sherri Harder at the Des Moines Vineyard and for their willingness to pilot this material as a curriculum in their church. The same thanks goes to Debbie Fooskas and

Mark Tindall of the Blue Route Vineyard. Your input and feedback and prayers really kept this project alive.

There are folks who in friendship have served and loved me so well and who support my life in other areas, making it possible to have the vision and imagination for such a project as this book. I am so grateful to Caleb Maskell, who has cheered me on and believed in the vision all along, and Michael Raburn, who has offered a ton of encouragement along the way. I am indebted to my friend and mentor David Nixon, who introduced me, first in spiritual direction and then in friendship, to the work I have now given my life to. Steve Summerell too has journeyed with me in a significant way, helping me pay closer attention to the Father's deep and lasting love for me. John and Kara Kim, thank you for your continued friendship and welcome in New York City, and for collaborating in nurturing the presence of God through spiritual direction. Sara Carlisle, thank you for your work in the Order of Sustainable Faith and in your commitment to the journey. Last, all the folks in our new faith community at Franklinton Abbey. You are too many to name. I love you and am forever changed by your willingness to uproot your lives and follow the lead of God's Spirit.

This book was not written in long or leisurely periods. It was written in the margins of an already full life of parenting, husbanding, pastoring, and teaching. This means that the margins were thinner elsewhere, and my wife, Jaime, has no doubt felt the extra weight. Thank you, Jaime, for your love and encouragement and willingness to serve me and our girls. You love well.

And finally, my girls, to whom this book is dedicated.

Rayli, you are bold and courageous and I am grateful for the laughter and connection when you and I are the only ones awake.

Talitha, you have a depth and a sweetness that you share generously with me. I am grateful for your hunger for God to speak and heal.

Sadie, you are one of a kind. Your laughter is contagious and your hugs are a fuel of comfort to me.

Josephine, you are a vision.

Notes

Introduction

[1] Evan B. Howard, *The Brazos Introduction to Christian Spirituality* (Grand Rapids: Brazos, 2008), 269.

[2] M. Robert Mulholland Jr., *Invitation to a Journey: A Road Map for Spiritual Formation*, exp. ed. (Downers Grove, IL: InterVarsity Press, 2016), 16.

[3] Spiritual direction, defined most simply, is a form of pastoral guidance that facilitates a believer's spiritual formation. Generally, a person will meet monthly with a trained spiritual director who helps the believer pay closer attention to their prayer life and God's invitation toward Christlikeness.

[4] Richard Foster, *Celebration of Discipline* (New York: Harper, 1978). The evangelical world has been warming up to many of the formational writings from our Catholic brothers and sisters, though even Foster's book has been met with quite a bit of resistance in many evangelical circles.

[5] James K. A. Smith, "Defined by Our Loves: A Liturgical Anthropology," *YouTube*, March 11, 2103, www.youtube.com/watch?v=ixKR7duSamU.

[6] For one perspective on the "stage theory" of spiritual development see Janet Hagberg and Robert A. Guelich, *The Critical Journey: Stages in the Life of Faith* (Salem, WI: Sheffield, 2005).

[7] James K. A. Smith, *Desiring the Kingdom: Worship, Worldview, and Cultural Formation* (Grand Rapids: Baker Academic, 2009), 68.

[8] For an excellent introduction to the *Spiritual Exercises* of St. Ignatius see Larry Warner, *Journey with Jesus: Discovering the Spiritual Exercises of Saint Ignatius* (Downers Grove, IL: InterVarsity Press, 2010).

How to use this book

[1] We've tested this material with children nine to twelve years old. There is something remarkable about the ages of nine to eleven in particular. Children these ages are old enough to be able to grapple with some significant questions and even wrestle through some abstract concepts. But they are young enough to have a sense

of *playfulness*, which makes these exercises more engaging. Each child is different. We've also received feedback about how this material has been used in retirement-aged small groups and Sunday school classes, which was an unexpected use of the material. Much joy (and tears) came to folks on the tail end of their lives, imagining their faith as a child would, perhaps for the first time.

[2]Dallas Willard, "Leadership and Spirituality," Regent College, May 15–19, 2000, Regent Audio.

[3]If you are using this material in collaboration with your local church, the material fits nicely within a nine- to ten-month school year.

[4]See James K. A. Smith, *You Are What You Love: The Spiritual Power of Habit* (Grand Rapids: Brazos, 2016).

[5]I love the Moleskine Cahier Journal, which comes in a set of three for less than $10. I buy the unlined blank journals for both myself and my girls, which allow for sketching, drawing, writing, and even some watercolor for those inclined.

[6]This volume doesn't attempt to be comprehensive. I've chosen to take six themes a little deeper rather than try to cover too much ground. I'd love to explore the following themes through imaginative prayer in another project: the kingdom of God, God's special power (Holy Spirit), the family of God (the church), following Jesus, doing what Jesus did, and partnering with God.

[7]The Westminster Shorter Catechism (1648) and the Heidelberg Catechism (1586), respectively.

[8]If this material is being used as part of an education program in your local church, we've put some additional resources into their hands to help you connect with how this material is being used in the classroom. For more information go to imaginativeprayer.com.

[9]For an audio sample of how these imaginative sessions are intended to be read, go to imaginativeprayer.com.

[10]To explore how your own vulnerability forms connection see Curt Thompson's *Anatomy of the Soul: Surprising Connections Between Neuroscience and Spiritual Practices That Can Transform Your Life and Relationships* (Carol Stream, IL: SaltRiver, 2010). Also, Brené Brown's work has helped me give voice to my own vulnerability in parenting. See her *How the Courage to Be Vulnerable Transforms the Way We Live, Love, Parent and Lead* (London: Portfolio Penguin, 2013).

[11]James Wood, *How Fiction Works* (New York: Farrar, Straus & Giroux, 2008), 237-38, cited in James K. A. Smith, *You Are What You Love: The Spiritual Power of Habit* (Grand Rapids: Brazos, 2016), 93.

1 God loves so many things

[1]Norman Wirzba, *From Nature to Creation: A Christian Vision for Understanding and Loving Our World* (Grand Rapids: Baker Academic, 2015), 32.

[2]Francis of Assisi, "The Canticle of Creation," 1225.

[3]These pauses are meant to feel like they are creating space and room for your child to slow down and transition from the other parts of their day. They provide, I hope, a slow unwinding. During these prayers we can create a habit of quiet and silence that your child will become more accustomed to over time. These tiny disciplines of silence are part of the process of formation.

2 He loves me

[1]David G. Benner, *The Gift of Being Yourself: The Sacred Call to Self-Discovery* (Downers Grove, IL: InterVarsity Press, 2004), 49.
[2]Thomas Merton, *New Seeds of Contemplation* (New York: New Directions, 2007), 75.
[3]I am grateful to my friend Michael Raburn for sharing this prayer with me.

7 God invites us to live a life of love

[1]Traditionally, lectio divina has four movements: read, meditate, pray, and contemplate. First a passage is read, then it is meditated on in a prayerful posture with a welcome for God to speak, followed by a period of quiet contemplation.

8 Love is patient and kind, and does not make a list of people's mistakes

[1]St. Ignatius included in his *Spiritual Exercises* a daily *examen* prayer that seeks to review and understand how God is working in one's life. The *examen*, when practiced regularly, can help us become more in tune with God's presence and action in our everyday life.
[2]Jacques Philippe, *Searching for and Maintaining Peace: A Small Treatise on Peace of Heart* (New York: Alba House, 2002), 55.

9 Love invites people who may be left out

[1]The number of refugees globally has surpassed twenty million people living displaced from their country due to war, floods, and drought. See "Global Forced Displacement for 2015 on Track to Break All Records, Topping 60 Million," *UN News Centre*, December 18, 2015, www.un.org/apps/news/story.asp?NewsID =52859.

11 We love others with the love that God pours into us

[1]"Water Cooperation: Facts and Figures," *UN Water*, accessed November 22, 2016, www.unwater.org/water-cooperation-2013/water-cooperation/facts-and-figures/en.
[2]Here are two great places to start: Blood:Water Mission (bloodwater.org) and World Vision (worldvision.org).

13 Forgiveness means we can have peace with God

[1]For a wonderful essay on our role of response see "Spiritual Formation in Theological Perspective" in Jeffrey P. Greenman and George Kalantzis, *Life in the Spirit: Spiritual Formation in Theological Perspective* (Downers Grove, IL: IVP Academic, 2010).

[2]This imagery is borrowed from a powerful scene in C. S. Lewis's book *The Voyage of the Dawn Treader*. In Lewis's story, Eustace, a young boy, struggles to believe in the goodness of Narnia. His bitterness and resistance lead him to a cursed treasure field where he is changed into a dragon for a significant duration of the story. See C. S. Lewis, *The Voyage of the Dawn Treader*, Chronicles of Narnia (New York: HarperCollins, 2007).

15 Forgiveness means God takes away our sin

[1]Thomas Merton, *No Man Is an Island* (New York: Harcourt, Brace, 1955), 204.

17 When we forgive, we will be forgiven

[1]Frederick Buechner, *Wishful Thinking: A Seeker's ABC* (New York: Harper & Row, 1973), 29.

18 Love and forgiveness make room for reconciliation

[1]For an excellent resource on the connection between forgiveness and reconciliation see Everett L. Worthington, *Forgiving and Reconciling: Bridges to Wholeness and Hope* (Downers Grove, IL: InterVarsity Press, 2003).

[2]Henri J. Nouwen, *Peacework: Prayer, Resistance, Community* (Maryknoll, NY: Orbis Books, 2005), 15-16.

19 Jesus is the king who came to undo the power of death

[1]Dallas Willard, *The Great Omission: Reclaiming Jesus's Essential Teachings on Discipleship* (San Francisco: HarperSanFrancisco, 2006), 71.

[2]Greg Boyd, "The Christus Victor View of the Atonement," Re/New (blog), 2008, http://reknew.org/2008/01/the-christus-victor-view-of-the-atonement.

20 Jesus is the king who came to defeat the power of sin

[1]Ronald Rolheiser, *Sacred Fire: A Vision for a Deeper Human and Christian Maturity* (New York: Crown Publishing, 2014), 83. Rolheiser gives a very readable description of the subtleties of sin in these classic forms.

21 Jesus is the king who came to defeat the power of the accuser

[1]See Gustav Aulén, *Christus Victor: An Historical Study of the Three Main Types of the Idea of Atonement* (New York: Macmillan, 1969).

[2]An excellent resource for looking deeper into this is Timothy M. Gallagher, *The Discernment of Spirits: An Ignatian Guide for Everyday Living* (New York: Crossroad, 2005).

[3]This bread, temple, kingdom formulation was picked up in conversation with my friend David Nixon.

22 Jesus is a faithful king, even when his people are without faith

[1]David G. Benner, *Surrender to Love: Discovering the Heart of Christian Spirituality* (Downers Grove, IL: InterVarsity Press, 2003), 15.

[2]Ibid., 59.

23 We have life with God through the faithfulness of Jesus the king

[1]John Wimber, *The Way in Is the Way On: John Wimber's Teachings and Writings on Life in Christ* (Atlanta: Ampelon, 2006), 39.

25 God made a new promise and it comes to us through Jesus

[1]An entire part (hopefully in another volume) could be devoted to the family of God, our adoption into that family, and how this new extended family is God's plan for the work of new creation.

27 The good news of God comes to us through the life of Jesus

[1]C. S. Lewis, *Mere Christianity* (New York: Touchstone, 1996), 171.

[2]Dallas Willard, "Leadership and Spirituality," Regent College, May 15–19, 2000, Regent Audio.

28 The good news of God comes to us through the death of Jesus

[1]For a wonderful overview of the richness of the meaning of the Lord's Supper see N. T. Wright, *The Meal Jesus Gave Us* (Louisville, KY: Westminster John Knox, 2002).

[2]Justin Taylor, "You Are What You Love: A Conversation with James K. A. Smith," *Gospel Coalition*, April 5, 2016, from https://blogs.thegospelcoalition.org/justin taylor/2016/04/05/you-are-what-you-love-a-conversation-with-james-k-a-smith.

29 The good news of God comes to us through the resurrection of Jesus

[1]Lyrics from Sam Yoder, "Let All Things Rise," Mercy/Vineyard Publishing.

[2]For an excellent exploration of the role of the body in spiritual formation see Tara M. Owens, *Embracing the Body: Finding God in Our Flesh and Bone* (Downers Grove, IL: InterVarsity Press, 2015).

30 We receive the promises of God when we choose to follow Jesus

[1]Appropriate vulnerability and disclosure are helpful. This is not meant to be an invitation to disclose every struggle to your child. There are some things you may be struggling with that might not be appropriate to share with your child. Sharing your relationship struggles or financial burdens, for example, may cause more harm than good. Be mindful of how your struggles may affect your child before deciding to share.

31 When we follow Jesus, we join the mission of God to bring his love into the world

[1]David J. Bosch, *Transforming Mission: Paradigm Shifts in Theology of Mission* (Maryknoll, NY: Orbis, 1991), 390.

[2]In several of his works, New Testament scholar N. T. Wright has described the role of the church as faithfully improvising the work of the kingdom. For a full look at this idea and, more particularly, how Scripture can inform our improvisation, see N. T. Wright, *Scripture and the Authority of God: How to Read the Bible Today* (New York: HarperOne, 2011).

33 The mission of God is to bring all things under the reign of king Jesus

[1]David G. Benner, *Surrender to Love: Discovering the Heart of Christian Spirituality* (Downers Grove, IL: InterVarsity Press, 2003), 58.

Scripture Index

About the Author

Jared Patrick Boyd is a pastor (Vineyard USA), spiritual director, and founder of The Order of Sustainable Faith, a missional monastic order for the twenty-first century. He is the author of *Invitations & Commitments: A Rule of Life*. He and his wife have four daughters, and are planting Franklinton Abbey, a new faith community on the west side of Columbus, Ohio.

jared@sustainablefaith.com
Twitter: @BoydJared
#imaginativeprayer
imaginativeprayer.com

formatio

TRADITION. EXPERIENCE.
TRANSFORMATION.

Formatio books from InterVarsity Press follow the rich tradition of the church in the journey of spiritual formation. These books are not merely about being informed, but about being transformed by Christ and conformed to his image. Formatio stands in InterVarsity Press's evangelical publishing tradition by integrating God's Word with spiritual practice and by prompting readers to move from inward change to outward witness. InterVarsity Press uses the chambered nautilus for Formatio, a symbol of spiritual formation because of its continual spiral journey outward as it moves from its center. We believe that each of us is made with a deep desire to be in God's presence. Formatio books help us to fulfill our deepest desires and to become our true selves in light of God's grace.